The Geopolitics of Nordic and Russian Gender Research 1975–2005

This book examines how a geopolitical grammar works in Nordic and Russian academic feminism and how understandings of a joint feminist "we", of "Nordicness" and ideas of an "East/West-Divide" shape the formation of gender research fields. In three distinct chapters, each with a different approach to theories, methods and source ma-terials, the book explores the implications of lan-guage, translation, and situated knowledges in the development of gender research as a geopolitical area and particular academic space during the mid-1970s until 2005, and considers feminist knowledge production as a field of power relations.

The Geopolitics of Nordic and Russian Gender Research 1975–2005

Ulrika Dahl, Marianne Liljeström & Ulla Manns

PREVIOUS TITLES

Sven-Olov Wallenstein & Jakob Nilsson (eds.),
Foucault, Biopolitics, and Governmentality (2013)

Norbert Götz (ed.), *The Sea of Identities* (2014)

Andrej Kotljarchuk, *In the Forge of Stalin* (2014)

Samuel Edquist & Janne Holmén, *Islands of Identity* (2015)

Jonna Bornemark & Sven-Olov Wallenstein (eds.),
Madness, Religion, and the Limits of Reason (2015)

Jonna Bornemark & Nicholas Smith (eds.), *Phenomenology of Pregnancy* (2015)

Annika Öhrner (ed.), *Art in Transfer in the Era of Pop* (2017)

Södertörn University
The Library
SE-141 89 Huddinge

www.sh.se/publications

Cover photo: Jonas Mathiasson
Cover: Jonathan Robson
Graphic Form: Per Lindblom & Jonathan Robson

Printed by Elanders, Stockholm 2016

Södertörn Academic Studies 66
ISSN 1650-433X
ISBN 978-91-87843-53-2 (print)
ISBN 978-91-87843-54-9 (digital)

Contents

MARIANNE LILJESTRÖM

Foreword

Ten years ago our research project "Translating and Constructing Gender Studies in the Nordic Region, 1975–2005" received funding from the Baltic Sea Foundation (Östersjöstiftelsen). The project consisted of three separate but interrelated studies conducted by three gender scholars with different academic backgrounds: one historian, one cultural anthropologist, and one historian of ideas. Our overall and dual ambition, as it was presented in the grant application, was to analyse the Nordic Region (Norden) and Russia as regional imagined communities in women's and gender research approximately between 1975 and 2005. In particular, we aimed to focus on regional identity formations, theoretical canonisation and feminist research practices in order to understand women's and gender research communities not only as knowledge producers but also as feminist spaces in which to act, work and live.

The end result, this book, is a testament to the passing of time and certainly reflects some of the many twists and turns that our discussions have taken in the past decade. It offers a situated contribution to on-going conversations about the directions and developments of gender research among feminist scholars. Many of our colleagues have contributed to this project in different ways, by sharing their own stories, offering critical readings, and above all by providing ongoing encouragement and enthusiasm over the past decade. We are grateful for feedback and support from our colleagues at Södertörn University and Turku University and to participants in several Nordic and European Feminist Conferences, including in Turku in 2007, Karlstad in 2009, Budapest in 2012, and Rovaniemi 2015. Additional and special thanks go to Kerstin Alnebratt, Solveig Bergman, Maud Eduards, Anna Viola Hallberg, Beatrice Halsaa, Clare Hemmings, Kaisa Ilmonen, Sari Irni, Liz Kella, Katie King, Katariina Kyrölä, Katarina Leppänen, Mia Liinason, Karin Lindeqvist, Nina Lykke, Anna Nordenstam, Bente Rosenbeck, and Annika Olsson. Last, but not least, we thank the Baltic Sea Foundation for funding this project and the Publications Committee at Söder-törn University for supporting its production and publication.

Huddinge, August 2016
Ulrika Dahl, Marianne Liljeström & Ulla Manns

Introduction

Ulrika Dahl, Marianne Liljeström, and Ulla Manns

> "Is English the feminist language?" a Russian speaker
> asked at a conference in Denmark on "Women in a
> Changing Europe" in the autumn of 1991. Her joke,
> which caused lively amusement, points to what seems
> to be a fact, at least to the Nordic countries: English is
> our key to the greater world.
> NORA 1st editorial (Nielsen and Steinfeld 1993)

This book is a contribution to a scholarly feminist discussion about the knowledge formation variously called women's and/or gender studies.[1] At its broadest, we study some aspects of the making of "Nordic" and Russian women's and gender studies from 1975 to 2005, in order to reflect on how the space of feminist knowledge is imagined, and what it means to gender researchers to be situated, epistemologically, and materially, in a particular region/location. At the same time, and more centrally, we ask how geographical regions and nations are constituted in and through institutional feminist knowledge production as an on-going process and practice. In so doing we trace how theories, ideas, people, and knowledge practices travel, and how they are translated into and from specific locations. Thus, we move beyond the literal translation of a text from one language to another and attend to the cultural and geopolitical practice of transference and transmutation of ideas, concepts, and theories, as well as the political economy of knowledge production.

---

[1] In this book, we use slightly different understandings of women's and gender studies in our respective chapters, but largely we understand it to include research and teaching about the meaning, impact and effect of sex and gender both within autonomous departments of women's and gender studies and as research conducted within specific disciplines.

Between 1975 and 2005, women's and gender studies came into being almost simultaneously in each of, as well as across, the Nordic countries (Norden),[2] and the field was variously established and institutionalised both via the creation of autonomous departments and as subfields of research within established disciplines. This period is also commonly understood as being marked by vast geopolitical changes, most notable through the collapse of the Soviet Union and the fall of the Berlin Wall, but also, and equally importantly for the formation of women's and gender studies as an increasingly transnational field, the expansion of the European Union (EU). It was a time of heated debates about feminism, gender (equality), sexuality, nationalism, migration, neoliberalism, and racism in and across the Nordic region and Europe. The knowledge formation called women's and gender studies reflects these broader concerns, and has been shaped by all these factors. Less an evolutionary narrative of the establishment of a new university discipline, then, this book aims to address the role of geopolitics and location in the production of feminist knowledge, using Nordic and Russian women's and gender studies as our cases.

One way to introduce the reader to the approach we take in this book is with a story about an arrival, namely that of the central concept of *gender*. In the late 1980s, gender as a category of analysis was making its entrance into Nordic women's studies (Hirdman 1988). According to most accounts, gender as a concept/term is not "native" to any Nordic language, but rather "arrived" with theories understood to originate in Anglo-American contexts, that eventually gained salience within welfare state policy about equality between men and women. At that time, Karin Widerberg, Swedish by nationality and a feminist scholar who had been working in Norway for many years, sought to start a discussion not only about the translation of concepts but also about Nordic scholars writing in English. She asked about the consequences of adapting concepts, such as gender, that were already positioned in certain political and theoretical localities (see also Braidotti 2002). At the same time, she was concerned with what happens to "Nordic" research through the use of such concepts and by addressing audiences in

---

[2] Norden includes Norway, Sweden, Denmark, Finland, and Iceland, as well as the self-governing areas Åland (a part of Finland), the Faeroe Islands and Greenland (which is a colony of Denmark), all of which are represented on the Nordic Council and the Nordic Council of Ministers. Norden is to be distinguished from Scandinavia, which consists of the three first mentioned countries. In this book, we use the terms "Norden" and "the Nordic Region" somewhat interchangeably. For a discussion of "Norden" as an imagined community, see for instance Bo Stråth and Øystein Sørensen (1997).

English. Widerberg (1992, 31) claimed that "when we write in English, we 'write ourselves into' a foreign discourse." Using non-native concepts or writing in what was presumed to be a foreign language, according to Widerberg, ran the risk of undermining Nordic specificity and academic self-confidence in a broader field dominated by Anglo-American research.

Widerberg's original article in Swedish, while frequently cited in historiographical accounts of the concept, did not result in much discussion, nor did her translated version of that argument: an article called "Translating Gender" published six years later in NORA, Nordic Journal of Feminist and Gender Research (1998). It could be argued that the lack of debate speaks to a "successful integration" of the concept of gender, perhaps that it was particularly well suited for a region where emphasis was placed on gender equality (Braidotti 2002), or that it found ways to coexist with other key terms for analysis and demarcation of the field itself, such as "woman" or "sex" [kön]. What might be seen as Widerberg's more crucial questions, namely how academic relations of power are maintained through language, how publication language facilitates or prevents the subsequent travel of ideas, how translations bring forth new meaning and how such matters shape belonging in an epistemic community, remain central to feminist practices, theories, and methodologies, including our own. This book is written in English in order to contribute to a broader discussion about what we will here call the geopolitical grammar of women's and gender studies in Nordic women's and gender studies. It carries the vexed dilemmas of "writing ourselves into a foreign discourse" insofar as it is difficult to ascertain what will be familiar and what foreign to our readers. It also critically assesses the meaning of "foreignness," to whom, how and when in terms of the production of knowledge.

For Widerberg, and probably for many of us, concepts and theories are often understood to be intimately tied to geopolitics, that is, they become assigned or are presumed to have national or regional belonging, as do the theorists who coin or use them. We can think only of how a theoretical school called "sexual difference" is sometimes described as "French feminist theory," how "queer theory" is often understood to originate in North America, or how "intersectionality" is understood to originate in US Black feminism. Like many others, Widerberg understands the Nordic region (Norden), to have its own shared genealogy of women's and gender studies, often explained as rooted in empirical facts, such as a shared history, culture, language and similar political systems. While Widerberg's point about language and the translation of concepts is polemical, and importantly draws attention to the geopolitical power relations of knowledge produc-tion, it is also a territorial argument. The extent to which she constructs a joint "we" (one that when written in English writes itself into a foreign dis-course) in an article written in Swedish, omits a range of complexities, such as the fact that, while there may possibly be a joint Scandinavian linguistic "we" – insofar as Norwegian, Danish, and Swedish are relatively similar – joint "Nordic" discussions have never been unified linguistically. Instead, a nor-mative "we" is often constructed, one in which the "native" language is in-evitably "Scandinavian" and in which English is "foreign" to all who inhabit this region. Furthermore, even as she makes her critique of the dominance of Anglo-American theory, Widerberg's Nordic becomes a matter of differ-ence, a non-normative "other" position that emerges primarily in relation to the very same imagined Anglo-American feminist, gender and women's studies community. In other words, the Nordic "we" inevitably emerges relationally and linguistically and thus appears as an investment.

The concern with difference in relation to an Anglo-American "norm" of women's and gender studies is not unique to the Nordic region or to authors such as Widerberg. In the introductory essay for *Thinking Dif-ferently: A Reader in European Women's Studies*, an anthology from 2002 that shows the growing European desire for geopolitical demarcations of the field, editors Gabriele Griffin and Rosi Braidotti situate the urgency of their book with an exercise in assigning territoriality to research(ers). The reader is asked to list "known" feminists who are not American, British, or French. They argue that, while feminists working in different European countries may have received some degree of recognition, "their local success has not received the international resonance it deserves" (Griffin and Brai-dotti 2002, 2). This statement reveals several things. First, it reveals that being "internationally known" drives (or should drive) academic feminism and individual scholars, which tells us something about the motivation and conditions for feminist work at this time. Secondly, it points to the role of language and geopolitics in shaping knowledge production and dissemi-nation, and to how a scholar's work is not understood to be sufficient in being locally relevant, but rather should aim to receive "international" resonance. A large part of the marginalisation of almost all "Europeans" in this logic concerns the very limits of translation to and from English. Brai-dotti (2002, 285) thus insists, "one of the assumptions and starting points for European cooperative work has been the recognition that both the terminology and the bulk of the scholarship in Women's Studies have been generated in English-speaking cultures and traditions." European cohesion in this anthology and a range of other publications is the effect of working across but through difference, a difference that is here constituted linguistically and conceptually in relation to "English-speaking cultures and traditions" (Braidotti 2002, 285). According to this narrative, Braidotti (2002, 285) contends, "Women's Studies as a term is in fact a North American invention; it was quickly and easily adopted by the Anglo-Saxon world because of the strong cultural ties existing between the two geopolitical areas. The North of Europe also followed." Whether this model for organising knowledge is applicable to other parts of Europe is questionable, according to Braidotti. The women's studies model has to do with linguistic, cultural, religious, and national differences – in short, what we would call geopolitical concerns. Somewhat paradoxically however, the very strengthening of regional cohesion through Europeanisation places a growing emphasis on international (most often English) publications.

Why should scholars interested in the history and futurity of a knowledge formation such as women's and gender studies care about these questions? Are we not better served by pursuing empirical work on the questions that feminist and gender research has centred on, namely inequalities on the basis of gender and discrimination of different kinds? In recent years, much theoretical attention has been paid to the politics of location and its significance for feminist space and knowledge production. Increasingly, questions about the implications of language, translation, and situated knowledges have been raised (Knapp 2005; Davis 2014). While these are productive theoretical exercises, hardly any empirical studies have been conducted on the implications of this seemingly taken-for-granted approach. In some ways, the contested question of language could be understood as itself something of a tradition within this field. Indeed, as the epigraph of this introduction suggests, the editorial of the first English-language feminist journal in Norden, *NORA*, described the first large academic interdisciplinary European women's studies conference in terms of language: Is English the feminist language?

In the last decade, it is clear at conferences, in publications, at European and Nordic network gatherings, and even in assessments of scholarly work, that the predominance of English as the *lingua franca* of women's studies and gender research is largely taken for granted, even if it continues to produce inequalities of different kinds. One effect of this emphasis is the rise of critical anthologies and readers such as *Thinking Differently* and journals such as *NORA*, publications that serve to strengthen the hegemony of English as an academic *lingua franca*, no matter how much the articles they contain seek to disrupt this hegemony. Symptomatically, in a recent assessment of high profile centres of gender research in Sweden, the importance of scholarly leaders who speak "with English 'native speaker' fluency" is one of three final comments made, but no longer with any reflection about the implications, translation problems or risks of cultural or intellectual and feminist homogeneity this might cause (Evaluation of "Centres of Gender Excellence" 2011, 37). The fact that such a comment *can* be made is perhaps indicative of the place and politics of women's and gender studies, of the neoliberal state of academia, and of how belonging in the broader imagined communities of knowledge is constituted. English was, and remains, a double-edged sword for some; on the one hand, a tool with which to discuss with a growing international field of women's and gender studies and, on the other, increasingly an expectation of scholars, including the three "non-native" English speaking authors of this book.[3] Grabbing that sword, we offer here our analysis of some of the events and discussions that make up the Nordic tradition of collaboration and contestation, and in effect contrast these with the Russian one, which, as Marianne Liljeström discusses, is shaped by different concerns and different relationships to "Western" knowledge formations. We also comment upon how they become part of constituting geopolitically demarcated knowledge formations.

As already alluded to, the question of language begs another one, namely who belongs in a Nordic, Russian or European "we"? An obvious answer is that such a cohesive "we," to a great extent understood as "different" from a dominant Anglo-American one emerges through translation and in conversation with that very same English-speaking audience. In other words, it is discursively constructed, constituted in knowledge production as a field of power relations. As Liljeström shows in her chapter, in contrast to a Nordic "we," which is often cast as "progressive," Russian feminist research

---

[3] The question of language remains centred on the degree to which "Scandinavian" can be understood to be a "common" language in the region. This is reflected, among other things, in whether or not "Nordic" journals such as *lambda nordica* should permit publications in English, a question first raised in the mid-1990s. It was also a sore point at the Nordic Feminist Forum that gathered tens of thousands of academics, policy makers, activists, and government representatives in Malmö, Sweden in June 2014. The language question has also been frequently debated at the Nordic women's and gender history conferences since the early 2000s. It is telling that, in the 2015 meeting in Stockholm, all plenary sessions were held in English. A more comprehensive study of the language question in and across all Nordic gender research settings remains to be done.

is caught in an East/West, or first and second world logic that is also characterised by a temporal logic which places Russia "behind" the West and with
little consideration of other (internal) differences. In both the Russian and
Nordic cases, the question of what difference is and to whom English is a
"foreign" or "native" discourse is more complex than reducible to national
or regional borders.

The discussion of translation of concepts and the critique of the "hegemony" of Anglo-American concepts that Widerberg was one of the first to
call for and that Braidotti and others have extended and to which we
contribute here, interestingly coincides with the "arrival" of difference in
feminist theorisation in both the Nordic and the Russian setting. As we shall
show in the chapters that follow, this was related both to changing demo-
graphics, to the expansion of the EU and the changing relations between
East and West. At the same time, we will show, the discussion of the origin,
translation and usefulness of concepts coincides with the "arrival" of poststructuralist approaches to gender and power and the very question of who
the subject of women's studies and feminism is. In the Nordic setting,
poststructuralist and deconstructivist approaches are often linked to the
introduction of queer theory and a critique of heteronormativity.[4] Interestingly, this "arrival," which is also related to a renewed discussion about
the meaning of gender tends to flatten out some of the initial critique made
by English-speaking Black feminists, which included a critique of that very
poststructuralism.[5] Embodied to a great extent by the growing centrality of
poststructuralism and its understandings of gender for the social constructivist and Marxist-based traditions in the Nordic Region (Norden), queer
theory is a body of work that also is largely presented as an (Anglo)Ame-
rican "import" (Dahl 2011, see also Mizielińska 2006 and Edenheim 2008).
Curiously, for Widerberg, it is the very question of difference that the term
gender opens up for that turns out to be the "foreign" problem that she does
not wish to address. Reflecting back, she writes:

> So when "we," in the 1980s, were criticised for not highlighting the dif-
> ferences among women, but instead producing an image of women as
> one and the same, we took this to our hearts and bowed our heads in
> shame. If we instead had looked inward and scrutinised our own re-

---

[4] We have deliberately chosen to avoid depicting changes as turns, eager not to reinforce
ideas about rapid, sudden or total changes in theorising.
[5] We thank Liz Kella for this observation.

search, we could have seen that this was simply not true for Scandinavian feminist research. (Widerberg 1998, 135)

As Ulla Manns' chapter in this volume elaborates, the imaginary "we" of the
1980s to which Widerberg refers to both here and in the original 1993
version, is never defined. It is taken for granted, and it implicitly seems to
suggest feminist scholars residing in Norden. Indirectly one learns that it is
a feminist collective that is criticised for not addressing difference. The
critics are not identified, nor the location from which they speak; and since
little discussion about "difference" occurred in the Nordic context at this
time, we might assume that this refers to a broader discussion of difference.
The reader can only infer that such critics are not "here" or part of a "we." It
is a "foreign" critique, that is, one that does not come from within, from
"us." The effect of critique, we learn from Widerberg in retrospect, is not
responsiveness or dialogue, but shame.

As Sara Ahmed (2004) notes, shame is narcissistic. It is an emotion that
turns us inward, returns focus to the self, one that stops flow. "Bowing
heads in shame" is here a powerful and gendered metaphor, for "women"
bowing in shame is recognisable as an act or symbol of subordination –
here, the subordination of a feminist collective. For Widerberg, "looking
inward" is not what stops flow, but rather what finds difference, internally;
"we" would find that difference was already there in "Scandinavian" feminist research. Following Ahmed, we might say that, in this way, shame
can be turned into (regionalist) pride through emphasising difference.
Widerberg insists that *kön* (the Scandinavian term for morphological sex or
sexual differentiation, in Danish *køn* and in Norwegian *kjønn*) already includes the differences that gender is understood to encompass, for instance,
in differences between women's labour or in the differences between urban
and rural living. While such differences could be understood as being significant, this book will show that the construction of a "we" in a Nordic feminist research context in this time period was constituted through recognising some forms of difference and not others, resulting in silence around
and othering of some forms of difference, especially those relating to
sexuality, race and migration, thus erasing that very difference between
women (cf. Mulinari 2001). Differently put, it seems that, in order to emphasise the difference that Nordicness presented, some internal differences
were highlighted and not others.

This discussion of Widerberg's rationale, which we suggest reflects a
broader understanding, is certainly not undertaken in order to engender

shame, nor does it wish to present contemporary women's and gender studies as either the outcome of a loss of a unified subject or the result of progress towards greater complexity (cf. Hemmings 2011). We look inward, but since our respective theoretical and spatiotemporal starting points are different from Widerberg's, the understandings of Nordic and Russian women's and gender studies that we find are different from hers.

Related to the question of translations of concepts, a central question for this knowledge field since the 1980s, and increasingly in the 1990s and early 2000s, has been the subject itself. What and who is the proper subject of women's and gender studies, and how should such a study be institutionalised? On this topic, it would be vastly reductive to diminish the "different" arguments made on behalf of either term simply to national or regional setting and thus produce a shared "context." Indeed, while the field has different names in the different Nordic countries (until quite recently called Women's Studies, naistutkimus, in Finland, Gender Research, genusforskning, in Sweden, kjønns- kjønsforskning, sex/gender research, in Denmark), naming practices also differ across institutions, disciplinary subjects, and theoretical traditions in all national settings. Curiously, however, like the concept of gender, introductions of theories of power related to the history of race and colonialism are often presented as originating elsewhere and arriving later as "foreign" in a historically "homogeneous" Norden, and are then often debated for their "relevance."

These brief examples illuminate how and why this book places the politics of translation, understood as being both linguistic and cultural, at the centre of the making of Nordic and Russian women's and gender studies. In the chapters that follow, we examine how the processes, effects and products of translation become central points of contestation and concern within the simultaneously national, regional and international construction of women's and gender studies, with which scholars in Norden are concerned. Of particular interest in this book is how ideas and theorists are assigned geopolitical belonging, how ideas and scholars migrate, and how they both transcend and reproduce national borders and hierarchies. Specifically, we investigate conceptions and understandings about a specific Nordic and Russian community of women's and gender studies from its emergence in the late 1970s until 2005. Taking into account the current emphasis on internationalisation in academia, we have chosen to examine the construction of Nordic and Russian on two levels: the interaction with other imagined communities, and the interfaces within the Nordic and Russian communities of women's and gender studies. This means, on the one hand, that we carry out three distinct case studies, each of which is informed by our respective routes through, and locations in, this field and, on the other, that we examine and deconstruct the often unproblematised, self-evident conceptions, and comprehensions within a research field under construction. To that end, we pay attention to, and attempt to map, some dimensions of the workings of scientific canonisation and epistemological categorisation: particular understandings of relevant research fields, objects, and analytic categories and how they are formed and legitimised. Conceptions and comprehensions of canonised theory and research practices are primarily studied at a Nordic level on the bases of joint practices of organisations, networks, publications, academic courses and discussions. This is done with a particular focus on texts that declare an explicit emphasis on the Nordic. Since we three authors are all nevertheless situated in the Nordic context, this level of canonisation is put in conversation with Russian gender studies, an academic research field that understands itself as being in the process of becoming and of becoming institutionalised, and to some extent, with Anglo-American women's and gender research, which is often understood as being the internationally most influential body of knowledge.

The context: Studying women's and gender research

Why, then, the starting point on the Nordic region (Norden) aside from it being our own "location" as scholars? Geopolitically, the Nordic countries inhabit an interesting location between the former socialist bloc of Eastern Europe and Russia, and Western Europe and USA. The fall of the Soviet Union and Eastern European communism eliminated one of the crucial touchstones of liberal Western identity. With the growth of the EU, heightened emphasis is instead placed on shared "Europeanness" (Shore 1993; 1995; Borneman and Fowler 1997) on the one hand, and on a strategic strengthening of regions, on the other (Hadjimichalis and Sadler eds. 1995). Following Benedict Anderson (2006), we contend that the boundaries of nation-states or geographic entities, such as the "West," the "East" and "Norden," have always been imaginary. Yet, at the same time, we attend to the material and semiotic effects that these entities have on the field of women's and gender studies. While contemporary media surrounds us with a constant global flow of images and objects that suggests an interconnected world, it also (re)creates and reinforces imaginative and real boundaries. Regional identities are discursively and repeatedly constructed, not least in knowledge production. They form everyday practices that emerge from various similarities and communities.

One intriguing and challenging question is how new circumstances contour contemporary political, social, and cultural life, and remould the dichotomies between East and West, North and South. Another equally intriguing question is how new conditions along with new forms of contacts and communication shape possibilities for transnational discourses and new forms of knowledge production within a certain region. Therefore, we ask how imagined regional identities are constituted by and constitutive of the field of European and Nordic women's and gender studies. How, in this multifaceted period and in the global context of seemingly all-encompassing Anglophone feminist knowledge production, are ideas of the European, the Baltic, the Russian and the Nordic articulated? In the light of the above-mentioned profound changes in the international political setting and climate surrounded by the European integrative processes, the current construction of Nordic commonality, we argue, is particularly interesting. At the same time, our approach to this vast and multilayered question consists of a significant and generally unexamined part of university history, Nordic women's and gender studies 1975 to 2005.

As a geopolitical setting, Norden forms both an imagined and a politico-administrative community of nations whose similarities are often comprehended as self-evident on the basis of historical, geographical, cultural, political, and religious proximity. This understanding prevails, despite differences such as language, large geographical distances, different experiences of World War II and questions about the historical and contemporary place of the indigenous Sami whose territory, Sápmi, spans the north of Norway, Sweden, Finland and Russia. In other words, Norden, like all regional and collective identities, is constructed at, and is the effect of, certain historical conjunctures and for specific aims (Stråth and Sørensen 1997; Aronsson and Gradén 2012). The conception of a united Scandinavia (that is Norway, Denmark and Sweden) emerged within student and artist milieus in the 1830s and to this day, this idea and its proponents rarely address the question of rule or "colonisation" on the part of any of the Scandinavian nations (including that of neighbouring lands). The interest in a particular Nordic past and the restoration of such a shared identity on the spiritual level was followed by political engagement, where political utopias were replaced by pragmatic cooperation. In the early 20th century, Nordic cooperation was built on the notion of complete national sovereignty, but the national state projects were ascribed "typical" Nordic characteristics

(Frykman and Löfgren 1987; Rosenbeck 1998; 2000; Hillström and Sanders 2014). In addition to being nations whose self-image includes the legacy of a strong Lutheran state church, the Nordic states are considered to have gone through a more harmonious process of modernisation resulting in strong welfare states. Much Nordic cooperation is based on these characteristics being understood as good criteria for collaboration. Today, we might say that cooperation has two principal directions: the generation of collaborative activities within national organs, and the foundation of Nordic organisations (*Den jyske historiker* 1994; Markkola 2001).

Alastair Thomas (1996) contends that the very concept of Norden has been crucial for Nordic cooperation. The Nordic Council is the body that has largely been responsible for shaping and producing the idea of a common Nordic identity since 1945. A Nordic identity has grown through inter-regional trade and migration, as well as through efforts to harmonise domestic legislation. According to Thomas (1996, 17), it is largely based on "extensive inter-Nordic cooperation and interchange of scientific, academic and cultural activity", as well as joint efforts around education (Thomas 1996, 25).

Given this history, it is perhaps not surprising that, since the mid-1970s, feminist scholars have found the idea of a Nordic community with shared features and problems, and differing research perspectives to be fruitful and interesting. Since both the women's movement and politicians by then had a profound tradition of cooperation on a Nordic level, working together with academic feminists in the Nordic countries did not seem to cause much of a problem for central actors in the early days of women's studies. As Manns discusses later in this volume, scholars soon began meeting both in multidisciplinary seminars and conferences, and within different disciplines. For instance, regular Nordic meetings were started in the early 1980s for scholars of women's history, women's literature, political science, and sociology. Academic journals (mainly *Kvinnovetenskaplig tidskrift* 1980–2007)[6] covering the Nordic research field were initiated. Several joint events are often emphasised as having been important for the organisation of women's studies and women scholars in the Nordic region at the time; these include the Nordic Summer University, which started in 1973, the founding of the Nordic Forum for Women's Studies, the 1983 Nordic Women's Studies Seminar, and the 1988 Nordic Forum (Rosenbeck 1998; 2000; Halsaa

---

[6] *Kvinnovetenskaplig tidskrift* [Women's Studies Journal] changed into *Tidskrift för genusvetenskap* [Journal for Gender Studies] in 2007.

2004; Manns 2009). In the 1990s and early 2000s, this collaboration is extended with the founding of NIKK: Nordic Institute for Gender Research, the founding of the Nordic Journal *NORA*, and, starting in 1991, the biannual conferences defined as both Nordic and European.

Women's and gender studies as an academic discipline, and the women's and feminist movements, are examples of the principal cooperation that Thomas describes. National and joint Nordic investments have above all been formulated as part of promoting gender equality (Rosenbeck 1998; Halsaa 2004; Liljeström 2009). This promotion and its achievements are constructed as a "typical" Nordic discourse and concern, thereby drawing distinctions between Norden and other European regions. The overall broad and active cooperation requires that it is the objective of ongoing motivation and encouragement, where the shared "Nordic elements" become reconstructed. Within this process, the comprehension of Norden and the Nordic is both confirmed and changed. Bearing in mind that Nordic women's and gender research has gained international attention in the 1990s, particularly attention which focuses on equality in politics and the labour force (Bergman 2000a; Bjerrum Nielsen 2000), our research goes beyond examining the translation of ideas and practices of equality into English. We instead examine the traffic of ideas and ideals within Nordic women's and gender research over time. We pay attention to what is meant by "Anglo-American" in arguments about the dominance of these ideas. We look into which particular theoretical and epistemological trajectories and authors have come to be assigned the category "Anglo-American," when and where. Liljeström's chapter on Russia provides an additional perspective on how such territorialised and widely circulated ideas are translated and disseminated. In addition, we ask how the making of European women's and gender studies has reconfigured understandings of power and language during the consolidation of the field. We ask how the broad international changes have affected ideas of a Nordic imagined community of researchers, as well as theoretical and methodological concerns. Stressing contacts and research exchange with Eastern Europe, and how the Eastern European is constituted in relation to the Nordic and the European, we highlight and analyse unexamined ideas of both Norden and Nordic women's and gender research, as well as the making of a feminist scholarly space within the Nordic feminist community.

On location: Previous research and the idea of studying women's and gender research

The primary aim of this book is not to offer a detailed chronological account of women's and gender studies as a discipline in various university settings, or at national and regional levels, but to examine the formation of women's and gender studies as a field of knowledge production. Four decades after the first informal groups of feminist researchers were formed at many of the universities in the Nordic region, women's and gender studies has become an established field of research and study in Norden. In terms of research, it has its own national, regional and international refereed journals and conferences, its own tenured positions and professors, its own Centres of National and European Excellence and a vast number of large research projects, with national, Nordic and/or EU funding. It is possible not only to gain an undergraduate degree, but also to pursue a doctorate within this field. In addition, if one of the most significant institution-building practices within any academic field is the establishment of a "canon," a particular set of texts which are understood to be shared by those in the field and with which one is expected to engage, women's and gender studies is no exception – despite its own engagement in critiquing *other* canons. As Katie King (1994) has rightfully noted, while a considerable amount of theory and knowledge is produced in classrooms and conversations, and perhaps particularly within critical research fields with strong relations to social movements and change, it is not until an idea or research finding is published and can be "cited" that it "counts." Thus, debates about the locations and languages of publication, as well as about circulation and citing, tend to be affective and engaged. They provide insightful opportunities to study the stakes and understandings of location. Indeed, in the introduction to the aforementioned anthology *Thinking Differently,* editors Griffin and Braidotti (2002) dedicate considerable discussion to the Anglo-Americanisation of the canon of European gender studies. They argue for an expansion of this canon to include more "European" scholars who, they contend, will contribute to a canon based on difference. At the same time, this canon is largely oriented around the concepts of sex and gender, how and when they are used and to what ends.

Along with the growing production of research, all of which engage in the practice of both citing and critiquing a canon, recent years have witnessed a growing interest in introspection into the field itself and into its historiography. Indeed, as the field continues to professionalise and institutionalise, a growing body of work is now committed to reflecting on historical and epistemological changes. Such studies and debates about "what happened" and which reflect on and analyse changing institutional, political, methodological, and theoretical changes are, we contend, a central part of both establishing, recognising, and legitimising women's and gender studies as a field in its own right. One obvious effect of the expansion of the field is that there are multiple versions and interpretations of the emergence of the field. As far as we see it, they continue to be both highly glocalised and contested.

This book on Nordic, European and Russian women's and gender studies is part of the contemporary trend of "introspection" and "remapping" (see also Christensen et al. eds. 2004). As stressed above, it aims to contribute to this research, specifically by attending to and examining some of the unmarked categories on which such analyses often rely. It seems to us that the geopolitical organisation of studies of "the field itself" reflects a few overarching methodological and epistemological tendencies that are worth pointing out as a way of situating our study. One immediate observation is that few analyses of the field are all-encompassing, in part because of varying understandings of the boundaries of an inherently interdisciplinary field, that is, what should be included in this field and on what grounds. There is a tendency, which to some extent we share, to base arguments on what we might call "exceptional examples" that are inevitably chosen for the purpose of highlighting a particular argument or critique. In the case of frequently cited works, this means that what might be specifically national or even local debates are read as general trends. While there are obviously shortcomings and limitations to the analyses we offer, one point of departure for us is that many works that aim to outline major theoretical developments seem to address the implications of a politics of location, but at the same time to obfuscate institutional specificities, including questions of translation, circulation, and the material and institutional conditions under which knowledge is produced. In particular, works that are produced within an "Anglo-American" framework tend (perhaps unintentionally) to speak for the development of feminist theory "as a whole," leaving the reader with an impression of a de-territorialised field of knowledge, a kind of imagined hyper-real community that is rhetorically shaped by the narrator's location. Another tendency in narratives about the history of the field is to take the nation as an unexamined unit of analysis (and comparable "difference") for granted.

Within the growing body of work on the Nordic and European field, we identify some overarching trends, at least in the moment of completing this book. First of all, there are plenty of shorter overviews and introductions to the field, some of which partly rely on primary sources. There are also a number of overviews and reports written by researchers and bureaucrats at Nordic and national coordinating institutions.[7] These provide an important background and complement to this book. A second dominant trend might be called "autobiographical" and consists of "pioneers" of the field "telling their stories" of professional coming of age.[8] These capstone works tend to centre on the personal and collective struggle and strife in male-dominated and hostile, misogynist academic environments. They also tend to focus on how the early days were characterised by an encompassing feeling of unity and joy that is often set in contrast to contemporary gender studies, which is depicted as more conflict-ridden, fragmented and less political. These memoirs offer interesting personal accounts and vivid description, but rarely deliver comprehensive analyses about the development of the field itself, nor do they reflect in any comprehensive way on the geopolitical politics of the authors' location.[9] Furthermore, they usually discuss the rise of and changes within the field without relating these to larger and changing trends within academia and society.

A third broader trend in the production of knowledge about the field of women's and gender studies focuses on theoretical and political changes in the field itself (for example Dahlerup 1998; Bergman 2002; Halsaa 2002; 2004; 2006; Honkanen 2004; Nordenstam 2005; Alnebratt 2009; Haavet 2009; Lindén 2012; Blažević 2015 Rosenbeck 2014). This growing body of work is interestingly situated, insofar as it in various ways is both a part of and critically reflects on the field itself. Attending to the particular ways that these stories are narrated and structured tells us something about the complex interaction between institutionalisation, professionalisation, and continued politicisation that will be discussed in this book.

---

[7] Some examples are Göransson (1987; 1989), *Kvinnovetenskaplig tidskrift* (1989), Bergman ed. (2000), Rosenbeck (1998), and Thurén (2002; 2003).

[8] Examples of this trend include the Norwegian journal *Kvinneforskning*'s special issue "My Way to Women's Studies" (1999), and publications such as Lützen and Nielsen eds. (2008) (which includes a longer interview with Bente Rosenbeck), Florin och Niskanen (2010) about women's studies pioneers, Hirdman (2007), and Witt-Brattström (2010).

[9] An interesting exception to this is the Norwegian historian Gro Hagemann's book *Feminisme og historieskrivning: Inntrykk fra en reise* (2003). She departs from the metaphor of a journey to reflect upon her own as well as the fields' transformation over the years.

A fourth and related broader strand of scholarship consists of doctoral dissertations in gender studies dedicated to the relationship between knowledge production, activism, and institutionalisation (van der Tuin 2008; Liinason 2011; Pereira 2011). The fact that it is possible to conduct doctoral research *on* the field of gender research itself shows how established this field has become. If we were to generalise, these doctoral studies tend to pivot around questions of whether or not the field itself has "lost its edge" (Scott ed. 2008), has got caught up in or become complicit with institutionalisation (Brown 2002; Wiegman 2008), questions concerning the "proper" objects and subjects of feminist theory (Wiegman 2012), and how stories about the field are narrated (Hemmings 2011).

Needless to say, these and other recent works also do other things that fall outside of this schematic presentation. It is almost impossible to do justice to the last decade's growing production of (post)disciplinary introspection and critical historicisation. What appeared to be an unmapped terrain when this project started almost ten years ago – the virtually unwritten story of where we have been and the intimations of directions to come – has quickly and increasingly become a matter of methodological, political and theoretical discussion, the subject of thematic issues of journals and editorials, and a debate that often reflects the work that the grammars of storytelling and the politics of narrative and citation practices do. Consequently, our book claims to be neither a completely original discovery nor a comprehensive account of the unfolding of a field. Instead, this book offers a considered geopolitical and historical analysis of the making of "the Nordic" within women's and gender research and of "Russian" gender studies, as well as of an analysis of the importance and implications of these developments. This book and our respective contributions pay loose attention to how geopolitical categories, in particular the category Norden, or the Nordic, are used within narratives of the field's development and constitution; narratives that in our view construct both space and temporality. While previous studies offer important insights into the nature of women's and gender research from different perspectives and time periods, thus far no extensive empirical studies have focused on the construction of Norden and the Nordic. In pursuing this angle, our approach both analyses and builds on all these broader trends, especially the last mentioned above.

Authors and readers

Our approach to previous research brings us back to the question of the situatedness of researchers and readers. Through the long course of working on this book, we have often discussed and imagined whom this book addresses and what kinds of reactions it might engender. Given the many years we have worked on this project and the growing number of scholarly works on this topic, this has changed over time. Taking into account the emphasis on the readers, we have inevitably had to contemplate both what it means to analyse timelines, circumstances and changes, and what we ourselves have influenced and been influenced by, and certainly what types of processes we have been – and still are – participating in. In anthropological terms, we are certainly studying "our own culture," a field to which all three of us belong. Our readers, whom we identify broadly as scholars and students interested in the geopolitics of feminist knowledge production, have also been dialogue partners, draft readers, and conference commentators along the way. The comments offered to us have also reminded us of how imagining an audience can stop a line of thought, a flow of thinking and make one unsure of whether one's bases are covered. As Clare Hemmings (2011, 191) notes, reader recognition is "saturated with affect." Partly we might argue that this is because, as Helene Cixous (1986, 148) once wrote, "one never reads except by identification." Feminist knowledge formations merge around affective readings of the past and present in which the individual feminist scholar always seems to be the central node. The power relations that continue to structure our research field, often coalescing around various understandings of belonging, resource distribution and circulation, are perhaps particularly rampant in a community that is both critical of inequalities and yet, due to its complicity within already hierarchical academic knowledge practices, cannot escape them (cf. McDermott 1994). In the field of critical knowledge, there is generally a strong tendency to consider critical reading as looking for absences, thin ground, or exceptions. Objections are not objectionable objects in themselves; indeed, identifying gaps and absences is a central driving motivation for funding and publishing new work. However, in scrutinising the feminist "we" of the 1970s and 1980s, investigating the geopolitical grammar of women's and gender studies in the 1990s, and challenging the taken-for-granted temporalities and directionalities of translation, we are aware that there are stories that challenge and supplement the arguments presented here.

Behind our particular research interests, there are always one or several stories of arrival at the place or topic (Ahmed 2012). Accounts of arrivals, Ahmed notes, often involve memories, incidents that have affected us, oriented us in particular directions and have made us ask some questions, and not others. Arrivals are, therefore, never just anywhere, rather they are at a particular place from which some bodies of flesh and knowledge might appear more than others. Arriving somewhere can also result in a dwelling there and yet our dwellings "here" in a research material that is also a home, inside rather than outside, are situated and partial ones (Haraway 1991). To that end, it matters to our respective approaches and academic styles. Manns, a gender historian trained in the history of ideas, was raised as a feminist activist by and in the budding Swedish and Nordic women's and gender scholar community in the 1980s. Thus, she "arrived" to the women's studies context as an undergraduate. Not having the opportunity to take any proper courses in women's or gender studies, but being part of a living, dynamic and sometimes antagonistic interdisciplinary network of feminist activist scholars was Manns' formative context. Her research circumstances and experiences over the years have confronted her with a range of questions concerning the construction of feminist space, its internal and implicit borders. Ulrika Dahl, who pursued her studies in the United States, took a dual PhD degree in anthropology and women's studies in the early 2000s. Thus, Dahl "arrived" in Nordic feminism and research at the end of the moment she investigates here (see also Dahl 2014; 2015). This project has offered her an opportunity to study a "recent" past she did not learn much about during her training in the USA. If, in the Nordic context, difference has often been cast as a more recent "arrival," in Dahl's training, it was central to feminism and gender studies. Liljeström obtained her scholarly training in history both in the Soviet Union and Finland at a time when feminist research was beginning. Since the mid-1990s, she has been an important part in the shaping of the formation of academic feminism in Finland as well as in the Nordic region, not least in gender history.

Building on and bringing together our different backgrounds and time-lines, this book proposes a shift of focus towards an analysis of feminist space and of intellectual and cultural kinship, as a way of approaching the formation of women' s and gender studies. In a way, we might say that we all have been guided by Hemmings' thought-provoking questions:

> But what if we do not "all know" the same things about what has happened in Western feminist theory's recent past; what if we were to

understand the "we" as inaugurated by rather than inaugurating this repeated certainty? (Hemmings 2011, 32)

A geopolitical grammar

To address bodies of knowledge in *geopolitical* terms is in this book a matter of invoking a concept that since the early 20th century has been used to address "actual distribution in space or with the actual interplay between people and space" (von Kohl *in* Lemke 2011, 13). It is also about the spatialisation of knowledge, something that of course is not unique to the field in question. Rather, while research networks and projects are encouraged to be "international," universities, and the bodies of flesh and knowledge that they produce and are produced by, are almost always taken for granted as symbols of both national pride and interest. A concern with geopolitics is, in this book, a way to consider women's and gender studies as fields of knowledge in ways that are not only genealogised and generative, but also spatialised and distributed. Here the geopolitical approach thus has a double implication – it means exploring *how* epistemic communities, variously called women's/gender/feminist studies or research, are constituted both in terms of *which* bodies are understood to belong to the larger body of knowledge (that is, how some bodies, and not others, are understood to geopolitically belong), and more importantly, *how* such an understanding of belonging is itself the effect of proximity and/or geographic, linguistic, and cultural distance (Ahmed 2000; Yuval-Davis 2011). In so doing, we depart from a wish to take seriously what happens when we insist on a broader idea that these communities are "projects of becoming, in process" (Griffin and Braidotti 2002, 27). Following Hemmings (2011), we wish to contribute to re-orienting the ways we map feminist knowledge-making. If constructedness is central to discussions about geopolitical and epistemological "we-ness," if "change" and proximity are key concepts with which communities are imagined, we ask: How are such changes understood and narrated? Who or what is presumed to undergo changes, and in what ways?

If women's and gender studies can be described as an epistemic community, that is, as "a network of professionals with recognised expertise and competence in a particular domain and an authoritative claim to policy relevant knowledge within that domain or issue-area" (Haas 1992, 3), then what does a focus on geopolitics offer? As many of those who teach introductory courses in feminist or gender studies know, a common method is to discuss the relationship between ideology, knowledge, and politics in terms of what it teaches us about gender and power (Wahl 1996). In introducing theoretical frameworks, we often discuss the context in which particular projects have emerged. This is because women's and gender studies are commonly described as both the effect of, and in dialogue with, feminist movements. With Millie Thayer's (2010, 204) formulation, social movements, including feminist ones, can be understood as bundles of relationships, constituted by relations with interlocutors such as academic institutions, politicians, policy makers, funding bodies and so on. In studies of the founding of Nordic women's and gender studies, what is often highlighted is indeed the close collaboration with state agents (Rosenbeck 1998; 2014; Alnebratt 2009; Liinason 2011).

As an epistemic community entangled with social movements, women's and gender studies has long understood itself to operate within both national and international structures. At the same time, in recent years, there has been a shift towards thinking in terms of transnational movements of ideas and bodies. But what remains, and what gets lost in translation? In different ways, we argue that it is precisely in its already discursive and institutional formation as an epistemic community, and through a *specific* bundle of relationships, that women's and gender studies reproduces ideas of representable, comparable national and regional differences that manifest in bodies of both flesh and knowledge (Sullivan 2006).

Hemmings (2011) offers a model for investigating stories of the recent past of feminist theory, that she calls the political grammar of feminist theory. This work has in different ways inspired all three of us. Bringing together *stories* or what Hemmings (2011, 227) calls "the overall tales feminists tell about what has happened," *narratives* and *grammar* "serve as narrative building blocks." This political grammar of feminist storytelling is "the stitching together of all these levels as well as the broader political life of these stories" (Hemmings 2011, 227). In a similar vein, this book's empirical materials include stories of the development of Nordic/European/Russian women's and gender studies. In various ways, we study patterns in how such stories are told (an emphasis on cooperation as tradition, for instance) and place a great deal of emphasis on grammar (the national as a comparable unit of difference and similarity, for instance). As Dahl shows in her chapter, taken together, this epistemological approach shows how both ideas and bodies are assigned *geopolitical* belonging; they are assigned degrees of "foreignness" depending on when they are thought to arrive in the Nordic region. Furthermore, Dahl argues that the Nordic imaginary itself is an effect of this geopolitical grammar.

While Hemmings clearly states that she sets out to analyse "Western" feminist theory, her own very illuminating account of competing versions of "our" recent past, as often cast in terms of either progress, loss or return in relation to an imagined original moment of inception, can be read as rather de-territorialised and, thus, by extension as a universal story. This opens up many possibilities of disidentification and critique, particularly for those who do not claim to belong in an imagined "Anglo-American" formation of women's and gender studies that is outlined in her account. At the same time, as Liljeström's chapter shows and as Allaine Cerwonka (2008) has argued with regards to Central and Eastern European feminist critiques of Western feminist theory, there is a tendency to critique this admittedly dominant discourse on the basis of being "located in another part of the world." Cerwonka (2008, 822) reminds us that the "critique of Western universalism is part of the larger (transnational) critical discourse about liberal feminist thought currently at the very centre of women's and gender studies." In this book, our work is motivated by a similar wish to challenge the idea of, as Cerwonka (2008, 825) writes "understanding the relationship of feminist ideas through a framework of difference and geographical separateness". Like Cerwonka, we are sympathetic to the idea of considering knowledge formations in terms of what Mary Louise Pratt (quoted in Cerwonka 2008, 825) describes as "co-presence, interaction, interlocking understandings and practices, often within radically asymmetrical relations of power." In the context of Nordic, European and Russian women's and gender studies, such asymmetrical relations of power are not always reducible to national or regional differences, but rather to the uneven distribution of resources and power across different networks and institutions. As Hemmings' (2011) convincingly argues, how feminists tell stories of our recent (theoretical) past matters for how we orient ourselves and are oriented by them. It seems to us that we must pay attention to the geopolitical grammar of women's and gender studies if we are to understand both the past, contemporary effects, and future orientations of the stories we read here.

Organisation of the book

In the first chapter of this book, "Re-Mapping the '1980s': Feminist Nordic Space," Ulla Manns analyses the construction of women's studies and feminist academic space in the Nordic region during its first dynamic years of establishment, approximately 1975 to 1990. During these years, national and regional cooperation was extensive. Women's studies drew heavily on ideas from and experiences of the so-called new women's movement. The new women's movement in the Nordic countries was to a high degree influenced by socialist ideas and ways of organisation (Eyerman and Jamison 1991; Dahlerup 1998; Rosenbeck 1998; Halsaa 2004). The early women's studies scholarly networks and organisations continued working along much the same lines, with open forums and flat organisations intended not only for scholars but for all (women) who were interested in networks, open seminars and reading groups (Manns 2009). The early years of women's studies are primarily analysed in relation to contemporary developments within academia, to social movements, to "politics of belonging" (Yuval-Davis 2011) and to state politics in the field of gender equality and higher education. Stressing the spatiotemporal dimensions of knowledge production, Manns' study explores how the core field of women's studies was constructed on its Nordic level of cooperation, and how it was described and explicated over time. Tracing the traffic in feminist ideas, her study examines how theories, methods, and approaches were picked up and emphasised. The influences and interactions of several milieus is important here; they include political movements, other contemporary critical research fields, and ongoing national and Nordic state policies concerning gender equality in higher education and research, and in society at large. Lastly, the study analyses how feminist scholars defined and constructed a distinctly Nordic field of women's studies. Special attention is paid to how and to what extent ideas and conceptions of Norden and the Nordic are problematised and scrutinised over the years. Because of the close ties to the women's movement of the time, a prior feminist tradition of cooperation and joint events seems to have been followed almost without hesitation. As argued in Manns' chapter, the unreflected notion of a joint Nordic women's studies "we" and the everyday making of that collective identity, created a certain feminist space in academia. However, several factors contributed to circumstances, which hindered the public performance of internal critique in these years.

In the chapter "Between Familiar Differences and American tunes: The Geopolitical Grammar of Nordic Gender Studies in an Age of Europeanisation (1990–2005)", Ulrika Dahl investigates the work that a geopolitical grammar does in women's and gender studies. In particular, she examines how the meaning of the Nordic, as well as the content and shape of Nordic women's and gender studies, are constructed in relation to an emerging and proliferating European women's and gender studies. Expanding on Hemmings, she attends to how "difference" is understood and discussed, and to how it takes shape in geopolitically demarcated knowledge projects as part of a storytelling grammar. The argument that there *is* something different about both the Nordic and the European, and that this difference in many ways is a geopolitical and linguistic difference (a difference from "Anglo-America"), has been postulated and critiqued again and again in the past two decades, paradoxically enough, often in English. Yet, what this difference is, why this matters and to whom, has been much less clear as both ideas and subjects are assigned geopolitical belonging. By looking at a couple of key constitutive moments, Dahl discusses how a specific form of "Nordic" cohesion is constituted through particular institutions and knowledge-making practices. What does "creating a strong Nordic community in a strong Europe" mean for an imagined community of feminist and gender researchers? In what worlds is the Nordic "different," and in relation to what? What is the "consensus" about "different European cultures"; what makes it deviate from the norm of the "American-based model," and why does this matter?

Marianne Liljeström's chapter "Constructing the West/Nordic: The Rise of Gender Studies in Russia," analyses the lively and innovative discussions about the perspectives of feminist scholarship and gender studies in Russia. Particular focus is on the adaptation of a "Western" apparatus of gender terminology. Liljeström examines how, in the Russian discussions and statements, Western/Nordic feminism is constructed from a variety of perspectives, rarely however, as a homogeneous and evolutionary concept based on some self-evident, consensual, taken-for-granted understandings of the content and stages of its development. In her view, the presumed dichotomy between East and West, though routinely mentioned, forms a point of departure for many accounts of the state of gender studies in Russia. In order to create national differences and features of national specificity, the West/Nordic becomes a monolithic entity in these accounts. Basing her analysis on a variety of feminist publications, conference proceedings, and journals published in Russia, Liljeström discusses how meanings of theories and concepts change and become displaced. This analysis emphasises the interconnectedness of "international" and national elements in the production of feminist meaning and knowledge.

Re-Mapping the "1980s": Feminist Nordic Space

Ulla Manns

When we talk about the past, we tend to structure and narrate according to decades, even though historical change rarely follows this format. Recent feminist historiography is no exception. It is often structured in precisely this manner, even though theoretical trends and empirical interests have emerged and developed irregularly, in fits and starts that sometimes overlap and sometimes occur simultaneously (Hemmings 2011). In this chapter, "the 1980s" refers to a conceptualisation of the time period between approximately 1975 and the early 1990s. The 1980s thus names a fifteen- to eighteen-year time period when women's studies and feminist research started to gain a foothold in, and to consolidate within, universities throughout the Nordic countries. Women's studies groups in academia and seminars started in large numbers and were most often organised locally. These groups generally expressed a strong and explicit affinity to different sorts of women's movement groups. As a result of the diversity of these liaisons and affinities, differences emerged in the organisation and research focus of the milieus of women's studies. As this predominantly new research field developed throughout Norden, the 1980s became a period heavily dominated by mobilisation. Scholars, students, supportive administration staff within the universities as well as allies outside of the academic world got together and organised in order to gain recognition for new research topics. As a consequence, a new kind of research area gradually gained legitimacy: the study of women.

This chapter is devoted to this intense time period, when women's studies entered academia as a loosely organised and not yet institutionalised field of research. The focus here is on the particular feminist space that Nordic collaboration among women's studies researchers generated. National specificities or differences between the Nordic countries will not be elaborated further.[1] From the point of view of university history, it is fascinating to see how quickly Nordic collaboration in women's studies research was initiated and how many areas of research were covered. What was the basis for feminist scholarly mobilisation within the Nordic realm? Why was Nordic collaboration chosen instead of other collaborations across borders? And, not least, how was the concept of Norden and Nordic commonality perceived? Finally, what particular effect did Nordic mobilisation have for the feminist space that took shape within women's studies?[2]

Women's studies scholars claimed the right to be acknowledged as a proper field of research, and joined the choir of other interdisciplinary researchers in a critique of positivism. As in other regions and countries, women's studies in Norden was explicit about its close affiliation to women's liberation and, therefore, presented itself as being part of the contemporary women's movement, aiming for social change and justice. As eloquently put by Robyn Wiegman:

> Academic feminism is constructed as much by the institutional organizations of knowledge as by the political demands that feminism has brought to them. (Wiegman 2010, 80)

Institutional organisations of power and feminist demands thus shaped academic feminism, but in order to understand the specific content of feminist space in Norden, it is necessary to consider a third factor: contemporary national and Nordic policies of gender equality. State policy in the Nordic countries showed great interest in issues of gender equality.[3] Early on, women's studies was given state financial and political support, because of its potential to improve gender equality in society. The Nordic Council of

[1] As in the entire book, this chapter differentiates between Scandinavia (Denmark, Norway and Sweden) and Norden (which also includes Iceland, Finland and the autonomous territories of the Faroe Islands, Greenland and the Åland Islands). Sapmí, the transnational Sami region that cuts across Norway, Finland and Sweden, usually remains invisible in presentations of Norden. Norden comprises a wider geopolitical and linguistic area than Scandinavia. For a more empirically detailed version of the analysis presented in this chapter, see Manns (2009).
[2] In this study, women's and gender studies refer to research performed both within women's and gender studies as an autonomous discipline and within other academic disciplines.
[3] Instead of "gender equality issue," the term commonly used at the time was equal opportunity or equal status issues, sometimes simply equality issues (referring specifically to equality between women and men).

Ministers, with representatives from all of the Nordic countries, played a major role in this respect. Since academia at large dismissed the critical and interdisciplinary research that women's studies represented, the field became heavily dependent on external support. The state-funded support, earmarked for women's studies, definitely helped to legitimise the new field of research, and in turn made possible regional research projects, conferences, and networks. This distinguished development in Norden, differed from many other places, not least the USA. At the same time, the support governed the type of research questions that could be explored (Halsaa 1996; 2004; 2006; Rosenbeck 1998; 2014; Bergman 2000a; Liinason 2011).

Early on, women's studies scholars chose to cooperate on a Nordic level, suggesting that such cooperation was deemed a strategic way to organise.[4] How are we to understand Nordic commonality within women's studies during this particular time period? How were Norden and the Nordic thought of and discussed in this newly organised community? What kind of collective identity came into being due to this particular way of mobilising, that is, in its specific geopolitical, historic, and cultural location? To use a 1980s formulation by Sandra Harding (1986), the "science question in feminism" had to be dealt with within the field of research, and it certainly had consequences for how and which feminist questions were made proper objects of study. How feminist analysis of women's oppression and women's conditions were translated into an academic setting affected who was considered a proper subject of knowledge as well as what was considered a proper object of research. In Norden, as elsewhere, the subjects and objects of feminism in academic research were not discussed out of their geopolitical context.

I argue that the translation of feminism from the context of the women's movement into the context of academia had a major impact on the particular kind of feminist space that gradually took shape within women's studies in its joint Nordic setting. My intention is to perform a critical reading of this context during the expansive and mobilising years up until the early 1990s, with the purpose to both understand and critically examine how a specific feminist space took shape within the women's studies community, during a time period when feminism was clearly felt to be "a living thing" (Wiegman 2010). Particular attention is paid to the effects of the

---

[4] Finland joined some years later, see Bergman (2000a) and *Women's Studies and Gender Research in Finland* (2002, 10).

35

close, even foundational, ties to the women's movement and to the early support given by state policies. The many political efforts to solve questions concerning social injustices and the subordination of women were extended to the realms of the universities when feminists from different backgrounds claimed the right to research and seek knowledge about women's lives and experiences. This project had to adjust to the new knowledge-producing context and the institutional framework of academia. I read this movement as a translation, a cultural translation from a local and in many ways historically familiar setting of the women's movement, into a new setting of the hitherto male-dominated academy. This chapter, then, historically and critically contextualises the travelling of theories and concepts in order to more fully grasp, re-map and, to cite Eva Bahovec and Clare Hemmings (2004, 336), analyse how and what "existing hierarchies are reproduced or challenged in particular conceptual travels" (see also Cerwonka 2008 and Davis 2014). This is done with particular regard to the cultural translation and travelling of concepts from a movement-based setting outside academia into a new setting within the academic community.

Furthermore, this chapter pays attention to the politics of belonging within a Nordic feminist space. Space is a concept with wide and somewhat various uses. In this study, space is analysed as a feminist scholarly community, an intellectual, political, and emotional community. Nordic feminist space is analysed as something partly real, partly imagined, as a context and a community of people who were working collectively for certain, but not always entirely shared or even specified, goals. How the collective knowledge-seeking of feminists outside academia was made possible within the new context of the university can be read as a cultural translation. Following Bahovec and Hemmings, I see this translation (of feminism into an academic, yet political setting) as a complex process that affects space – that shapes its borders, fills it with meaning, stretches it – but that, vice versa, is also affected by existing and experienced space, which sets the conditions for the translations that were made. When concepts and collective actions are set in a new context they change, they are transformed. Sometimes they are even abandoned and left aside. These processes have effects on the new milieu, the feminist space in which women's studies scholars act, think, and live (Bahovec and Hemmings 2004, 334). Expanding on Benedict Anderson's (2006) understanding of the nation, I consider space as grounded in implicit ideas of familiarity. According to Anderson, (national) space is to a large extent imaginary, not least because the members of the community are not likely to ever know or meet all their fellow-members. Despite this, "in the minds of each lives the image of their communion" (Anderson 2006, 6). Sara Ahmed (2004, 1) formulates the key issue about familiarity and familiar narratives in social discourses: precisely because of their familiarity, they need close and careful reading (see also Ahmed 2006). Space is thus analysed as something real and imagined, familiar and peculiar. In its specific social movement context, it is already filled with ideals, emotions about, and feelings of, belonging. In the case of women's studies, it is loaded with political and feminist investments, dreams, and visions (Wiegman 2010; Hemmings 2011).

During the 1980s, the close relation between academic feminism and the women's movement was repeatedly stressed in several ways. Women's studies was conceptualised as an integral part of the women's movement; research was inspired by feminist politics, and women's studies was often viewed as belonging to a particular stream of the women's movement (the new leftist part).[5] Visions were often far-reaching, but not always fully elaborated, neither in texts, nor in discussions. The dream of a profound change in society was nevertheless stressed – an equal and non-repressive world for all women. Women's studies were to offer a corrective to male-based knowledge production; it was to bring about an epistemic paradigm shift, to establish a new and critical field of research, as well as to integrate women's studies into already existing scholarship (Manns 2006; 2009). Because of these far-reaching and grand ambitions, as well as the collective character of women's studies, the visions as well as emotional and political investments made by scholarly activists differed. The feminist space was, therefore, on one side a shared space, a women's studies collective, and on the other side, it was experienced as a space with limits and hidden norms. In women's studies as elsewhere a centre and a periphery existed. As Ahmed (2007; 2011), among others, has argued, the limits of a shared space within social movements can be brutally manifest when unexpected things happen: when disorientation occurs, for example, on the basis of disagreement, or when certain (read non-white) bodies arrive, that is enter space and cause disturbance. Space is shaped by the very bodies inhabiting it and their (re)actions and orientations. In addition, we are shaped by the different spaces we inhabit, try to enter, and exist in. We might not always be aware of the particular content or exact borders of space when feeling at

---

[5] Bryld and Lykke (1985), *Kvindeforskning i Danmark* (1978), Davis et al. (1980), Westman Berg ed. (1979), *Nytt om kvinneforskning* (1980), are but some examples.

ease. However, as Ahmed (2011, 152; 2007, see also 2004) writes, we certainly become aware of borders and internal orders when we experience feelings of disorientation and discomfort. Belonging is about feeling at home in some sense, but it does not necessarily mean feeling entirely warm or comfortable when there, at home (Yvual-Davis 2011, 10). All kinds of social movements produce feelings of belonging, as well as social and ethical norms about political ideals and expected conduct. Nira Yuval-Davis explains:

> The politics of belonging involves not only constructions of boundaries but also the inclusion or exclusion of particular people, social categories and groupings within these boundaries by those who have the power to do this. (Yuval-Davis 2011, 18)

This is done within a global as well as in a local and regional context and has to be analysed from an intersectional perspective.

On sources and method

There is a wealth of source material from this time period. National journals and/or newsletters devoted to women's studies were quickly established, often with readers throughout the Nordic countries.[6] A number of pamphlets, articles in other academic journals, monographs, anthologies, posters, flyers, conference reports and other texts were produced. Many official documents from Nordic networks and associations are also available today. These documents form the basis for my analysis, and have been complemented with interviews.

---

[6] The women's studies journals in the Scandinavian languages were read throughout Norden, providing their readers with information about coming activities throughout the region. The largest journals were *Forum for kvindeforskning* (started in Denmark in 1981), *Nytt om kvinneforskning* (started in Norway in 1977), and *Kvinnovetenskaplig tidskrift* (started in Sweden in 1980). The Finnish journal *Naistutkimus/Kvinnoforskning*, started in 1988, was intended to be bilingual but only occasionally published articles in Swedish. An important newsletter was the Danish *Kvindeforskning*, started in 1987 to which anyone could subscribe for free. In Sweden the local organisations for women's studies scholars all had newsletters of their own where not only information concerning local and regional issues were disseminated. Regular information about articles in the many international women's studies journals the organisations subscribed to was published. This was usually done by simply photocopying the table of contents of each journal and adding it to the newsletter.

My point of departure for examining Nordic feminist commonality and feminist space has, furthermore, been nurtured by the many and increasingly harsh controversies today about the very subject – feminist space within women's and gender studies in Norden.[7] What has become of women's studies and gender research, what trajectories have been, and are to be, chosen, and how shall we estimate the ongoing institutionalisation of the research field? What effects have issues of sexuality and intersectional understandings of power relations had on theorisations of gender, equality, and power? I read today's many disagreements as different kinds of reactions to an imagined, long-felt feminist community; some mourn what they perceive as the passing of that community, while others are trying to open it up and change it. In my view, the contentions show the existence of a (prior) feminist hegemony that is now either defended or criticised. Space, one can say, is made visible through these disagreements. Critiques about a history of neglect of certain questions, about internal borders and implicit norms, are put forward and met with defence from persons who seem to fear the decline of woman-focussed, feminist unity. Those who react to the critique are often, but certainly not always, scholars who were holding prominent positions in women's studies in the 1980s and 1990s.[8] In order to avoid misunderstandings or repetitions of what has already been commented upon in the introductory chapter, these contestations ought not to be read as generational conflicts. The disagreements rather concern important feminist questions about the conceptualisations of gender, power, and knowledge. In short, different perspectives on feminist and scientific/scholarly core questions are discussed today in a way that makes visible the borders of our recent past. I contend that the controversies of today can serve as important means to grasp implicit meanings and internal borders of the feminist space during the early years of consolidation, if read with care and historical sensitivity. If historicised, they help us to probe deeper into implicit, even denied, conditions and borders of feminist space in our recent past. To speak with Joan W. Scott (2011, 47–48, 51): careful attention to

---

[7] See discussions in the different Nordic gender studies journals, and in the joint Nordic journal *NORA*. These discussions are also often shown at conferences and in comments made later in social media.

[8] I will here limit my empirical examples to Swedish debates. At the centre of the debates has been the role of an intersectional perspective on gender and power, and a discontent about women's and gender studies as an autonomous discipline. See de los Reyes et al. eds. (2002), Witt-Brattström (2006; 2007), Hirdman (2007; 2008), and Edenheim (2010). See also Liinason (2014), and Lindén (2011).

space and the situatedness of narratives helps us avoid an unconscious "retrospective identification" of a past that was already grounded in a selective representation when produced. This kind of reading improves our ability to see what was present at the time, but not always manifest in the historical sources we work with.

Narratives of the early mobilising days, of theoretical changes, of who felt at home within women's studies back then and why, differ considerably depending on who is given the opportunity to speak. The stories told also differ depending on how research about the past is conducted: which problems do we address, how do we contextualise, and not the least how do we historicise? Hemmings' (2011) careful analysis of narrative structures in the story of feminist theory in recent decades shows how citing practices and poor contextualisation colour much of our understanding of that which is close to us in time. By evoking feelings of recognition and familiarity, certain statements are received as "true," whilst others are overlooked. This "political grammar" of the stories produces implicit truth claims, which are difficult to recognise as such, but which are nevertheless forceful in the production and reproduction of feminist grand narratives (Hemmings 2011, 227).[9] Following Hemmings, I am using some of the "stories" told today as a heuristic tool for a further critical reading and historicisation. My intention is to capture some of the volatile space and geopolitics of Nordic women's studies during the 1980s. By focusing on the particular space that took shape within a partly real, partly imagined Nordic women's studies community, my ambition is to contribute with a reading of a recent past many of us were, and still are, emotionally invested in, often without really paying close attention to how this investment might have affected, and might still be affecting, us. In this study, I thus try to grasp and understand a partly shared past that, when investigated and remembered, is highly contested today.[10]

---

[9] As discussed in the introduction of this book and in the chapter by Dahl, this grammar is not least of a geopolitical kind.

[10] Controversies about how to understand our recent feminist past exist not only in Norden (Manns 2009, Edenheim 2010, Lindén 2011, and Larsen 2013), but also in Europe and the USA (Wiegman 2000; 2008; 2010, Brown 2002, Hemmings 2005; 2007; 2011, and Torr 2007).

The taken-for-granted Norden

Nordic space in women's studies during this time period is not easy to grasp. At the time, the meaning of the Nordic were seldom discussed and reflected upon, neither was the importance of regional collaboration.[11] The consequences of the vast, rapidly expanding collaboration and the ongoing institutionalisation on a national as well as on a regional level were usually seen as entirely positive among women's studies scholars. These developments appear to have been regarded as both crucial and self-evident, as reinforcing the newly born field of research, and as important to help legitimise women's studies (Rosenbeck 1998; Manns 2009). Before the 1990s, when Nordic women's studies became more institutionalised with journals such as *NORA: Nordic Journal of Women's Studies*[12] (1993–), and NIKK: Nordic Institute for Women's Studies and Gender Research (1995–2011), the meaning of the Nordic was to large extent implicit and un-problematised (see further Dahl in this volume).[13] As a taken-for-granted entity, self-evident in its content, form, and function, Norden thus appears as the imagined community that Anderson (2006) sketches; a community built on assumptions about proximity, linguistic similarities, and shared historical, cultural, and political (feminist) experiences.[14] The concept of Norden, as well as the attitude to Nordic collaboration within women's studies, was similar to already existing ideas of Nordicness in regional state politics, social movements, and cultural institutions (Stråth and Sørensen 1997; Liljeström 2009; Manns 2009; Aronsson and Gradén 2013). Furthermore, as Peter Aronsson and Lizette Gradén (2013) contend, the imagined Nordicness is performative. They describe Nordicness as an ongoing performance, repeated and manifested over and over again in different regional and national arenas.

[11] Exceptions are, of course, to be found concerning the relation to state policies on gender equality. See, for example, the theme issue on gender equality in *Kvinnovetenskaplig tidskrift*, in which Maud Landby Eduards (1986) warns women's studies scholars and women in general against becoming passive consumers of welfare, and urges them to retain a critical stance towards gender equality politics and its maintenance of male privileges.

[12] Since 2008 NORA: *Nordic Journal of Feminist and Gender Research*.

[13] NIKK has undergone several changes due to organisation and assignment. In 2006, it changed to NIKK: The Nordic Gender Institute. Since 2012 it is located in Gothenburg, Sweden, under the name, NIKK: Nordic Information on Gender.

[14] Linguistic proximity only applies to the Scandinavian languages (Danish, Norwegian and Swedish).

After the Second World War, Nordic collaboration in general became stronger. The Nordic Council was established in 1952, and in the early 1970s, the Nordic Council of Ministers was initiated (and serves under the Nordic Council). The non-contested and ongoing production of Nordicness and the imaginary of Norden as a long-lasting and well-functioning regional community were strong, not only at a state political level. Social movements such as the labour movement, the left-wing movement, and the women's movement shared this imagination, all movements having prior experiences of Nordic collaboration. In general, it was regarded as a familiar and well-functioning form of political activism, originating from the Scandinavian movement of the 19th century (Rosenbeck 1998; Hillström and Sanders 2014). This helps explain why ideas and ideals about the Nordic and Nordicness were seldom elaborated. There was simply no real need to explain the Nordic in detail to its inhabitants (Aronsson and Gradén 2013). When described (usually in addressing people outside Norden, but with effects on conceptualisations of the Nordic within), the Nordic usually ended up as self-referential, simply as "the Nordic." That is, it was uncritically understood as a region comprising five culturally similar nation-states: Norway, Denmark, Finland, Sweden, and Iceland (cf. Stråth and Sørensen 1997). The five nations were usually depicted as one community, as a unit sharing ideals such as social welfare and democracy, gender equality, and peace in a "fairly problem-free" way, as Marianne Liljeström (2009) phrases it. Thus, those who lacked a deeper knowledge of Norden received a simplified and "uniform image" of it (Liljeström 2009, 233–234), an image that overlooked geopolitical and national differences (such as membership of the EU and NATO, national World War II experiences, different migration policies), linguistic differences, etcetera. As Dahl (2011) notes about today's queer studies, the production of "family resemblances" (borrowing the term from Ahmed 2007) still goes on. In women's studies during the 1980s as well as in queer studies today, Norden is closely tied to constructions of naturalised assumptions of shared national and regional values. When these levels conflate, there is a great risk "of placing both ideas and bodies that are not understood to be of Scandinavian 'origin' outside the frame" (Dahl 2011, 154–155, see also Keskinen ed. 2009).

Against this brief historic backdrop, I place my main research questions: How can we understand the making and translation of feminism in the specific Nordic setting of women's studies during the first years of mobilisation, intervention, and state financial support? Since so many initiatives were taken on a Nordic level, how are we to understand the operations of meaning about regional commonality? As a women's movement historian and engaged feminist, I try to understand without overlooking the factual circumstances or making a-historical, simplifying conclusions. I read with a desire to historicise the present situation, a time of increasing internal disagreements both within the field of gender research, and in the feminist movement outside of academia. Four different aspects of the commonality of Nordic women's studies' will be addressed. I first discuss the relation between the research field and the contemporary women's movement. The Nordic inter-state stage and its concern with gender equality and research policies will then be presented briefly. The international (primarily Anglo-American) women's studies context will thereafter be contrasted with the Nordic one. Finally, two particular aspects of Nordic women's studies will be discussed: the absence of lesbian studies and the translation of gender as a category of analysis.

A feminist stance: Research and women's liberation

Early uses of pictures, symbols, and statements made by women's studies scholars often showed a clear feminist stance – one that stressed proximity to the women's movement and, in particular, to the Nordic left-wing, new women's liberation movement. In an early Norwegian publication, the overall aim of women's studies was stated in a way that was common throughout the region:

> Women's studies represent a corrective to the hitherto male-dominated and male-centred research. It carries with it promises of cognitive innovations of transgressive or revolutionary character. This is because old ways of explanation that fail to explain women's lives and conditions may be on the wane, to the benefit of more comprehensive theories that also can account for women. (Wetlesen 1976, 12–13)[15]

Numerous explications similar to this one can be found. Others, however, were more elaborated and eager to make distinctions between revolutionary

---

[15] My translation. Quote in the original: "Kvinneforskningen representerer et korrektiv til den tidligere mannsdominerte og mannssentrerte forskning. Den bærer løfter om erkjennelsesmessige nydannelser av grenseoverskridende eller revolusjonerende karakter. Dette beror på at gamle forklaringsmønstre som ikke forklarer kvinners liv og situasjon, kan komme på vikende front, til fordel for mer omfattende teorier som også fanger inn kvinner."

women's liberation and reformist women's emancipation in relation to women's studies.[16] The Swedish journal *Kvinnovetenskaplig tidskrift* (which started in 1980)[17] had a Nordic readership and was by far the largest women's studies journal during the 1980s. In its first issue, the editorial board was explicit about the ideological differences within the contemporary women's movement and about the position of women's studies. The editors stated that women's studies belonged to the socialist part of the women's movement. Gender equality research and sex-role research were presented as pro-change but reformist, quantitative, and less critical than women's studies (Davis et al. 1980). Even though sharp distinctions between women's studies, on the one hand, and gender equality/sex-role research, on the other, were made, the space of Nordic women's studies soon proved to be much wider (Rosenbeck 1998; Halsaa 2004; Manns 2009). All kinds of research that aimed to improve women's lives and in some way to critically engage in producing knowledge about women counted as women's studies. This broader and more inclusive notion of women's studies therefore opened up space for different trajectories and perspectives within the research field. A quick look at Nordic networks, working groups, and conferences shows a great variety concerning empirical research about women. However, empirical breadth and feminist inclusiveness did not necessarily entail theoretical exploration along lines of differences between women and power regimes. Even though considerable attention was directed at the gender division of labour and its impact on equality and women's agency, on a theoretical level "woman" nevertheless came to be regarded as one monolithic category.[18] Debates concerning sameness and difference (in relation to men) burgeoned, but they did not

[16] See Silfwerbrand-ten Cate ed. (1975), Støren and Wetlesen eds. (1976), Ravn et al. (1978), Westman Berg ed. (1979), Aniansson ed. (1983). The discussion is also based on interviews with Kari Melby (August 18, 2008), Eva Borgström (November 23, 2007), Birgitte Possing (August 19, 2008), and Drude Dahlerup (2009).
[17] From 2007, *Tidskrift för genusvetenskap* [Journal of Gender Studies].
[18] Even though much attention was given to the relation between class and gender, and critical readings of Marxist theories of oppression were plentiful, the absence of bringing other oppressive systems into discussions unintentionally, it seems, resulted in a reinforcement of the idea of women as a single category. See, for example, Ravn et al. (1978), Carlsson et al. (1983), Jónasdóttir (1984; 1985), and Ganetz et al. eds. (1986). Critique was heard, but did not seem to have had much influence until later. See Lundgren (1987), Widerberg (1987), and Peterson (1987).

generate questions concerning racism or heterosexuality as a norm in relation to gender, justice, and equality.[19]

The material indicates that a combination of an open, inclusive feminist space and, simultaneously, a lack of readiness to theorise the category of women in terms of multiple power regimes greatly contributed to a culture of consensus within women's studies. Within the imagined community, no one was supposed to be critical! For example, it is striking for a reader today, that hardly any critical or negative reviews in women's studies journals are to be found. Internal scholarly debates were rare and seldom concerned theoretical issues about gender.[20] The culture of unity and consensus was probably a result of a common and collective feeling of fragility, since women's studies was not yet legitimised as a field of research. At the same time, there are indications that the culture became regulatory as well. Internal debates were to be avoided. Indeed, the norm of consensus was already strong in Nordic academic culture in general; one was simply not supposed to disagree.[21] Beatrice Halsaa (2006) shows in her study on Norway that, as a contrast to the harsh male academy, women's studies was eager to be perceived as a comfortable and welcoming space. The ambition to be experienced as a warm and welcoming space was in turn dependent on unity and solidarity among women studies scholars regardless of any disagreements. Considering that women's studies was not yet recognised as a proper field of research, this most certainly contributed to strengthening feelings of the importance of mobilisation and feminist unity. The need for unity, I believe, has in the long run fed ideas of feminist familiarity across national, political, and disciplinary differences. A general perception at the time seems to have been that dissentions concerning theoretical and political issues were likely to threaten a fragile unity that was needed in order to gain a foothold in academia. Therefore, disagreement was put aside easily, even though there

---

[19] See, for example, conference reports from 1986 in Denmark (Fredriksen and Rømer 1986), in Hässelby 1989 (*Kvinnohistoria i teoretiskt perspektiv…* 1990), and at the interdisciplinary Nordic conference Kvinnouniversitetet 1982 (Anianson et al. 1983).

[20] Based on a review of the Nordic women's studies journals, 1975 to 1990. See also Halsaa (2006).

[21] Several studies claim that the culture of consensus and compromise in politics as well as in the academy is significant for Nordic collaboration. See Stråth and Sørensen (1997), Aronsson (1998), Aronsson and Gradén (2013).

were large differences between standpoints on aims, objects, theories, and methods.[22]

The newly organised field of research fought to remain independent from Nordic state governance. At the same time, state funding and support was gladly accepted. Scholars were, however, by no means unaware of the risks of government intervention (Liinasson 2011). Many tried to navigate between the agenda they set themselves and political demands and expectations from politicians and the women's movement. This was not an easy course to follow, since obligations towards the women's movement occasionally collided with state political interests in improving gender equality in areas such as the labour market, politics, research, and higher education.[23] Nevertheless, the inclusive strategy was regarded as a strategically sound one, despite the risk of becoming disciplined and too closely linked to state-approved gender equality research. This strategy reduced the possibility of clashes between feminist intervention and state political interests, and state support helped establish and legitimise the broad and diverse field of women's studies in Nordic academic life (Bergman 2000a; Alnebratt 2009; Liinason 2011).

Despite the overall positive attitude to state support in the 1980s, Nordic women's studies scholars did take a rather united stance against state intervention in naming the field of research. The label quickly became a delicate issue. Nordic and national state policy kept insisting on the term "equal opportunity research,"[24] or occasionally "sex-role research," whilst the vast majority of women's studies scholars fought for the right to call it "women's studies". At the time, sex-role research held a prominent position in Nordic sociology, to some extent also in the field of literature and history (Halsaa 2004; Nordenstam 2005; Olsson 2011). Even though much Nordic sex-role research, in Norway not the least, became critical, and distanced itself from American sex-role research during the 1970s, "sex-role research" was a term that was denounced by many (Halsaa 2002; 2004). As a feminist statement, the term "women's studies" was preferred (*Forskning om jämställdhet* 1978). When arguing for their own definition, scholars referred to affinities

---

[22] Telling examples are the already mentioned editorial in *Kvinnovetenskaplig tidskrift* and the Norwegian key scholar Harriet Holter's (1980) article in the same issue.

[23] See, Ravn et al. (1978), *Nytt om kvinneforskning* (1980), and *Organisering av jämställd-hets-/kvinnoforskning i Norden* (1984).

[24] As mentioned at the beginning of this chapter, the more established term later became "gender equality research." See Alnebratt (2009) for an elaborate analysis of this change in Sweden.

to women's studies in other countries, as well as to its roots in the women's movement (Rosenbeck 1998; Halsaa 2004; Manns 2009). Concerning the right to label the field of research, one prominent scholar explained:

> [F]or us women's studies scholars it played a major role. Women's studies belonged to us, it was all about us as women, we were in the centre. And now we experienced that they tried to take it away from us and make it into something else that they would gain influence over and take control over (not everything is gender equality research). (Widerberg 1986a, 36)[25]

As Halsaa notes about Norway, the overlap between the women's movement and early women's studies is hard to overlook. It was as feminists that students and scholars acted in academia:

> What the young feminists did as students or as activists could hardly be separated, the feminist identity was shared. The urgent need for feminist theories to guide the elaboration of political strategies was quite adequately taken care of in higher education. Writing course papers, participating in seminars and during lectures and preparing for exams were all part of the feminist struggle. [---] The literature scrutinized during political meetings and study circles were the same as focused during academic seminars. The women's liberation aims were similar, the symbols, slogans, concepts and perspectives were similar inside and outside academic institutions. (Halsaa 2004, 91–92)

Nordiskt sommaruniversitet (NSU) [Nordic Summer University] was one of the Nordic spaces for left-wing feminists, prior to their mobilisation as women's studies scholars. Founded in 1973, NSU played an important role not only as a pioneering institution for Nordic collaboration among left-wing intellectuals, but also for its early interdisciplinary approach (Arnfred and Syberg 1974; Rosenbeck 1998, 350–1; 2014, 140–141; Halsaa 2004; Göransson 2010, 194; Dahlerup 2010, 38). Early on, a feminist study group was established, focusing on women's oppression under capitalism. Already in 1974, the group published a book, *Kvindesituation og kvindebevægelse under kapitalismen* [Women's Condition and the Women's Movement

---

[25] My translation. Quote in the original: "[F]ör oss kvinnoforskare spelade det en stor roll. Kvinnoforskningen var vår, den handlade om oss som kvinnor, vi stod i centrum. Och nu upplevde vi att man försökte ta den ifrån oss och göra den till något annat som de skulle få inflytande och kontroll över (allt är inte jämställdhetsforskning)."

under Capitalism] (Arnfred and Syberg eds. 1974). In an initial phase, the group was in contact with Juliet Mitchell, the British left-wing feminist activist and scholar, who was invited to their summer meeting (Rosenbeck 2014, 140). Even though the editors commented on the importance of the Nordic scope, no remarks were made about the specific Nordic construction of NSU. Nordic collaboration seems to have been regarded as self-evident, unnecessary to comment upon. Several of the participants in the group soon became prominent women's studies scholars.[26]

Nordic mobilisation, gender equality, and research policy

Collaboration within the Nordic realm was not a new form of feminist activism. This was just one more historically familiar area in which to work collectively (Rosenbeck 1998). Around the turn of the 20th century, the early women's movement held joint conferences and cooperated to a great extent on questions such as women's suffrage, citizenship, and reforms of the marriage laws. During the 1960s and 1970s, Nordic activists also met frequently (Dahlerup 1998; Bergman 2002; Melby et al. 2006; Ingström ed. 2007; Isaksson 2007; Schmitz 2007; Hallgren 2008; Larsen 2013). Women's studies scholars started to organise networks, seminars, conferences, PhD courses, and organisations on a joint Nordic level during the late 1970s. The similarity of the Scandinavian languages facilitated collaboration as well as the dissemination of information and knowledge, at least among those who mastered any of these languages.[27] A brief look at the many activities in only a couple of years shows a great variety of content and trajectories. Nordic networks in a wide range of disciplines such as history, political science, sociology, literature, medicine, urban development, law, and criminology were built, alongside interdisciplinary seminars and conferences on feminist methodology. National newsletters and journals all had a Nordic scope, addressing and informing readers throughout the region (Rosenbeck 1998; Manns 2009). Several joint Nordic research projects were initiated. Examples are the project in political science starting in 1977 and resulting in

---

[26] The editors Signe Arnfred and Signe Syberg, as well as Birte Siim, Anita Göransson, Margot Bengtsson, Irene Iversen, and Drude Dahlerup all belonged to this group.

[27] People from Iceland were often fluent in one of the central Scandinavian languages, usually Danish. Finnish scholars most often used Swedish. Many Finnish scholars at the time also belonged to the Swedish-speaking minority in Finland. At Nordic meetings today, English is more commonly used.

the 1983 anthology *Det uferdige demokratiet: Kvinner i nordisk politikk* (Haavio-Mannila ed. 1983) (published in English in 1985, *Unfinished Democracy: Women in Nordic Politics*),[28] the research project *Nordisk kvinnolitteraturhistoria* [Nordic History of Women's Literature] (5 volumes 1993–2000), starting in 1981, and the project BRYT, aiming at changing the gender-segregated labour market in the Nordic countries.[29] These activities all contributed greatly to the dissemination of feminist issues and new knowledge about women and women's conditions in the past and present. Joint Nordic efforts helped legitimise the field of knowledge across national borders and, as Halsaa (2004, 82) points out, "undoubtedly encouraged the process of institutionalising" the field of research. Bente Rosenbeck's (1998, 353) remark about the importance of Nordic research collaboration, that only "by thinking beyond the boundaries of each individual country has it been possible to bring together sufficient numbers of researchers in comparable fields," still constitutes an accurate assessment.

Despite reluctance and criticism from parts of the academic community, the new field of research paved its way into universities throughout Norden. The rapid development was made possible by a large amount of feminist activism, and financial and ideological support from Nordic governments, from the Nordic Council of Ministers in particular. It is interesting to note that the funding from the Nordic Council of Ministers came from the Gender Equality area, not from the Ministers of Education and Research.[30] Women's studies was, it seems, first and foremost considered as belonging to gender equality policies, not to the area of higher education and research.

Several initiatives were taken by the Nordic Council in order to help women's studies scholars organise. Already in 1981, women's studies scholars organised in Nordic Forum for Research on Women in the Nordic Countries. The group soon received sponsorship from the Nordic Council of Ministers, and was able to initiate a Nordic coordinator. In 1996, the coordinating function became institutionalised as NIKK: Nordic Institute

[28] The project started as a network in 1977. The Nordic Council of Ministers gave economic support for the group to meet, see introduction and a short presentation by the main editor, Haavio-Mannila (1985). The book has been given a seminal status and was published in all the Nordic languages in 1983. See Bergqvist (2001), Halsaa (2001), and Dahlerup (2001).
[29] *Nordisk kvinnolitteraturhistoria*, main editor Elisabeth Møller Jensen, has now been digitalised. The so-called BRYT project was financed by the Nordic Council of Ministers.
[30] We still lack detailed knowledge about how the academic community handled the situation at a local, national, and regional level.

49

for Women Studies and Gender Research, based in Oslo. Nordic Forum also arranged two large interdisciplinary conferences, in 1981 and in 1988, both times with financial support from the Nordic Council of Ministers (*Skrivelse från Nordiskt Forum* 1984; *Kvinneforskning i Norden* 1988; Bergman ed. 1991). In addition, the national research councils organised conferences and meetings on the topic (cf. Manns 2009). Nordic politicians did not seem to take much offence at the way in which many women's studies scholars distanced themselves from sex-role and gender equality research. On the contrary, women's studies and research from a "women's perspective" was soon regarded as crucial for improving gender equality in society. As the Swedish Equality and Migration Minister Anita Gradin (1984, 111) stated at a Nordic conference about gender equality in the early 1980s, "[a]cademic women's studies is a necessary part of gender equality work." She continued by explaining that women's studies, with its specific women's perspective, was a necessary condition for high quality gender equality research in general. That is, gender equality politics was dependent on critical and feminist research: women's studies. This conference was yet another activity sponsored by the Nordic Council of Ministers, financed in order to promote gender equality in the region.

Within this specific context, hardly any explications or discussions of the content of the Nordic are to be found. Women's studies scholars by and large adhered to common ideas about Norden and Nordicness, as shown in one of the few descriptions to be found expressed by the Nordic Women's Studies coordinator in 1991:

> A large number of historic, socio-economic and linguistic similarities tie the Nordic countries together. The pattern of life for women in this region has developed along roughly similar lines. [--] However; the above picture does not imply that Nordic women have attained real social power or influence either in the public, or in the private sphere. (Bergman ed. 1991, 5)[31]

---

[31] In an analysis of the editorial in *NORA* 1993 no. 1, Nina Lykke (2004a, 80) remarks that the politics of location in this particular editorial implicitly constructs a Nordic "we" against another "them." The editorial addresses readers "out there" with the aim to "show the many qualities of Nordic feminist research." Like many other brief or lengthier presentations of Norden, the editorial simplifies and reduces, and thus helps to maintain the imaginary of Nordic commonality.

Regional commonality, viewed in terms of linguistic similarities, shared values, socioeconomic conditions, and history, were repeatedly taken for granted and rarely commented upon. The text quoted above is no exception. Similar ideas underlie publications such as *Kvindesituation og kvinde-bevægelse under kapitalismen* (Arnfred and Syberg eds. 1974), *Det uferdige demokratiet* (Haavio-Mannila ed. 1983), reports from Nordic seminars on theory and method,[32] as well as *Nordisk kvinnolitteraturhistoria* [Nordic History of Women's Literature], and the first editorial of Nordic women's studies journal, *NORA*, in 1993. The first volume of *Nordisk kvinnolitte-raturhistoria* went even further than most publications of the time, explicitly referring to a common Nordic identity. The very opening words, formulated by the chief editor, stated this clearly:

> *Nordisk kvinnolitteraturhistoria* is about women's writing and it is about Norden. Even if the Nordic countries each have had its own historical development, the sense of a particular community, a Nordic identity, is part of the self-perception of the majority of Nordic people. In the work with texts by women writers, the Nordic point of departure has proved to be productive. Features that have isolated one woman writer in her country often recur in women writers in other Nordic countries. An authorship that has fallen outside of conventional literary categories in one country finds a natural habitat in a Nordic context of women's writing. Subjects, themes, and aesthetic features coincide and establish new Nordic patterns. (Jensen 1991, 11)[33]

Karin Widerberg's critique of homogeneous representations of women in Norden in 1985, discussed in the introduction to this volume, is one rare and also early exception. Why, Widerberg asked at a Nordic conference, is sexuality and heterosexuality as an institution usually overlooked in Nordic feminist scholarship? She refers both to theories of women's oppression

---

[32] See, for example, *Metoder och problem i kvinnoforskningen* (1982), and *Kvindespor i videnskaben* (Bryld and Lykke eds.1985).
[33] My translation. Quote in the original: "*Nordisk kvinnolitteraturhistoria* handlar om vad kvinnor har skrivit och den handlar om Norden. Även om de nordiska länderna var för sig har haft sin historiska utveckling, är känslan av en särskild gemenskap, en nordisk identitet, en del av de flesta nordbors uppfattning om sig själva. I arbetet med texter av kvinnliga författare har den nordiska utgångspunkten visat sig vara fruktbar. De särdrag som har isolerat en kvinnlig författare i hennes land återfinns ofta hos kvinnliga för-fattare i andra nordiska länder. Ett författarskap, som fallit utanför gängse litteratur-historiska kategorier i sitt land, finner i ett nordiskt kvinnolitterärt sammanhang sin naturliga plats. Motiv, teman och estetiska drag sammanfaller och bildar nya, nordiska mönster."

such as the ones stemming from Heidi Hartmann's dual system theory, widely discussed and elaborated by Nordic scholars, and the lack of interest in institutionalised heterosexuality in empirical studies (Widerberg 1985, see also Rosenbeck 2014, 144).[34] In her most fully elaborated discussion, published in 1987, Widerberg criticises Nordic scholars for not paying attention to women's differing participation in upholding women's oppression. Widerberg claims that this neglect results from an under-problematised woman-centred theorisation dominating Nordic feminist scholarship. She points out the reductionist representation of Nordic women in women's studies research, where sexuality is almost absent:

> In Nordic women's studies women have become strangely sex-less and heterosexuality as a force is absent. Women emerge as beings without sex in their activities. They work and work – as if we women lived by and for labour alone! (Widerberg 1987, 60)[35]

Widerberg (1987, 61) states further, the focus on labour (no matter paid or unpaid) makes Nordic women's studies scholars unable to recognise the role heterosexuality as an institution plays, in private life as well as in social structures.

Nordic familiarity

Nordic women's studies scholars were well acquainted with much research within women's studies in other western countries. West German, US, and British scholars were frequently invited to seminars and conferences, and their work was widely read and often translated. Particular attention was paid to the relation between women's oppression and class. The works of Heidi Hartmann, Ulrike Prokop, and Juliet Mitchell were all soon translated

---

[34] Widerberg, a Swedish-born sociologist, long active in Norway, repeated this critique on several occasions. See also Widerberg (1986a).

[35] My translation. Quote in the original: "Inom nordisk kvinnoforskning har kvinnorna blivit underligt könlösa, och heterosexualiteten som kraft saknas. Könlösa framtonar kvinnorna i sina olika verksamheter. De arbetar och arbetar – som om vi kvinnor levde av och för arbete allena!" Widerberg does not use the term gender (in Swedish *genus*), instead she deliberately chooses what she considers to be the much more ambiguous term *kön* (approximately "sex" in English). Widerberg has continued to critically discuss the concept of gender in terms of translation and adaptation, pointing to the geopolitical difficulties of theoretical and conceptual translations. See Widerberg (1992; 1998).

into the Scandinavian languages.[36] Literary scholars such as Sandra Gilbert and Susan Gubar, thinkers associated with what soon came to be labelled "French feminism," such as Julia Kristeva, Hélène Cixous, and Luce Irigaray, became widely read and acknowledged, not least because of the book *Sexual/Textual Politics* from 1985 by Toril Moi, a Norwegian literary scholar working in the USA (Lindén 2008; Rosenbeck 2014). References to anthropologists such as Gayle Rubin and Sherry Ortner, as well as to philosophers Sandra Harding and Carolyn Merchant, are often seen in publications from this period. Alongside these, the French feminist triad Julia Kristeva, Hélène Cixous, and Luce Irigaray with their psychoanalytical trajectories attracted the attention of many others, literary scholars and the already cited sociologist Widerberg.[37] Women's studies journals published abroad (primarily but not entirely in English) were easily accessible at the women's studies offices, which often included a small library.

Several contemporary debates held outside Norden resonated throughout Norden, but some did not. Notable is the absence of critique from Black feminists and Chicana feminists. Publications such as bell hooks *Ain't I a Woman? Black Women and Feminism* from 1982, the anthology by Gloria Hull, Patricia Bell Scott and Barbara Smith *All the Women Are White, All the Blacks Are Men, But some of Us Are Brave: Black Women's Studies* also from 1982, as well as articles such as Valerie Amos and Pratibha Parmar's "Challenging Imperial Feminism," published in 1984 in the journal *Feminist Review*, received little attention from Nordic women's studies.

---

[36] Juliet Mitchell's texts were quickly published in Scandinavian languages. Her seminal article "Women: The Longest Revolution," in *New Left Review* 1966, was translated into Swedish in 1969, and into Danish in 1971. *Women's Estate* from 1971 was translated into Danish and Swedish already the following year and into Norwegian in 1973, her book *Psychoanalysis and Feminism* from 1974 was published in Danish, Norwegian, and Swedish in 1977. *Women's Estate* was also translated into Finnish in 1973. Heidi Hartmann's article "Capitalism, Patriarchy, and Job Segregation by Sex," in *Signs* 1976 was translated into Swedish and published in *Kvinnovetenskaplig tidskrift* in 1981, Ulrike Prokop's book *Weiblicher Lebenszusammenhang* from 1976 was translated into Danish in 1978, and into Swedish in 1981, when an extract from her book was also published in *Kvinnovetenskaplig tidskrift*.

[37] Sometimes lists with suitable readings and extensive bibliographies of women's studies within different areas of study were attached to publications. These provide an insight into, though not a full picture of, the topics and geographical areas that were recognised. See, for example bibliographies in the report from a Nordic conference on method, *Metoder och problem i kvinnoforskningen* (1982) and Jónasdóttir (1984). Translated articles in women's studies journals also support the statement made above.

I read the absence of commentary or critique as a cultural translation, indicating what counted as relevant at the time. It might seem unreasonable to expect all feminist issues to resonate within Nordic women's studies. However, there are at least two reasons for examining the lack of discussion about these specific issues. First, the intention is to help disrupt common narratives about feminist theory and research in Norden during this period; more precisely, it is to disrupt the idea that race and ethnicity came "late" to women's studies and feminist theorising (that is, not until postcolonial reactions in the 1990s, cf. Hemmings 2011). Second, the intention is to show that academic (and activist) oppositions, exemplified by the above-mentioned texts, were published in journals and books known to and available to a Nordic feminist academic readership. Thus, the lack of reaction to the internal critique that these publications delivered can be understood as an act of a selective cultural translation of, and an adaptation to, certain theoretical and political standpoints already established in Norden.[38]

In 1984 Valerie Amos and Pratibha Parmar's article "Challenging Imperial Feminism" was published in *Feminist Review*. The authors addressed essential questions of gender, power, and race in feminist scholarship. The internal feminist critique resembled in many ways the critique formulated by contemporary Black feminists in the USA (bell hooks, Angela Davis, and Patricia Hill Collins to mention some). Worth stressing is that, in a footnote, Amos and Parmar particularly point to the problems within socialist feminism, the very kind of feminism theoretically dominating Nordic feminist scholarship and theory. Well-known publications such as *Beyond the Fragments: Feminism and the Making of Socialism* by Sheila Rowbotham, Lynne Segal, and Hilary Wainright (1979), and *Women and Revolution: A Discussion of the Unhappy Marriage of Marxism and Feminism*, edited by Lydia Sargent (1981) were given as examples of recent publications which failed to take racism into account. Since both women's studies scholars and the women's movement in Norden struggled greatly with the shortcomings of Marxism in relation to women's oppression, an article such as "Challenging Imperial Feminism" could be expected to have

---

[38] Later, in 1998, Karin Widerberg once again started a debate. She criticised Nordic women's studies for not paying enough attention to what effects unreflected uses of American feminist theorising could have, not the least for conceptualising and translating central concepts such as "gender." I strongly agree with my colleague Ulrika Dahl and others that the labelling of certain theories as "American" is itself a reductive narrative of what counts as American. See Dahl in this volume.

caught the interest of Nordic scholars. It did not. Had it done so, their argumentation might have contributed to elaborations on the theoretical and methodological problems that were so often addressed in Nordic women's studies.[39] Instead, a Nordic counterpart to the anthology *Women and Revolution* was published, *Feminism och marxism: En förälskelse med förhinder* (Ganetz et al. eds. 1986), one that did not pay attention to the questions posed by Amos and Parmar.

The next example concerns the relation between racism and institutionalised heterosexuality in feminist analysis emphasised by Cherríe Moraga in her well-known article "From a Long Line of Vendidas," published in 1983 in the anthology *Loving in the War Years*. Reprinted in the acclaimed anthology *Feminist Studies/Critical Studies* in 1986 (edited by Teresa de Lauretis), it was once again made available to a Nordic readership. Like Amos and Parmar, and other feminists who criticised the feminist agenda within US and British women's studies, Moraga received little attention in the Nordic women's studies community. In 2010 Karin Lützen, one of the few Nordic scholars conducting lesbian studies during the 1980s, recalls her first encounter with Moraga's article. When she reread Moraga's article, the reprint in the anthology edited by de Lauretis, she was surprised to note that she hardly paid any attention to the article when stumbling upon it in the 1980s. Instead, she explains, the contribution in the anthology by her "favourite women's historian" Carroll Smith-Rosenberg was full of notes (Lützen 2010, 67). These two examples illustrate how certain ideas, trajectories, and feminist visions caught the interest of Nordic women's studies scholars in the 1980s, while others did not. Some questions seemed considerably more relevant than others did in the Nordic context at the time.[40] Questions of racism were not given much attention, as scholars have since pointed out.

---

[39] The need to further develop new and useful concepts, theories, and methods in general, and to overcome the shortcomings of Marxist theories of oppression in particular, was often commented upon. See, for example, *Kvinnovetenskaplig tidskrift* during the early years of the 1980s, *Metoder och problem i kvinnoforskningen* (1982), *Kvindespor i videnskaben* (Bryld and Lykke eds.1985), and Jónasdóttir (1984).

[40] Much interest was shown in theories about women's oppression within a socialist and social constructivist framework, as the ones about patriarchy and capitalism, gender, gender socialization, and gender division of labour, also epistemological and methodological discussions as the ones brought forward by some feminist standpoint theories. Again, only parts of the debate within feminist standpoint theory reached Norden. bell hooks, Patricia Hill Collins, and Uma Narayan, were by and large left uncommented du-

THE GEOPOLITICS OF NORDIC AND RUSSIAN GENDER RESEARCH

In 2000 Diana Mulinari, a sociologist and gender studies scholar in Sweden, reflected on the lack of importance accorded to race and ethnicity in Nordic theorising on gender and power. In fact, she referred to race and ethnicity as the "elephant in the room": something not acknowledged, but felt by many. Her keynote "'Race'/Ethnicity in a 'Nordic' Context," delivered at a national Swedish women's and gender conference, stirred a lot of feelings, not least of discontent (Manns 2009). The critique of long-term neglect was explicit, and Mulinari demanded answers. Her line of thought went well together with a similar critique formulated by another Swedish-based researcher a few years earlier. In 1997, Paulina de los Reyes presented a paper at a national Gender Historian Meeting criticising gender history in terms of hegemony. She contended that the neglect of ethnicity reproduced theories and conceptualisations of gender that naturalised certain belongings and made invisible, even denied, others (de los Reyes 1998).[41] At the conference in 2000, Mulinari asked why earlier efforts to make feminist scholars aware of the importance of ethnicity and sexuality had failed:

> Critical voices have asserted that class but obviously also "race"/ethnicity and sexuality are central landscapes through which gender(s) identities and feminist consciousness are lived and acted upon. An adequate theory of gender (as an adequate theory of class) – it was suggested – must simultaneously be able to incorporate other forms of social inequality. (Mulinari 2001, 7)

Why did not anything happen? In her view, the alleged lack of interest was due to a particular conceptualisation of women and gender in Nordic feminist research in general, and in Swedish research in particular. She claimed that gender was comprehended as monolithic and was a dominating focus in much research about women in relation to the Nordic welfare states, that is, within one of the dominating research fields. Mulinari (2001, 22) concluded that the feminist research community not only needed a better understanding of how specific gender regimes functioned, but it also needed to "confront its own history of exclusion and silence within the area of 'race'/ethnicity and racism. In this sense what I am arguing for is a need of a disciplinary crisis." In her view, Nordic women's and gender

ring the 1980s, while Dorothy Smith, Hilary Rose, Nancy Hartsock, Sandra Harding, and Allison Jaggar were well-known.
[41] The article was reprinted in de los Reyes et al eds. (2002).

studies had a long history of exclusion and neglect, of legitimising only certain areas of study, only certain bodies of knowledge, only certain ways of analysing discrimination and social inequalities. The imaginary of an inclusive, all-welcoming field of women's studies was severely questioned.

An implicit imaginary of a Nordic feminist "we" seems to have dominated during the early mobilising years, despite certain theoretical disagreements (for example to what extent poststructuralist theorising could work in favour of the emancipatory goals of women's studies, and the discussions about sameness and difference). The implicit feminist "we" appears as one closely related to the socialist feminist community in Norden in which gender was related solely to class (or rather, to labour), and women were seen as one universal category. The monolithic concept of womanhood seems to have grown out of the close entanglement between women's studies and the women's movement in its historical and geopolitical Nordic setting. Furthermore, the still non-consolidated and therefore fragile position of women's studies in the academy during the 1980s most certainly played an important role, enforcing a feeling of vulnerability. It became important to stick together in order to retain a foothold and to be perceived as strong, and to succeed in making women's studies a legitimate field of research. In this respect, unity became crucial.

The Swedish gender historian, Yvonne Hirdman, explains in a text what made women's studies activists and scholars mobilise during these years – a collective urge to intervene in male-biased knowledge production, and to oppose the continuing neglect of women's oppression in left-wing theorisation. She writes:

> To say "we" was a political act. To look for unity among women was like breaking a taboo – a taboo stating that women and men could not have diverging interests. And we were out looking for women's *common* interests, shared experiences regardless of class, ethnicity, place on earth or in the labour market. [---] We were in the process of trying to shape a powerful, politically unified "we" – we as in "women." (Hirdman 2008, 39)[42]

[42] My translation. Quote in original: "Att säga 'vi' var en politisk handling. Att söka det som enade, det som var det lika var som att bryta igenom ett tabu – det tabu som sade att kvinnor och män inte får ha skilda intressen. Och vi var på jakt efter kvinnors *gemensamma* intressen, gemensamma upplevelser, gemensamma erfarenheter, oavsett klass,

This kind of feminism is what today's critique has targeted: a dominant, hegemonic feminism based on a vision that is seen as too narrow, a vision that is blamed for not having encouraged and given space to any kind of theorising beyond a monolithic conceptualisation of gender. As Nordic postcolonial feminists in the late 1990s came to address the problem of universal, monolithic categories of gender, their theorisation differed considerably from earlier theorisation. First of all, they directed a critique straight at their own feminist community, which was unexpected in women's and gender studies. The critique stressed eurocentrism and pointed to an unexamined and neglected situatedness of knowledge production. Postcolonial feminists further claimed that a lack of interest was in fact an unwillingness to listen to internal opposing voices, which in turn contributed to the maintenance of women's oppression. In a text from 2002, the editors write with particular address to Sweden:[43]

> Feminist attitudes in Sweden towards differences are [...] strange. When differences in women's lives and strategies have been noticed, these have been defined as questions of "diverse experiences" or "difficulties within sisterhood." Such an approach allows the power dimension in the relationship between women to be ignored or turned into a question subordinate to the one about inequality between women and men. A consequence of this is that women's and gender research in this way contribute to the construction of a notion of womanhood where subordination and oppression of different groups of women do not fit. Feminism is constructed on an idea of "womanhood" as homogeneous and free from conflicts while formulating policies seemingly beyond women's race, ethnicity and/or class experiences. (de los Reyes et al. eds. 2002, 12)[44]

etnicitet, plats på jorden eller på arbetsmarknaden. [---] Vi var i färd med att söka forma ett slagkraftigt, politiskt enande 'vi' – vi som i 'kvinnor'."

[43] *Maktens (o)lika förklädnader* (de los Reyes et al. eds. 2002), was a publication in honour of Wuokko Knocke, researcher in migration, gender and labour, and has been reprinted several times since its original publication.

[44] Quote in original: "Den svenska feminismens förhållningssätt mot olikheter är [...] betänksamt. I den mån att skillnader i kvinnors levnadsvillkor och strategier har uppmärksammats har dessa definierats som en fråga om 'skiftande erfarenheter' eller 'systerskapets svårigheter.' Ett sådant förhållningssätt gör att maktdimensionen i relationen mellan kvinnor ignoreras eller också görs ojämlikhet mellan kvinnor till ett problem som underordnas ojämlikheter mellan kvinnor och män. En följd av detta är att kvinno- och könsforskning på detta sätt bidrar till att skapa en föreställning om kvinnlighet där underordning och förtryck mellan olika grupper av kvinnor inte får plats. Feminismen konstrueras utifrån en uppfattning om 'kvinnlighet' som homogen och konfliktfri sam-

Lesbian studies and the translation of gender

Publications show that lesbian studies in Norden did not prosper at the time. Worth noting is that women's studies was perceived of as quite an open space for students and scholars living openly as lesbians or bisexuals (Manns 2008; 2009). Today queer feminist research holds quite a firm and prominent position throughout the Nordic field of women's and gender research (Berg and Wickman 2010; Dahl 2011; Rosenbeck 2014).[45] However, when *Kvinnovetenskaplig tidskrift* launched a lesbian issue in 1985, Nordic scholars in the field were hard to find. This was the case even next time in 1990, when the theme issue "Sexuality" was launched.[46] According to the editors ("Från redaktionen" 1985), scholarship on same-sex relations and heterosexuality as a social institution was considered neither suitable nor relevant to Nordic women's studies in 1985. The editorial even accused the community of occasionally being a homophobic milieu.[47] One of the editors, Eva Borgström, remarked several years later in an interview that, even though women's lives and experiences of all kinds were said to be important (as in the well-known and frequently used slogan "the personal is political") and therefore legitimate to analyse, lesbian love and lives came to be regarded as too personal to fit into women's studies. According to Borgström, the field of research was seen as too intimate, embarrassing, and therefore unsuitable for feminist research.[48] Rosenbeck states that Nordic scholars sought elsewhere, outside Norden, for networks where lesbian studies could be conducted.[49] Even though lesbian studies did not flourish, the Nordic women's studies context is remembered and narrated as quite a comfortable one to live and act within. When asked, several (but certainly not all) scholars emphasise that it was a space open to non-heterosexual

tidigt som den formulerar politiska strategier till synes bortom kvinnors ras, etniska tillhörighet och/eller klasserfarenheter av förtryck."
[45] During the late 1990s, Judith Butler gained an almost hegemonic position within Nordic gender studies (in Sweden not the least), particularly her theorising about the heterosexual matrix.
[46] The Lesbian issue was inspired by the one in *Signs* 1983, see "Från redaktionen", editorial 1985.
[47] The term homophobic was also explained in the text, indicating that it was unknown for the readers ("Från redaktionen" 1985, 3). See also Lindholm (1985, 56) where she says that lesbian issues are controversial particularly in Swedish women's studies.
[48] Interview by author with Eva Borgström, 2007. See also Edenheim (2008), and Mulinari (2009).
[49] Private conversation with Bente Rosenbeck.

existence, even if research about lesbian love and same-sex sexuality was not encouraged, or even regarded as suitable to talk about (Manns 2008). In this respect, the Nordic women's studies space did not seem to have differed much from other European ones. As Nina Lykke (2001a, 276) contends, women's studies in Europe have not been a place for carving out "conceptual and discursive spaces for emerging lesbian subjectivities and lesbian voices." In this respect, the Nordic feminist community was one of many European ones, which overlooked lesbian love and life as a legitimate field of study. The Nordic conceptualisation of gender did not help to alter this much.

Early on, Nordic feminist scholarship elaborated on gender as an analytical category, particularly in relation to male dominance and structural discrimination. Hirdman (1988) elaborated on what she called the gender system: a structure in society, which functioned according to two principles. First, women and men were regarded as two distinctly different kinds and kept apart, and secondly, the system was hierarchical, with women and femininity subordinated to men and masculinity. Her writings were widely read and used in Norden, together with Joan W. Scott's (1986) article "Gender: A Useful Category of Historical Analysis" Like Hirdman, Scott elaborated on the construction of gender and the reproduction of social inequality throughout history in terms of women's subordination to men as a power relation and as working within several social institutions.[50] Their work gained almost hegemonic status in Nordic scholarship, particularly in Swedish gender history (Rosenbeck 1998; 2012; 2014, 144–145; Hagemann 2003; Manns and Östman 2008; Haavet 2009; Mulinari 2009; Manns 2012; Edenheim 2012). Little attention was paid to the differences between Scott and Hirdman. In many scholars' ways of using them, the two went well together in what seemed like a specific Nordic, and Swedish-dominated, understanding of gender and power. Somewhat paradoxically, the dominance of their thinking about gender nearly resulted in a failure to critically conceptualise gender, not because of the understanding of gender as a power structure and relational, but because gender in the Nordic adaptation strengthened already existing tendencies to regard women and men as two separate and distinct social categories without paying attention

[50] See particularly Scott's article "Gender: A Useful Category of Historical Analysis" (1986), originally published in *American Historical Review*. The article is still (in May 2016) the most cited one in the journal. See particulary Hirdman's articles "Genussystemet" (1988) and "The Gender System" (1991). Hirdman furthermore located a number of gender contracts, empirically based in modern Nordic welfare states.

to the relevance of other power regimes at play within each category. Both Hirdman and Scott stressed gender as a social construction and a power relation. However, neither of them probed deeper into the role of sexuality or ethnicity, nor did scholars in the debates that followed. The debates primarily focused on whether a gender system-thinking à la Hirdman was suitable for early modern history, whether a structural approach had the capacity to fully grasp women's agency, and whether the poststructuralist mode of Scott was a reliable tool for feminist intervention (Gemzöe et al. 1989; Carlsson Wetterberg 1992; Hagemann 1994; Sjöberg 2000). Hardly any researchers commented on these texts' failure to problematise hetero-sexuality, ethnicity, and structural racism. A group of anthropologists did comment on Hirdman's reductive reading of Gayle Rubin, but their remarks were not picked up in the debate. Scott's lack of theorising sexu-ality went largely uncommented as well. Exceptions were Widerberg's critique, mentioned earlier, and "Institutionalized Heterosexuality and the Category of Gender," an article by the Finnish historian Marianne Lilje-ström (1990). Published in the Sexuality-issue of *Kvinnovetenskaplig tid-skrift* in 1990, the article attempted to put heteronormativity at the centre of discussions about gender and social order.[51] Like Widerberg, Liljeström attributes the lack of problematisation of heterosexuality to a dominant Marxist tradition and an emphasis on women's work in Nordic theorising. Liljeström writes:

> With only a slight exaggeration, I contend that the Marxist tradition [...] has led to a prioritisation of studies on different aspects of women's work, and to an idea of sexuality as a "second-tier" issue. The cherishing of this tradition might hinder the development of feminist thought in Norden. Let us therefore also here, at these latitudes, involve ourselves more deeply in the discussion about sexuality/heterosexuality within feminist theorising. (Liljeström 1990, 18)[52]

[51] The title of the article in the original, "Institutionaliserad heterosexualitet och under-sökning av könssystem," explicitly relates to the Swedish term "gender system" as well as gender, but the author argues in favour of the Swedish word *kön* [sex] instead of gender.
[52] My translation. Quote in the original: "Med en mild överdrift påstår jag, att den marxistiska traditionen [...] lett till en prioritering av studier om kvinnoarbetets olika aspekter samt till en uppfattning om sexualitetsproblematiken som en 'andra rangens' fråga. Omhuldandet av denna tradition kan utgöra en broms för utvecklingen av femi-nistiskt tänkande i Norden. Låtom oss alltså även på dessa breddgrader djupare invol-

Scott and Hirdman's respective ways of reasoning enriched theorisations of gender and power in Nordic feminist research. Scott furthermore functioned as a bridge between a poststructuralist, deconstructive strand, and a more empirical, often under-theorised field of gender history. However, Hirdman and Scott were read in ways that helped to strengthen the already dominant conceptualisation of women as a monolithic category. Despite their important contributions and despite many studies' focus on women's work and the gendered division of labour, the effect of the homogeneous reading of these two theories reinforced an already present mode in much Nordic, and particularly Swedish, feminist research, a mode that viewed women as one homogeneous category, and men as another. The conceptualisation and cultural translation of gender and power did not make dominant trends in Nordic theories of oppression and inequality more prone to develop theories that took material and social/economic differences between women (and between men) seriously into account. To emphasise my argument, this particular way of conceptualising gender unintentionally came close to one already established in Nordic gender equality policies. It was also close to a way of thinking the category of women that had been dominant in the women's movement, namely a way of thinking about gender and gender inequality that tended to repeatedly misjudge the importance of the interaction between different power regimes and its effects on life (Isaksson 2007; Velásquez 2007; Alnebratt 2009).

As shown above, at the turn of the millennium, postcolonial scholars harshly criticised Nordic feminism for its reliance on an understanding of womanhood as homogeneous, and for its avoidance of internal debates around feminist core issues. A brief look at the debates during the late 1980s and early 1990s about gender as a category of analysis confirms the accuracy of this critique. The debates circled around how to get proper knowledge about gender and power, and how to translate the very word gender, rather than around the homogenising and universalising tendencies at work in the social construction of femininity and masculinity.

vera oss i diskussionen om sexualitets/heterosexualitetsproblematiken inom feministiskt teoretiserande."

Conclusion: Nordicness, feminist space, and belonging

In theorisations of women's oppression and the translation of gender from a women's movement context into an academic (yet political) setting, the concept of gender gradually lost its meaning in Nordic and national gender equality policies. The ambition to remain independent of state governing, stressed in the early years proved to be much more difficult to achieve than expected. As Kerstin Alnebratt (2009) shows, during the 1990s the term gender was adjusted (back) into prior conceptualisations of equal opportunities/equal status between women and men (regarded as two separate categories). Gender as a concept gradually became compatible with a political vision about gender equality, as in equality between two distinct groups (a monolithic group of women and an equally monolithic group of men). This vision was not much concerned about ethnic discrimination or heteronormative oppression (Alnebratt 2009, 206–209). Alnebratt (2009, 209) concludes that gender simply became a new way of saying *jämställdhet* [gender equality], and therefore became a way of performing gender equality policy, without much regard to feminist theorising about it. I have shown that the lack of internal debates and critical elaborations within Nordic women's studies during the 1980s about different discriminating power regimes paved the way for and contributed to a geopolitically specific translation of gender. This translation/conceptualisation was, as Alnebratt shows, quickly adopted in gender equality policies, which in turn affected women's studies research.

As concluded, at the centre of attention was the literal translation of the word gender in the Nordic countries. The selection of the word was considered crucial to the usefulness of the concept in its geopolitical and historical setting. Widerberg (1992; 1998) proposed that the already existing and more widely used concept of *køn/kjønn/kön* (approximately "sex") in Scandinavian languages, ought to be maintained in order to avoid an untenable binary opposition between sex and gender she found in much US theorising. Hirdman (1988) also aimed at overcoming this binary, but argued strongly in favour of the term *genus*. While *genus* [gender] soon gained a firm foothold in Sweden, the terms *køn/kjønn* and "women" lingered on in the other Nordic countries. According to Kari Jegerstedt (2000), the three different words in Nordic feminist scholarship: *genus* in Sweden, *køn/kjønn* in Denmark and Norway and *naisten* and *kvenna* [woman] in Finland and Iceland, all tried to avoid getting captured in an untenable distinction between sex as biological and gender as a social construction.

The role of heterosexuality in the oppression of women was, as stressed, notably absent in much Nordic feminist theorising during its formative years. This is not the least the case in discussions about gender as a category of analysis. Hardly anyone commented upon this matter.[53] This is somewhat striking, since both Hirdman and Scott took their point of departure in Rubin's article "The Traffic in Women: Notes on the 'Political Economy' of Sex" from 1975. Rubin's theory about the social organisation of sexuality and how sexuality is moulded in a compulsory heterosexual matrix simply fell out of focus in much Nordic reading of Scott's and Hirdman's definitions of gender and power. Hardly any critical comments on this are to be found, even though Rubin's article was an often-cited text. Instead, scholars focusing on sexuality from a critical perspective were inclined to turn to queer theory in the early 1990s, particularly using Eve Kosofsky Sedgwick and Judith Butler (Edenheim 2008; Berg and Wickman 2010).

As argued here, the translation of gender (where femininity and masculinity first and foremost became understood as a social construction within an unproblematised heterosexual matrix) went neatly together with dominating ideals in gender equality politics, a policy that tended to see women and men as two distinct and universal categories. This was the case, even if several feminist scholars were critical of the lack of in-depth thinking about power and male dominance in the policies of gender equality. I contend that the lack of reflection about heterosexuality as a social institution and of ethnicity and racism concerning gender and power within Nordic women's and gender research in the late 1980s and early 1990s, did contribute to a particular and everyday production of Nordic commonality. What feminist scholars contested was the imaginary of Norden as a woman-friendly welfare state. It was not, they claimed. In fact, it failed to turn formal possibilities into real ones. The discrepancy between the ideal and the real, it was argued, was wide throughout Norden (as stated in Haavio-Mannila ed. 1983). In contemporary critique of policies of gender equality, and occasionally also in critique of research about it, few comments were made about regionally dominating, underlying ideas of a universal womanhood. In regard to an ongoing construction and performativity of Norden and Nordicness, this stance was quite clearly expressed in the first editorial in *NORA*, the joint Nordic Women's Studies journal, started in 1993.[54] In the

---

[53] Exceptions were as mentioned Gemzöe et al. (1989), and Liljeström (1990).
[54] This mode of thinking remained during the 1990s. See Dahl in this volume.

editorial, women in Norden once again were depicted as a homogeneous group regardless of class, ethnicity, or sexual orientation:

> The Nordic countries have been termed "laboratories of equal rights policy," with reference to the lifestyle of Nordic women, their high level of education, their sexual emancipation, their employment rate and, not least, their political activity and positions. [---] Viewed from the outside, such phenomena support the supposition that the Nordic countries are models of successful application of policies of gender and social equality. Viewed from the inside, the enthusiasm has been somewhat more moderate, as our consciousness about the difference between formal rights and women's everyday lives is sharpened, and certainly also because the welfare state not only fulfils needs but also promotes a radicalization of them. (Bjerrum Nielsen and Steinfeld 1993, 1-2)

Lykke (2004a, 80) later comments on this very editorial and its specific politics of location. She states that the editorial was first and foremost eager to present Nordic women's studies as a research field of high quality, to readers outside an imagined Nordic community. This implicitly did not only produce a firm "them," the readers, but also a firm "we," Nordic women's studies scholars of a particular sort.[55]

Several aspects have been taken into account in my own translation of this time period and its everyday making of Nordic familiarity. Feminist space within women's studies on its Nordic level seems to have had at least two significant characteristics. It functioned by and large as an open, welcoming space for many kinds of women's studies scholarships. Even though women's studies was presented as feminist and more radical (politically and/or feminist) than sex-role and gender equality research, practically all kinds of studies of women's conditions and lives were included, as long as the research embraced some kind of critical perspective (often referred to as the woman's perspective) on gender and power. A kind of extended do-it-yourself culture stemming from the women' s liberation movement and the all-embracing character encouraged empirical diversity. This empirical diversity was important for implicit conceptualisations and imaginaries of Nordic familiarity in women's studies, and helped produce a certain politics of belonging. The empirical heterogeneity shows one side of Nordic feminist scholarly space, its open and inclusive side. It shows the aims of intervention, as well as the scholar's capability to form broad and innovative

[55] This editorial and others in *NORA* are further discussed by Dahl in this volume.

collaborations across national and disciplinary borders, with or without financial funding. Simultaneously, the space was clearly limited as shown in the examples about lesbian studies, the specific translation of gender, and in the lack of interest in internal discussions about racism and ethnicity. The performativity, the everyday doing of feminist Nordic familiarity did, therefore, contribute to and reinforced the production of assumptions of regional feminist commonality. This commonality concerned ideas and ideals about who belonged to women's studies as a proper subject of know-ledge, and also what counted as proper objects of study. Today's comments about, and reactions to, allegations of exclusionary practices and hegemonic feminism within gender studies are many. This definitely shows that our feminist scholarly space has changed over the years. How we react and respond to these changes, where and how we position ourselves in the field and with whom we seek to collaborate differs for many reasons. How we relate to our recent past and envision our future matters, because as Robin Wiegman (2010) puts it, feminism is a living thing.

Between Familiar Differences and American Tunes: The Geopolitical Grammar of Nordic Gender Studies in an Age of Europeanisation

Ulrika Dahl

> The Nordic countries have a long tradition of working together. This is also reflected in the lively Nordic collaboration within the field of Women's Studies. This kind of crossnational and regional cooperation, encompassing both Women's Studies researchers, teachers and administrators, is quite unique from an international perspective. (Bergman 2002, 16)

This chapter explores what counts as Nordic and European in women's and gender studies and how such imaginaries are constructed, circulated, and given meaning around the millennium, or 1990 to 2008. Rather than tracing a particular "development" or "progress" of Nordic gender studies as it becomes increasingly established as a scientific discipline or research field, that is, an account steeped in a naturalised notion of historicity (cf. Honkanen 2005), the chapter instead asks some broader and seemingly self-evident questions: How and why does a knowledge formation such as women's and gender studies, with diverse theoretical, methodological, disciplinary, and interdisciplinary dimensions as well as epistemological contradictions and conflicts, come to find a cohesion, a sense of "we-ness" and belonging in geopolitical terms and what counts as Nordic? What work does such an imaginary of "Nordic" or "European" do in an increasingly "global" era?

As we point out in the introduction, the past decade has witnessed the arrival of a range of historiographical studies of the field of women's and gender studies, most of them told from within and about the West as in Anglo-American women's and gender studies. Many such accounts rely on historicity, what Kattis Honkanen (2005, 293) describes as "a mode of thought that enables the entity history to become an object of science, for instance, or to become a personal investment, or a shared horizon of reality, or a narrative." As she points out, history is part of the way we think, and often accounts that are considered "historical" rely on chronological order and thus on ideas of causality, the notion that one thing leads to another (Honkanen 2005, 291). Accounts of women's and gender studies are also often construc-tivist, insofar as they make clear that stories matter in the creation and orientations of this meaningful and radical knowledge formation.

Informed by some aspects of feminist historiography but far from a "properly trained" historian, I instead place at the centre of the analysis in this chapter questions about what I, with inspiration from Clare Hemmings (2011), will call a *geopolitical grammar*. Thus, I do not simply wish to add a locally situated story "from the Nordic region," but rather I wish to show how and why geopolitics, as short for a complex of historical, cultural, linguistic, and politico-economic context is both presumed and produced through the (re)making of women's and gender studies in this region.

The epigraph by Solveig Bergman, director of NIKK, Nordic Institute for Gender Research in 2000 illuminates, what Ulla Manns' chapter has already shown; namely that the idea of (regional) cooperation, as well as a cooperation of different actors, both individual, institutional, and national is commonly understood as a "Nordic tradition" in women's and gender studies, and is often highlighted as a unique feature of Nordicness itself. While the content of the tradition and the effect of cooperation vary across accounts, the importance of stressing such a "tradition" itself is rarely called into question. In contrast, I will argue that, around the turn of the millen-nium, the need to identify and account for Nordic specificity, largely nar-rated through sameness as in homogeneity (always a matter of looking back, of historicising), came to matter in renewed ways. As we shall see, the mil-lennial decades are often described as marked by extraordinariness first of all in terms of broader historical changes that, following the fall of the Berlin Wall and the proposed "end" of the Cold War and the beginning of "Europe-anisation," are understood to be cartographically, culturally, politically, eco-nomically, and technologically "transformative" for the world, and for Europe and thus the conceptualisation of the Nordic in particular. In short: the bor-ders and content of the Nordic and the European are reconsidered and given (re)new(ed) significance and meaning (cf. Mulari 2015).

With the onset of neoliberalism, the role of the welfare state, so central to feminist projects centred on equality between men and women in the Nordic region, also began to shift. After decades of political and intellectual work for the purpose of legitimising feminist research in relation to non-feminist disciplines, as a general trend women's and gender studies were increasingly transformed into degree-awarding programmes and sub-fields within established disciplines in many national contexts. Furthermore, professional journals and conferences were established and participation in and contribution to those have increasingly become ordinary dimensions of academic feminism – even if access to and participation remain unevenly distributed between and available to individual scholars, institutions, nations, and regions in Europe and "Norden".[1] At the same time, and especially with the arrival of "poststructuralism," queer theory, and what is often summarised under intersectionality, the question of who and what the proper objects and subjects of this field are, came to be debated. Who and what, in short, were to be the subjects of this research? This chapter is located at the intersection of these processes and explores how the status and content of Nordic and European scholarship is rearticulated, with an eye to how the conversation about these matters is shaped by discussions about what constitutes its uniqueness, origins, and orientations. My over-arching interest is in how and why ideas and theorists are assigned geo-political belonging and who is said to belong where. What work does such assignations do?

This chapter takes as its case the (re)making of Nordic women's and gen-der studies around the turn of the millennium, and it does so to ask broader questions about how a geopolitical grammar works in the production of (feminist) knowledge. The chapter centres on three themes. Following a discussion of the rationale behind the chapter's analytic framework, metho-dological approach, and source materials and a partial sketch of some factors that may be seen as "contextual" or as a "setting," I first analyse nar-ratives that discuss characteristics of "Nordic" and "European" women's and gender studies drawn from and produced between 1990 and 2008. Rather than outlining an *a priori* field called the Nordic and giving it a set of predetermined features (as much of the source material does), I show how shared Nordic or European features are presented, and attend to the sym-bolic significance of the utterances "our" and "we" and to which audiences are imagined and addressed. I then discuss a series of conferences, and the

---

[1] In this chapter, I have opted to use the term "Nordic region" rather than the Scan-dinavian term "Norden," in part as a reminder, because the Nordic region linguistically and geopolitically exceeds that of Scandinavia, which is not always made evident in narratives *about* this geopolitical region and in part, and certainly tellingly, because the former is more commonly used in the English source materials.

shape that they took as examples of what I call "constitutive moments" that demarcate the meaning of the Nordic. Next I turn to showing how the "arrivals" of new bodies of flesh and knowledge, and of new subjects, become crucial in the (re)making of an imagined Nordic or European "we." In the final part of the chapter, I consider the political ecology of institution building, with academic journal formation and particularly editorials as the key examples of collective enunciations of a Nordic "we." In the conclusion, I return to the value of attending to a geopolitical grammar for redressing the meaning of a politics of location, and for studying and thinking critically about what knowledge formations might do, specifically for feminist knowledge practices.

The approach here, it should be stressed from the outset, is *not* one of comparing and contrasting women's and gender studies with other academic fields and/or their histories. The starting point is that feminist worlds are meaningful worlds, not only in comparison to, or as refuge from, other worlds. While individual subjects may have chosen feminist worlds to escape from other worlds or due to the lack of a place within other academic worlds, this is a contribution to a *feminist* discussion about what makes the world of feminist research liveable and to whom, and, subsequently, about what Nordic and European mean in this particular context. To that end, it also largely relies on feminist theories to make its arguments. Among those are a feminist deconstructive reading which, according to Honkanen (2005, 292), "traces the possibilities and places for 'outsides,' and seeks to find the textual places where history or historicity is used as a foundation – elsewhere."

An anthropological approach to feminist story-telling

In attending to *geopolitical grammar* which can also be explained as a kind of *logic* in stories of the origin and development of Nordic and European women's and gender studies, I first and foremost build on anthropological and feminist theoretical approaches that suggest that stories are central for shared cultural imaginaries[2]. In the time period under study, significant institution building takes place, and my approach to women's and gender studies does therefore not primarily consider its relationship to social

---

[2] I will develop the argument of how kinship becomes a part of this grammar, or logic, elsewhere.

movements or its intervention into the "ivory tower" as such. Rather, it aims to take the becoming-institution seriously. As Sara Ahmed has argued:

> [T]o explain institutions is to give an account of how they emerge or take form [...] a way of describing not simply the activities that take place within institutions (which would allow the institution into the frame of analysis only as a container, as what contains what is described rather than being part of a description), but how those activities shape the sense of an institution, or even institutional sense. (Ahmed 2012, 20–21)

Thus, rather than investigate knowledge produced and circulated *in* a predetermined place as always already a reflection of a collective and co-herent body, I study the activity of narrating the (history of the) field itself in order to understand how place, or the meaning of the Nordic, becomes an *effect* of knowledge produced *through* a geopolitical grammar.

Needless to say, there are many ways to approach the question of institu-tionalisation, and as Mia Liinason (2011, 55) argues, the term itself is contested within a range of academic disciplines. In this chapter, institu-tionalisation is understood as the process of providing a robust and en-during material base for research and education on a particular, and in this case, interdisciplinary topic in the form of an institutional unit, complete with (academic) staff, courses, journals, conferences, and other reproductive technologies of knowledge production. Like Liinason, I am primarily interes-ted in how institutions reproduce themselves. In my understanding, as an institution, women's and gender studies is a body of flesh and knowledge; it consists of actors, texts, and institutional and political contexts that frequently travel and are brought together. The very coming-into-being of Nordic and European women's and gender studies is not only the effect of political and economic changes and interventions, which provided the grounds for considering this knowledge formation to be important and worth funding. Equally importantly, it is an effect of the stories that both underpin and recount such processes, and indeed those stories matter (Hemmings 2011). The production of stories about the institution and its history is thus not only an activity that takes place "in" the institution, but storytelling with Ahmed's understanding, actively makes and shapes the institution and its "we-ness." On an overarching level, we could argue that a central dilemma for women's and gender studies is one that concerns whether institutionalisation itself is a good idea for a field that was founded on the very critique of academic institutions.

For the purposes of my analysis here, I argue that we can approach women's and gender studies anthropologically and thus as a cultural formation that, like a society, has a worldview and a particular organisation. As such, it has its own cultural belief-based system for authorising stories about itself and its own origin and development.[3] Here I follow feminist anthropologists Sylvia Yanagisako and Carol Delaney (1994) in proposing that cultural analysis can be done not only through participant observation but also by attending to narratives. They particularly stress the significance of *origin stories* because such stories concern "notions of 'coming-into-being,' which are simultaneously physiological, social, and ontological." Furthermore, "stories of origin are told to every generation and thus shape how people imagine themselves to be" (Yanagisako and Delaney 1994, 2–3). Indeed, all teachers and students know that part of apprenticeship in a scholarly tradition involves studying/knowing our histories and situating and orienting ourselves in relation to such stories of origin (and development), and Hemmings' powerful argument that *how* we tell stories matter, supports this argument. In her book *Why Stories Matter,*Hemmings (2011, 16) explains that she aims to "flesh out the substance of Western feminist stories and to intervene by experimenting with how we might tell stories differently rather than telling different stories." She introduces the idea that stories of feminist knowledge have what Hemmings calls a "political grammar" and she suggests,

> [I]f we can identify the techniques through which dominant stories are secured, through which their status as "common sense" is reproduced, that political grammar may also offer a rigorous point of intervention through which Western feminist stories might be transformed.
> (Hemmings 2011, 20)

One example of a dominant story that is central to the substance of Western feminist stories is that of origin; where an idea or a thinker "originates" and

---

[3] By system I here mean both the educational and the promotional system that assigns authority to rank and degree and its reliance on a system of peer review. While it is a fascinating topic, it lies beyond the scope of this chapter and project to account for the complex workings of (institutional) power that makes up this system, but it is clear that the "truth value" of an account is understood to be linked quite literally to the authority of the author. A PhD examination of the field's historiography contributes new knowledge and often brings new perspectives, but the stories based on "experience" are often understood to be both more authentic and more accurate.

how a knowledge formation comes into being. As Yanagisako and Delaney (1994, 2–3) put it, "origin stories are a prime locus for a society's notion of itself – its identity, its worldview, and social organization." In other words, narratives of how and where "it" began, of who was there and what was done, shapes directions and organisations. Furthermore, Yanagisako and Delaney (1994, 2–3) contend that, anthropologically speaking, whether an origin story of particular society, institution or cultural formation is true or false is of secondary importance; the central significance is the work that such stories do as *representations* of origins.

Through close analysis of the materials at hand I have been especially struck by origin stories which are accounts of what Katie King (1994, 2) calls, "constitutive moments" in the (re)making of Nordic and European women's and gender studies. A "moment," in King's conception, can be a text, a location, or a historical shift, what she calls "local moments defined by specific strategies and stakes." I am less interested in the degree to which "constitutive moments" are "historical facts" and more in how they are narrated and recounted; how they become part of tradition. In this chapter, constitutive moments are conferences and the reports, networks and orientations they engender, as well as the journals and new topics that are presented as constitutive of the field or its turns. In order to denaturalise taken-for-granted geopolitical points of departure for understanding knowledge, I do not look at moments "in" a setting but rather focus on how conferences, organisations, and networks marked as European or Nordic *become* "locations" that work as constitutive moments. I also attend to how "new" topics in women's and gender studies, such as masculinity, age/generation, ethnicity, and sexuality are articulated and to debates about the "usefulness" of theories understood as new, foreign or challenging of the field's boundaries.

An all-encompassing coverage or close analysis of all texts written in and about Nordic/European women's and gender studies in the given time period of roughly 1990 to 2005 is near impossible, especially in a short chapter. First of all, the field expanded rapidly, with new departments and programmes established in most universities in the Nordic countries, and the volume of scholarly work in women's/gender studies produced during these years makes defining a diversifying field an epistemological challenge. At the same time, in this period the difference between the entire field of gender research, that is research on and with gender, and the field of *gender studies*, a designated discipline where both theory (development) and education play key roles, is gradually becoming distinguishable.[4] Boundaries between these two bodies, research and studies, are porous and at the same time, institutionally quite firm at times. Above all, as I have already mentioned, my primary concern is neither an empiricist one nor one concerned with outlining a chronology of facts.

My main source materials are conference and project reports, editorials and retrospectives, newsletters and magazines, all of which reflect and address themselves to and speak as "Nordic" and "European" in this time period. In particular, I focus on the text production of the NIKK, Nordic Institute for Gender Research and the journal *NORA,* as well as some from *European Journal of Women's Studies.*[5] Clearly, the choice and perspective of an authorised storyteller are of the utmost importance to how a story is told and received. The merits of the stories presented here thus lies in their narrative similarities and citational frequency. That said, it is important to stress that I look at stories that appear in print. Needless to say, the (collaborative) work and necessary demarcations required to produce the account is often concealed by the seemingly smooth published story. Such circulated and cited stories become central to the identity and worldview of the field itself – at least until challenged by other stories. Through their circulation and citation, written accounts of events and processes become enmeshed with "what really happened" and they demonstrate a certain "world-view."

Obviously, feminist knowledge comes in a range of forms, but that which is produced in the university holds a particular status and is often understood to be in the service of the wider society (McDermott 1994, 3). Analysing academic journals is one way in which scholars have studied the field of women's and gender studies (cf. McDermott 1994; Lykke 2004a). As Patrice McDermott (1994, 3) notes, a focus on journals offers a view on the institutional and discursive history of a field, as well as a way to identify themes in politics and scholarship, and I would add, it is part of a self-ref-

---

[4] At the same time, as women's and gender studies gains status in the academy as a discipline, the relationship to the diversifying women's movement and other social movements also changes in this time period. There is some mention of this relationship in this chapter, but for the most part, I focus on what goes on *in* the academy. For a closer analysis of feminist movements and their relationship to knowledge production in this time period in the Swedish context, see Mia Liinasson and Marta Cuesta's ongoing research project, funded by the Swedish Research Council.

[5] Most of these materials are available on line. In addition to project colleagues Ulla Manns and Marianne Liljeström, I am particularly grateful to Solveig Bergman, Nina Lykke, and Beatrice Halsaa for their assistance with materials and stories.

lexive practice. Clearly, a focus on published articles (and we might add, reports) only reveals the tip of an iceberg. Attention to the process of selection and exclusion in such practices, as well as to what never gets printed or circulated and why, is a study in itself. However, to gain access to such "data" requires inquiring into referee systems and formal and informal decision-making processes or, if you will, studying the micro-dynamics of power. Such a study is certainly worth doing with incisive care but it is not the one done here. Here the premise is that published stories are authorised stories and thus they carry weight in a community of peers; they get cited. While I have paid particular attention to the academic journal as the enabler and producer of feminist knowledge, we also need to attend to the gate-keepers of conventions and a reflection again of position and networks. Claiming belonging in the academic "family" means that to some degree one has to agree to participate in a system, which values research over teaching and publication in refereed journals over other kinds of publishing, and it is not a system all scholars wish to or can participate in.

Between American tunes and European difference:
(Re)defining the Nordic

> I think Europe is a bit of a colony in the realm of women's studies.
> (Braidotti *in* Braidotti and Butler 1994, 30)

If, as Kattis Honkanen (2005, 293), a Finnish women's studies scholar who trained at the University of Utrecht has suggested, historicising is part of how a "we" that consists of feminist social constructivists think, so is the idea of contextualisation, the idea that the context, or circumstances for an event or object, matter for our understanding of it. The choice here to focus on geopolitics and on a geopolitical grammar is obviously not random; rather it reflects both the approach and training of this particular researcher and the conversations she has been following and participating in during the course of this project. That said, I also hope to show that it is particularly fruitful for this study at this time. Before we turn to more in-depth analysis, in this section I want to offer a sketch of some key actors, events, and debates in the time period under study in order to illuminate the broader context in which this grammar emerges. I begin by locating Nordic women's and gender studies in a broader European "context" and by discussing the changing meaning of the Nordic in the aftermath of the fall of the Berlin Wall and how this relates to institutional support for women's and gender studies. As an instance of "globalisation" of knowledge, I then turn briefly to debates about language and translation of concepts and terms. This leads me, finally, to situate Nordic discussions in the larger setting of European women's and gender studies.

In this section and in the chapter as a whole, I want to take seriously the statement in the epigraph of this section, expressed in an often-cited conversation between Rosi Braidotti and Judith Butler (1994). Why and how does Europe, with its own imperialist and colonialist histories and powerful place in a global history, come to understand itself as a "colony," an "other," in a "realm" known as women's and gender studies in the time period of concern here? For Braidotti and other advocates of the import-ance of outlining a distinct "European" women's studies, the answer is that Anglo-American concepts have "colonised" the rest of the world's know-ledge formations, and that Europe, including the Nordic region, under-stands itself to be subordinated, peripheralised and even a kind of "other" to the "centre" of feminist knowledge production. This argument, which might be presumed to be an effect of a "context" in which postcolonial theory increasingly gains salience in women's studies and where the idea of a "colony" is that of a distant settlement closely linked to Edward Said's (1994, 9) idea of imperialism as "the practice, the theory and the attitudes of a dominating metropolitan center ruling a distant territory" is quite power-ful, if not paradoxical. The idea of "speaking back" to an imagined Anglo-American (cosmopolitan) centre of women's and gender studies has in turn motivated collaboration, joint productions, networks, and significant fun-ding for the establishment of a distinct field of "European" women's and gender studies, rendered possible by the 1990s expansion of the European Union. As we shall see here, the idea of the Nordic is understood to be both part of, and different from, such a formation. Furthermore, it is clear that the idea of Nordic cohesion is both produced in "European" stories and in the Nordic region's stories about itself.

As Nikki Sullivan (2004, 1) contends, "regionality, as a categorising logic that makes meaning and identity possible, does so in and through the instituting of boundaries." It is clear that such boundaries are not static, even if their existence is often legitimised by making transhistorical claims; it was "always" this way. As we noted in the introduction, Alastair Thomas (1996) contends that the very concept of the Nordic region has been crucial for Nordic cooperation and that the Nordic Council is the body that has largely been responsible for shaping and producing the idea of a common

Nordic identity since 1945. Perhaps the single most central actor is the Nordic Council of Ministers, founded in 1971 as a body for regional governmental collaboration; a vision, which like the UN and the origins of the EU has roots in the post-World War II context of a desire for stronger international collaboration in order to prevent war and conflict.[6] According to Thomas (1996, 17), the successes of this collaboration "rest more on shared culture and common objectives and values than on integrating institutions." According to Thomas, the 1990s were marked by a deep concern for the crisis of the Nordic community, largely as a result of the growth and institutionalisation of the EU. Following the "fall" of the Berlin Wall, the Council also oriented itself eastward and began closer collaborations with the (re)formed states across the Baltic Sea. In women's and gender studies terms, my research suggests that, crisis or not, the EU and the growth of "European" women's and gender studies might both threaten and strengthen the cohesion of "Nordic" commonality (cf. Rosenbeck 2000; Lykke 2001b). Thomas (1996, 16) also argues that in reality, "Nordic integration has been characterised by numerous small links, often at an inter-personal level and few of them are of major importance singly," and in many ways what appears as "Nordic" is in fact the coming together of "representatives" of different nations in joint research projects and networks. Thomas proposes that it is when listed by the Nordic Council and presented in such a manner that these small links appear in the form of "Nordic cooperation." Not only has a Nordic identity grown through interregional trade and migration, and through efforts to "harmonise domestic legislation," according to Thomas (1996, 17), it has also largely based on "extensive inter-Nordic cooperation and interchange of scientific, academic and cultural activity," and joint efforts around education, some of which are officially encouraged and many of which are sponsored by Nordic associations (Thomas 1996, 25).

The Nordic Council's mission has also come to include research and in 1995, this meant the funding and establishment of NIKK, Nordic Institute for Women's and Gender Research (today called the Nordic Gender Institute) with its office in Oslo, Norway. The main aim was to be "a bridge between Nordic gender research and equality politics,"[7] which also served to establish both a real and an imagined intimate tie between the field of women's and gender studies and state and regional gender equality policy.

[6] This is a story told on the website that promotes Nordic collaboration: www.norden.org (last accessed 2014-08-10).
[7] http://en.wikipedia.org/wiki/Nordic_Gender_Institute.

We can infer that, at this time, the idea of "gender equality" had already become part of a Nordic "tradition." While it later supported particular research themes, such as research on pornography, sexual violence, and masculinity, in the early days the main task of NIKK was sponsoring conferences, producing newsletters, and supporting journals promoting women's and gender research. In other words, NIKK was a key actor in both the institutionalisation of women's and gender studies in the Nordic region, and in the direction that the field took. Throughout the millennial decades, NIKK showcased theoretical and empirical development and diversity of research in various accounts of new themes across its publications. Indeed, Bente Rosenbeck (2000, 6) argues that it is the Nordic Council that has provided the key framework for Nordic collaboration and engendered possibilities for joint institutions while simultaneously "normalising" Nordic collaboration.

From its inception and through the period under study, NIKK also produced many stories of the development of Nordic collaboration and promoted the idea of an imagined Nordic community, in the form of editorials, research reports, and newsletters. At the same time, the changing name and mission of the institute tells us something about the changing definition of the object of study: women's and gender research. Initially called an institute for women's and gender research, in 2000, seven years after its founding, the institute is presented as a "coordinating organ for feminist, women's, men's, gender and gender equality research in the Nordic region" that aims to encourage, initiate, coordinate, and inform about gender and women's research in and outside of the Nordic region (*NIKK Magazine* 2000). Thus, NIKK as an institution reflects the larger changes in ideas of what the proper subject for a field called women's, gender and/or feminist studies around the millennium should be. This suggests that the Nordic is not "different" on the level of subjects and naming, but rather that NIKK is a central actor in attempting to establish a distinctly *Nordic* and thus perhaps "local" version of a larger imaginary.

Indeed, NIKK also presented itself as a common platform that aimed to make Nordic research more internationally visible, premised on the idea that regional collaboration would give "more value than particular national tasks" and would link research and work for gender equality. A year later, the aim of NIKK is presented as "a platform for Nordic cooperation in relation to nearby areas, Europe and internationally" and by issue 2 of 2001 as a platform for Nordic collaboration with the near areas of the Baltic states and Western Russia, Europe, and internationally. This expanding understanding of NIKK's aim reflects the Nordic Council of Ministers' growing interest in, and expansion of, what counts as Nordic, which increasingly also extends to the Baltic region. When NIKK and the Council of Ministers funded a Nordic Research school in Interdisciplinary Gender Studies in 2004, this consortium also included university partners in the Baltic States and in Western Russia. By largely following the Nordic council's narrative about the Nordic, NIKK and its researchers thus start from and deploy a geo-political grammar in which a story of Nordicness originates in a post-World War II context and yet is created through invoking an imagined "shared history" which also resembles that of an imagined "Baltoscandia" that originated in the late 19th century and gained renewed salience when the Baltic states sought entry into the EU in the early 2000s (cf. Moisio 2003).

The complex production of such an imaginary is reflected in how the boundaries of the Nordic and the aims of the institute shift through this period in ways that resonate with broader political discourses at the time. When NIKK launches its newsletter in English, intending to reach beyond the Nordic region, in 1997 a new story about regional collaboration is presented:

> The collapse of the Soviet Union and the establishment of three, auto-nomous Baltic states have created new possibilities for interaction with the East. This has made an impact on the vision of Nordic co-operation and also on NIKK. Our focus is thus to be intra-Nordic and European, with an emphasis on cooperation with "adjacent areas," including the Baltic Sea region, the Arctic and the Barents Sea region. Broader inter-national networking is also to be important however, echoing the general trend within women's studies world wide. (News from NIKK 1996, 2)

The changing state of the world and of Europe thus also affected both the borders of the Nordic region, its politics, economics, and culture, as well as the methodologies of women's studies.

For women's and gender studies, the relationship between the Nordic and the Baltic regions was especially brought into focus at a Nordic con-ference in Turku, Finland in 1994 (Bergman 1994, 62), and this event gives us an indication of how geopolitical change articulates with ideas of who the subject of women's and gender studies is. Writing under "Solveig's Corner" and reporting on this upcoming Nordic Forum under the rubric "Women's Life and Work – Joy and Freedom," director Bergman's account points to how difference and belonging was conceptualised. She writes:

> [I]n addition to women from the Nordic countries, the organizers of the
> Forum also look forward to the participation of women from the three
> Baltic republics of Estonia, Latvia and Lithuania and warmly welcome
> the positive input of women from other parts of the world, too.
> (Bergman 1994, 62)

This formulation points to the centrality of "Nordic" *women*, secondly
women from the Baltic republics are invited to *participate*, and lastly "positive" input is warmly welcome from "women from other parts of the world."
The centrality of Nordicness as the norm is unchallenged. In addition,
through this address, "women from other parts of the world" *reside* elsewhere
and critique is, it seems, made impossible; only "positive input" is welcome if
it is to be from "other parts of the world." The title of the column is "New
Challenges to Nordic Women," and in 1994 such challenges are not those of
the "crisis" of feminism's subject (as is often stated in accounts of the
1990s); rather, cutbacks in the welfare state as a result of economic reces-
sion, and backlashes against women and feminism were highlighted (cf.
Mulari 2015). In 1994 then, "women" in the Nordic states are understood to
have a common agenda and identity, one that in effect remains "different"
from that of women "from" other parts of the world and at the time, it is
largely one concerned with gender equality. On the other hand, the decades
around the millennium are characterised by a growing theoretical debate
concerning theories of gender, coupled with a broader one on difference
and a growing consensus that, indeed, the subject of feminist theory and
politics, Woman, may not be a unified subject, but rather a deeply differentiated one; as reflected in the change in name, among other things.

NIKK's mission to promote Nordic women's and gender research outside the region, in part via a regular newsletter in English (started in 1997)
points to one of the most heightened discussions of the (re)making of the
field itself. Indeed, the first editorial of the new English-language journal
NORA, established in 1993 for the same purpose, namely of promoting
"Nordic" research beyond the region, states that English is "the" feminist
language "at least to the Nordic countries: English is our key to the greater
world" (Bjerrum Nielsen and Steinfeld 1993, 1). As we outline in the introduction, English remained a double-edged sword in this period. On the one
hand, it was a tool for communication amidst a growing international field

and on the other, its use became increasingly dictated by the demands of institutionalisation and internationalisation.[8]

In relation to this, one of the most significant themes of both Nordic and European women's and gender studies is its relationship to what is perceived as the linguistic and conceptual-theoretical dominance of "Anglo-America" in the international field of women's and gender studies, a theme that is reflected in Braidotti's words from the opening; the idea that Europe is a colony" in women's studies. The perceived dominance of Anglo-American ideas, scholarship, models, names, and theories carries over from the period analysed by Manns in this book. There appears to be complete agreement about the Nordic region's perceived proximity to "Western" or Anglo-American traditions, and yet the relationship is ambivalent. In one report on twenty years of Nordic women's and gender studies, Rosenbeck (2000, 11; my translation) notes that "so far, Nordic women's studies has had a closer connection to Anglo-American Women's Studies than to Women's Studies in other European countries." Rosenbeck (2000, 11; my translation) notes that "this too is changing in these years of stronger European integration," and insists that "we in the Nordic countries should manage our geographical location between Anglo-Saxon and continental intellectual currents much better and more assertively." Rosenbeck does not offer any specific examples of this Anglo-American "connection," nor what European integration has actually meant, or why "we" need to manage our location. However, this story, as both one of origin and one of development, points to how the changing nature of Europe is also affecting the location of the Nordic within a broader "international" field; which is the central theme of this chapter.

The feeling/perception of Anglo-American dominance (and the subsequent need to challenge this) is repeated in many stories about Nordic and European women's and gender studies, and it is related to questions of translation, circulation, and citation of key theories. In such stories, ideas, theorists, and institutions are interchangeably constituted as agents vested with (intellectual) colonialising powers or "dominance," but it is presented

---

[8] In the Nordic context, the question of language also concerns the degree to which "Scandinavian" can be understood to be a "common" language in the region, among other things, as a new generation of scholars in Finland do not necessarily speak, or wish to speak, Swedish. This is reflected, among other things, in whether or not "Nordic" journals such as *lambda nordica* should permit publications in English; a question raised in the mid-1990s.

more as a "feeling" than as something that can be evidenced. In such stories, "American" (and sometimes "Anglo") concepts and theories are understood to originate in, and travel from, North America, and to become imported, imposed or translated into different contexts which are often understood as "different"; or alternatively, the Anglo-American origins of these concepts are disputed through insistence on their prior, "European" heritage; such as with poststructuralist or queer theory. Reading across a range of book reviews, journals, and conference programs/reports, one might argue that what is inferred by this dominance is first of all the "import" of the term gender (Widerberg 1998), and secondly the "arrival" of theories that go under the names queer or intersectionality (see also Dahl 2011). Both reveal the linguistic dimension of the translation of ideas, which in turn unsettles ideas of Nordic "women" as sharing a commonality, which also motivates cooperation. The geopolitical grammar reflects and reproduces the ongoing dilemma of the Nordic region's position in global relations of power and a kind of territorialisation of knowledge that reminds us of the salience of ideas of sovereignty.

The sharpest critique of the "Anglo-American dominance" via language and concepts is in the often-cited article, "Translating Gender" (1998), discussed briefly in the introduction to this book. In this article, Karin Widerberg sharply questions what she perceives as an Anglo-American "norm." As she reflects both on the idea of translating the term "gender" into the Scandinavian languages and on her experience of translating an article about the use of the terms "sex" and "gender" in Scandinavia into English where an editor had asked her to make the article "more general" and less Scandinavia-specific, Widerberg gives an account of an affective response:

> My spontaneous reaction was: of course! We were "special," weren't we? The deviation from the "norm"? The others, particularly the Americans, were the "general," the norm for any story within feminist research. (Widerberg 1998, 135)

Widerberg's article suggests that the Nordic "we" is exceptional, and she objects to the ideas that the American is the general, as well as that "American" ideas are relevant for Scandinavia. To her, difference from the American "norm" is positive. For Widerberg, the very discussion of difference is made "foreign" to the Nordic context, as the quote from the introduction to this book suggests:

> [W]hen "we," in the 1980s, were criticized for not highlighting the dif-
> ferences among women, but instead producing an image of women as
> one and the same, we took this to our hearts and bowed our heads in
> shame. If we instead had looked inward and scrutinized our own
> research, we could have seen that this was simply not true for Scan-
> dinavian feminist research. (Widerberg 1998, 135)

A couple of things happen in this passage. First, the "we" is a joint
Scandinavian one, and thus does not include Finland and its linguistic difference or territorial location east of the Baltic Sea. "Scandinavia," in Widerberg's narrative, has a shared legacy and history, and when challenged on
the issue of "difference," this Scandinavian "we" is shamed. Upon "inward"
scrutiny, however, difference (from the American norm) is found and
shame is turned into pride. The origin of the critique is unclear, but presumably, it is the Anglo-Americans who had asked her to be less "specific."
Shame does a lot of work in feminist settings and here Elspeth Probyn
(2005) usefully points out that, in order for there to be shame there has to
be interest; in this case, such interest might be a desire to be recognised by
some unnamed but "powerful" force. For Widerberg, pride is restored by
finding the regional research tradition that is valid on the given terms; by
finding "difference" there. While her reaction may be "valid," Widerberg's
(1998, 134) main argument in this article is that as Scandinavians "we"
should "stick to our own native concepts." The way this "norm" is understood to work is through rendering the "Nordic" foreign in the context of
Anglo-American feminist theory and by arguing for nativeness. Difference
thus becomes a parameter produced in relation to the very norm it seeks to
disavow. If, as queer theorists have argued, norms are the effect of discursive repetition (Butler 1990), attending to the work that stories of "Anglo-
American" hegemony does in feminist community making and story-telling
about the recent past sheds light not only on global academic relations of
power, but also on more local epistemological tensions. Here the Nordic
emerges as "in between" traditions and as in greater need of articulating its
own specificity in this time.

Debates about the translation of terms, the definition of the field and
about English as "the feminist language" also take place in Europe and in
European women's studies. More than anyone else, Braidotti has taken on a
more than a decade-long task to challenge Anglo-American dominance and
to argue for European "difference," not in a unified but a differentiated
plural sense. One example is the often-cited essay, "The Abuses and Uses of

the Sex/Gender Distinction in European Feminist Practices," (2002) where Braidotti explains:

> [O]ne of the assumptions and starting points for European cooperative work has been the recognition that the bulk of scholarship in Women's Studies has been generated in English-speaking contexts and traditions. (Braidotti 2002, 285)

European difference is here constituted linguistically and conceptually in relation to "English-speaking cultures and traditions." For Braidotti, the very name "women's studies" is an import; a North American term, readily adopted by the "Anglo-Saxon world because of the strong cultural ties between the two geopolitical areas. The North of Europe also quickly followed." (Braidotti 2002, 285) The proposal that the Nordic has a closer proximity to the Anglo-Saxon is in a range of publications explained in part by the relative ease with which the concept gender was introduced in its various Nordic language forms. Above all, Braidotti contends, in Europe,

> [T]here exists a consensus, therefore, that it is important to be alert to the differences in culture, religion, politics and educational practices which mark the different European cultures, which make the American-based model of women's studies one that is not necessarily universally applicable. (Braidotti 2002, 285)

While stressing the benefits of differences within Europe, the European consensus that is discursively produced here ultimately revolves around its difference from what is perceived as "the American." To my mind, there are many different theoretical trajectories and conversations happening simultaneously, and not all of them are captured by a geopolitical assignment.

I want to argue that attending to the geopolitical grammar of women's and gender studies and research, allows us to examine the effects that slippages have on the politics of knowledge production. If Nordic debates about what constitutes the Nordic are largely characterised by finding commonalities, European women's studies are steeped in discussions about the importance of difference. Yet, while Nordic discussions about the field tend to be focused on what makes Nordic culture and history different (from the American, as in the case of Widerberg) and shared (as in the case of Bergman's various texts), European critiques of the Anglo-American dominance of the field of women's and gender studies are more preoccupied with the status of scholarship and with claiming or distinguishing which theories and scholars count as European.

These discussions about difference take place in a time period when this field of knowledge is characterised by several other important shifts that are often discussed in the source materials. One is the degree to which the *lingua franca* of academia in general and women's and gender studies in particular increasingly becomes English, as among other things the increasing numbers of English-speaking and internationally oriented journals and anthologies and the number of conferences held in English attest to. Another is the multiple shifts brought on by institutionalisation, professionalisation, and formalisation and the difference these processes make to the production of knowledge; a topic that has taken up a significant amount of scholarly and administrative energy (cf. Wiegman ed. 2002; Lykke 2005; Liinason 2011).

The effects of Europeanisation in the form of standardisation are evident in many ways; one is in the countless evaluations, workshops, reports, and research papers that reflect on the development and institutionalisation of the field itself. One example is the EU Commission's evaluation of the field of women's studies in the EU, published in a report on behalf of the Advanced Thematic Network in Activities in Women's Studies in Europe (ATHENA) in 2001. Here the external reviewer reflected on the very possibility of comparing institutional developments in Europe as characterised by two dilemmas: First, is women's studies a field in and of itself and secondly, how should it be named? (Michel 2001, 14) While the name elicited a lot of discussion, the geopolitical demarcations did not. In this ATHENA report, the process of institutionalisation is defined as,

> the existence of autonomous or faculty-based Women's Studies *centres,* the academic standing of the *staff* involved, the size and variety of the *programme* of courses, the possibility of obtaining a *degree* in the field, the number of specialized *chairs* and lectureships, and their character: permanent or temporary the *finances:* amount of funding; structural or temporary, the number of *disciplines* involved, variety of themes. (Michel 2001, 15; emphasis mine)

Institutionalisation is thus characterised by autonomy, funding, and knowledge produced and disseminated according to a reproductive and hierarchical logic. Fields of academic knowledge are understood in nationalised and territorialised terms (autonomy, funding, self-governance), at the same time as they are also naturalised as national units in comparative frameworks. In this report, Sweden and Denmark get to stand in for "the Nordic countries" and the region is described as having high degrees of institutionalisation (Michel 2001, 16).

In this report, Nina Lykke, one of the editors and from 2001 to 2005 also the managing director of AOIFE (the Association of Institutions of Feminist Education and Research in Europe), an organisation whose membership consists of some 80 European universities that offer various kinds of programmes in women's, gender, and feminist studies, makes a case for the need for women's studies as an institutionalised and interdisciplinary field of knowledge. Drawing on Bruno Latour's famous example from *We Have Never Been Modern*, she contends:

> [T]he focus of Women's Studies, the intersections of gender, ethnicity, sexuality, age, class etc. is obviously also a hybrid network of relationships which, like the hole in the ozone layer or health, makes visible the contemporary need for multi-, inter- and transdisciplinary approaches. (Lykke 2001c, 20)

Reflecting on debates around institutionalisation in the Nordic countries, Lykke follows Marjerie Pryse (2000) and argues that disciplinary belonging often remains strikingly important to scholars in the field of gender and women's studies. Lykke (2001c, 22) argues that, while identities have been subjected to rigorous deconstruction, disciplines have not, but should. Following a section where she likens "Academia" to a town and institutionalisation to a house with a name plate on it, and making her position very clear, Lykke states that she,

> would never dream of questioning the politics that leads to institutionalization. It was and is a very important way to make women's lives visible and to create platforms for feminist rethinkings of theories, methodologies and epistemologies of existing disciplines. (Lykke 2001c, 22)

Here Lykke's account evidences how stories of an institution are part of the making of an institution, and points to the narrative tactics of bringing together theoretical developments, institutional politics, and geopolitical concerns in the same story.

Lykke stresses the importance of naming, another key concern in this period. For Lykke, women's studies works as an umbrella term for women's, gender, and feminist studies. In the comparison of academia to a town with houses in it, the insights of the "postmodern" feminism that she endorses for its important deconstructions of the category of woman, Lykke's metaphor makes little room for multiple identifications or places of belonging. Thus, her very discussion about institutionalisation points to the dilemma inherent in the need to agree on a name and simultaneously be assigned a *place*. Lykke (2001c, 21) stresses that there are many approaches to doing women's studies, and transdisciplinary ones, to her mind, are those that "go beyond disciplines and beyond existing canons." Examples of transdisciplinary issues to which women's studies have given attention according to Lykke (2001c, 21) include "the relationship between sex and gender and between constructionism and essentialism." As one example, she argues that Donna Haraway's idea of situated knowledges is a trans-disciplinary issue. In Lykke's account, the transdisciplinarity of women's and gender studies rests on the identification of key debates as constitutive to the field itself and, in some regards, on the possibility of a kind of meta-theoretical canon. The reports on the making of European women's studies, as exampled by Lykke's account, are some of the most significant origin stories produced in this time period, and I want to argue that they produce both collective cohesion and a sense of direction.

As all the narratives in this chapter point to, joint ventures that go under the rubric or umbrella (as Rosenbeck 1997 calls it) of "Nordic" or "Euro-pean" often acquire the shape of institutionalisation through key dedicated actors who through their positions, often also as nodal points in networks, on editorial boards, in (university) organisations have been able to generate joint projects which in turn produce these effects.[9] These regionally defined

---

[9] One perhaps exceptional but also very concrete example of this is the significance of Nina Lykke's institutional and theoretical work in the (re)making of Nordic/European women's and gender studies in this period. Lykke was trained in literature in Denmark, and in 1999 became Professor of Gender Studies at Linköping University in Sweden. In the period studied here, Lykke, among many other tasks, served as the Danish national representative on the European Network of Women's Studies, as a member of Network of Interdisciplinary Women's Studies in Europe (NOISE), board member and managing director of the Association of Institutions of Feminist Education in Europe (AOIFE), was part of the leading team of European Women's and Gender Studies (ATHENA) funded by the EU's Socrates programme, and was a member of the international pro-gramme committee and co-organiser of all European Feminist Research Conferences (discussed in part II), and the founding director of the Nordic Research School in Inter-disciplinary Gender Studies. In terms of contributions to the expansion of the field itself, Lykke has edited pioneering issues of journals on themes such as lesbian studies (Lykke 2001a), feminist methodologies, feminist technoscience studies, and among many other themes in this era alone. These institutions are all part of the geopolitically based proces-ses of professionalisation of the field that emerge in this time period and this list alone

areas of women's and gender studies thus organise themselves according to a logic of national representation on the one hand and, on the other, a commitment to interdisciplinarity in the production of academic knowledge that both maintains relations to social movements and contributes to them. Here it seems that (feminist) academia remains institutionally *international* rather than theoretically *transnational,* insofar as universities are funded nationally and the migration of students, scholars, and funding remains regulated by the nation state and by status within the EU. Even as the EU funds large research projects, it often invokes a comparative and representative framework, where "research output" that can be "put to use" in the Union is of importance.

The last point, to which I shall return below, is that in this time period what is perceived as a specific form of Nordic cohesion is increasingly challenged by a series of arrivals of what is perceived as "new" bodies of flesh and knowledge that press upon Nordic women's and gender studies in particular ways. Indeed, for narrators of Nordic women's and gender studies, it tends to be the arrival of *others* into the "Nordic" formation that calls the self-evidence of location, belonging, and tradition into question and unsettles a sense of a Nordic specificity. The argument that there *is* something different about both the Nordic and the European and that this difference is in many ways a geopolitical and linguistic difference (a difference from "Anglo-America" more precisely) has been postulated (and critiqued) again and again in the past two decades of feminist debate, interestingly enough often in English. Yet, what this difference is, why this matters and to whom, or what bodies of flesh and knowledge are constituted as the carriers of difference has been much less clear, as both ideas and subjects are assigned geopolitical belonging. In the materials analysed in this chapter, "difference" is most often understood to be working on the national level, which in turn is tied to how ideas and thinkers are territorialised in the making of European and Nordic "difference." As Ahmed has argued:

> [I]t is by "knowing strangers" that the "we" of the epistemic community is established, even though that "we" is called into question by the very

points to the significant ways in which particular actors such as Lykke have been able to contribute to, and perhaps even shape, the bodies of knowledge of concern in this chapter (see Lykke; all).

proximity of "the strangers" through which it comes to know. (Ahmed 2000, 5)

Following Ahmed, I would argue that it is precisely by encountering others that the Nordic becomes (re)made, even if the question of who belongs in and to the Nordic continues to be subject to discussion.

Interestingly, for Widerberg (1998) it is particularly the critique against an alleged white middle-class subject of feminism and women's studies that is understood to be American and thus not Nordic and also not relevant for a Nordic context at this time (even if this changes a few years later). For European critics such as Mary Evans and Kathy Davis, the dominance of American scholarship extends to include also those critical of this very norm, for they contend:

> [E]ven the critics of the hegemony of US feminism – feminists of colour and postcolonial scholars – enjoy a privileged existence in European scholarship, often replacing the more home-grown variety of the same critique. (Evans and Davis eds. 2010, 1)

In these conversations, steeped as they are in a seemingly homogenising notion of national origin, discussions of internal differences become subordinated to a broader understanding of the Nordic and the European as what Braidotti would call a colony (of the USA). As we shall see below, as the subject of "intersectionality" arrives in discussions that are demarcated as "Nordic," it is more often through citation of "Anglo-American" sources than of postcolonial scholars based "in" the Nordic region.

To conclude this section then, I wish to suggest that attending to the geopolitical grammar with regards to the central themes of the language debate and the assignment of territorial belonging to ideas, shows how epistemic communities (variously called women's and gender studies and/or feminist research) are constituted around an idea that some questions and bodies belong in the larger body of knowledge and not others. That is, some bodies and not others are understood to belong *geopolitically* and that this has to do with tradition and culture. Furthermore, it seems that the very assignment of geopolitical belonging, rather than the processes of circulation, language, and translation is the source of its power or status. Such an understanding of belonging, I argue, homogenises both national and regional identity and the ideas on which they rest.

Nordic family resemblances and the "arrival" of difference

> If we are concerned with women's studies in the Nordic context in relation to the rest of the world, the similarities in Nordic women's studies are prominent. If we on the other hand are concerned with women's studies in one of the countries compared to the others, there are many obvious differences. What kind of discursive and material conditions contribute to the similarities in Nordic knowledge-ing in *our* field? (Halsaa 2001, 71; my translation and emphasis mine)

In this section, I continue to examine how a geopolitical grammar is constructed and deployed in the making of Nordic women's and gender studies, and what it does by attending specifically to accounts of the Nordic. The above quote, drawn from "the Norwegian answer" to this question offered at/published from a conference entitled, *Gråt gärna – men forska* [Do cry, but also do research], in 2001, points to a key theme, namely how the idea of Nordic similarities indeed "depends on the perspective" (Halsaa 2001, 71) and on a kind of scaling and comparison with "the rest of the world." While it can certainly be read as an argument for a differential notion of women's studies what interests me in this section is this relational and institutionally supported understanding of the Nordic in relation to the European and to the world. Rather than defining the Nordic then, I ask what work the work of definition does.

Questions, such as the ones asked in the above quote, often become orientation devices; they point in particular directions. In the 1990s and early 2000s, the question "is there a Nordic feminism," both gave direction and served as an organising metaphor and theme for a range of conferences, anthologies, and discussions. While approaches differ somewhat, stories in response to this question share a set of features that can be clustered around commonality, proximity, and inheritance. Well aware that the Nordic region is an "imagined community" (Anderson 2006) and that it may be impossible to find a universal subject of (Nordic) woman, Rosenbeck (2000, 6) contends that women's studies researchers have not given up their efforts. As I showed above, for both Nordic and European women's and gender studies, relations to an imagined Anglo-American "canon" of feminist theory and other perceived others, are central in answering this question.

Halsaa (2001, 71) asserts that, when set in relation to the rest of the world, the Nordic is "relatively homogeneous, societies shaped by a Lutheran, secular, social democratic and liberal political culture and close and trusting ties between society, individuals, and collectives." The Nordic is also characterised by its modernity; an intimate relationship between movements, science, and state institutions, a historical tradition of establishing archives, public support for research, and a rapid spread of ideas. She points to how globalisation, notably exemplified by the increasing importance of the EU, including funding, shapes research. This, she argues, makes Nordic cooperation "vulnerable"; "it can mean reduced possibilities for maintaining and developing our historically important sociocultural community" (Halsaa 2001, 74; my translation). In anthropological terms, we might call this a heightened emphasis on the locally specific within an increasingly global imaginary and power structure. For Halsaa, the Nordic, where modernity is tradition, runs the risk of disappearing in the European and thus of losing its history and identity. Insisting on the importance of building Nordic institutions, Halsaa illuminates the material and semiotic construction of a Nordic that is both forward looking and deeply rooted in something "historical."[10] If a key driving force for the building of the EU was "reinventing Europe" by way of recasting its history as one of commonality, the effect seems to be quite the opposite: it heightens the importance of regional historical, socio-political, and cultural difference.

The production of regional similarity repeated through intra-regional national difference is key to descriptions of the Nordic in this time. According to Bergman (2001), who here represents Finland at the same conference/report, what characterises Nordic feminism and a Nordic women's and gender studies is, among other things, being "well read" and well situated in the international literature and in local feminist traditions, which she contends makes the Nordic a "melting pot" of feminist discussions. Bergman also points to "care" as a form of labour, as a key theme in Nordic feminist research, thus signalling the tradition of Marxist and materialist theories of gender. Like many others, she notes that women's studies have been more significant to public policy than to theoretical de-

[10] Examples of narratives similar to Halsaa's abound in this time. Widerberg (2006, 136) similarly contends that "characteristic for the Nordic countries is political support and support from the research funding bodies," and in an article that draws on accounts of the field's development and institutionalisation produced by other researchers, she argues that "it is obvious that Women's Studies in the Nordic countries benefits from intra-Nordic comparisons, competitions and collaborations. What one country achieves, the others can also demand." (Widerberg 2006, 137) Beginning from the polemic "Old Questions, New Answers?", this article narrates what she calls "women's studies" in a comparison between Sweden, Finland, and Norway. She concludes by declaring that "the smaller the country, the closer are also the connections between researchers and politicians" (Widerberg 2006, 136).

velopments in established disciplines in the Nordic region and, moreover, that it was concerned with collaboration across national boundaries "long before internationalisation became the word" (Bergman, 2001, 67–68; my translation). Other common formulations are that "by European and international *comparison* the Nordic countries are in several respects *predecessors* in the area of gender equality," arguments that "one unique *trait* of Nordic women's and gender research is its breadth," or stories of how Nordic cooperation has characterised women's studies "from the beginning." At this juncture, I ask who is included in the story of modernity, literacy, and inheritance presented here? How does a geopolitical entity acquire traits and how do such traits become shared?

The anthology *Is there a Nordic Feminism?* edited by Drude von der Fehr, Anna Jónasdóttir and Bente Rosenbeck (1998) sets out to explore the question of feminist research within something called "the Nordic." As is often the case with edited volumes, it began in response to interest from a publisher – in this case significantly, a British one – and is the result of six years of work that coincides with the transition into the EU for several of the Nordic countries. Published in English, the book has an imagined "international" audience and it was widely publicised in the Nordic region. The focus is explicitly geopolitical – it addresses the national, regional, and cultural specificities of the Nordic for feminist research. The Nordic region is here defined as the five Nordic countries, and "represented" by scholars from the humanities and social science. The premise for the book is corrective; "the Nordic," it is argued, has been obscured by an over-emphasis on Anglo-American perspectives.

Despite its name, however, the book does not engage much with the question of whether there is a "Nordic" feminism or what the Nordic might mean. Nordic feminist research in this volume is the work carried out by women researchers *in* the national contexts and which, we might conclude, put together make up the Nordic. The individual contributions engage "international" debates to varying degrees, not concerning particular concepts but rather in the form of examples; empirical historical and social scientific work that has been done by scholars located in the region. According to one report, *Is there a Nordic Feminism?* is a response to a moment of change and is concerned with,

> some of the complex cultural and societal changes taking place in the Nordic countries today. There is concern in the Nordic countries about these changing conditions which alter modes of living, loving, working,

acting, thinking and writing among women in this part of the world.
(News from NIKK 1997, 14)

A summary that nearly verbatim repeats the first lines of the book's preface. All chapters are written by "Scandinavian" authors and, despite insisting on "diversity," they do not address any questions pertaining to, for instance, the changing composition of the population nor of the politics of the "Nordic" in a "European" era. Instead, the Nordic is the accumulated effect of national similarities that emerge in relation and comparison to an imagined "outside," which might be English, Dutch, or French. At the same time, the book's title and content departs from and reproduces a set of shared "Nordic" characteristics.

Following this trajectory of setting up a "Nordic" specificity relationally, is a range of texts produced by NIKK, including a pamphlet about "efforts and collaborations" in women's and gender research in the Nordic region over the past twenty years. In her contribution, entitled, *"Kvinne- og kjønns-forskning i Norden"* [Women's and Gender Research in the Nordic Region] Harriet Bjerrum Nielsen (2000) begins with the formulation of the unique position of the Nordic countries compared to both Europe and the rest of the world when it comes to equality between the sexes. Her narrative relies on a geopolitical grammar of comparison in which hierarchy through standardised measurement is (re)produced. Bjerrum Nielsen (2000, 21; my translation) argues that "the anchoring in Nordic reality and cultural tradition has made Nordic women's studies from the start more strongly orientated toward sameness thinking than continental European women's studies." According to Bjerrum Nielsen this also explains why education, work, politics, and everyday life has been more central to Nordic research than sexuality, the body, identity, and socialisation as well as the intimate connection between research and politics in the Nordic region, or so called Nordic state feminism. Under the rubric *Kjønnsforskning* [Gender Research], Bjerrum Nielsen (2000, 22; my translation) argues that only relatively recently have attention occurred to how the "category gender interacts with other social and cultural categories such as class, sexual orientation, ethnicity, religion and generation" and also to "how the process of gender equality creates new differences between women." Her story is one of increasing complexity, moving away from the unified woman to looking at more relations of power and yet, she argues that the strongest contribution of Nordic gender studies to what she calls "a changing Europe" is its emphasis on equality between men and women. Difference is at this point located elsewhere, and the central concept is gender.

Again, we see the Nordic as constituted through an understanding of "proximity" and relations to a broader context, as with Rosenbeck's (2000) report and Braidotti's (2002) article on sex/gender discussed above, where the connection to Anglo-American women's studies is assumed to be "closer." Reading across book reviews, journals, and conference programs/reports produced at this time suggests that what is inferred is the "import" of the term gender and the "arrival" of theories that go under the names "queer" or "intersectionality" (see also Dahl 2011). Here, the geopolitical grammar used reflects the ongoing dilemma of the Nordic region's position in global relations of power and a kind of territorialisation of knowledge that reminds us of the salience of ideas of sovereignty.

Over the past two decades, these stories become fairly standardised and they increasingly form an address and a sense of "we-ness" in some formations of Nordic women's and gender studies. In 2008, NIKK sponsored the conference *Genusrelationer och förändringsprocesser: Nordisk feminism och genusforskning 2008* [Gender Relations and Processes of Change: Nordic Feminism and Gender Research 2008], and returned to the question "Is there a Nordic feminism," with a panel of its editors.[11] While this invitation stressed that neither "Nordic" nor "feminism" have "clear references," it also offered a description that in 2008 – and thus obviously beyond the explicit focus of this chapter – was quite familiar:

> [T]he Nordic countries have had a long tradition of political, cultural and scientific cooperation. There has also been a tendency toward a Nordic profile in the field of women studies, which has consisted of an interest in every day life, the material, equal rights, the welfare model, and welfare state reforms. In addition, Nordic feminism and women studies have had a stronger connection with Anglo-American women studies than the other European countries.

Whether this is a descriptive or a proscriptive statement could, of course, be debated, but for a discussion about the geopolitical grammar of Nordic women's and gender studies, it seems to me that the familiarity of this narrative is of some importance for the creation of a field which has a shared

---

[11] Conference invitation, Karlstad University, October, 6–8 2008, on file with author.

history, set of interests, and specific connections. Here a Nordic commonality is again founded on tradition and specifically on cooperation, which is both cultural, political, and scientific. To be Nordic is to be strongly connected to particular research interests and questions (everyday life), theoretical traditions (the material), political projects (equal rights), and the particular form of governmentality that countries in the region have had for the past 100 years (welfare states). According to this narrative, as according to many others, the connection with the Anglo-American tradition is stronger in the Nordic countries than in other parts of Europe. Furthermore, the Nordic is distinguished from the European – again positioned as non-Anglo-American. A geopolitical grammar both builds on and reproduces ideas of proximity; to belong together is to have a strong connection.

The questions from which this conference departed were familiar to the making of the field of "Nordic" women's and gender studies as simultaneously consisting of people who are "from" the Nordic countries and/or who research the Nordic, and included:

> Which are the future possibilities and challenges? Which changes have occurred in the last decennium? What can we say about the present situation? It is time for gender researchers to get together and make these questions the focus of critical assessment and analysis.

Among the conference's fifty-three abstracts were three papers dealing with "intersectionality," one on "heteronormativity," and four dealing with cross-cultural comparisons and/or engaging postcolonial theory. The remaining forty-five or so paper abstracts suggest that those who in fact felt most strongly summoned by such a call dealt with gender – men and women, gender and work, and gender equality in a variety of permutations. Thus, while the conference call invited "Nordic gender researchers to a conference on feminism and gender research in the Nordic countries," it appears that those who feel summoned by the name "Nordic" and who do research in the Nordic region felt invited. Keynote speakers were with one exception[12] from "outside" the Nordic context; more specifically "Anglo-American" feminist scholars. According to the conference call, these scholars "share an interest in the Nordic context and its gender research." Attending to the geopolitical grammar of accounts of how conference calls

---

[12] Eva Magnusson, then a staff researcher at NIKK.

define Nordic and in turn how this is folded into that of the European shows that the Nordic is an effect of the coming together of some bodies of flesh and knowledge and not others. It also shows how the arrival of new or differently defined bodies of flesh and knowledge reconfigures the "we-ness" of territorialised knowledge production.

What is perceived of as a specific form of Nordic cohesion is challenged largely through a series of arrivals of what is perceived as "new" bodies of flesh and knowledge that press upon Nordic women's and gender studies in particular ways. The first overarching parameter of Nordic and European women's and gender studies' distinctness is constituted through its relation-ship to the linguistic and conceptual-theoretical dominance of "Anglo-America" in the international field of women's and gender studies and the feeling of such a dominance is repeated over and over; sometimes as friend-ly proximity and sometimes as invasion. This paradox is reflected in the simultaneous invitation and frustrated sense of dominance. Common to all stories about the development of the field are attempts to capture change, movement, and expansion. In them ideas, theorists, and institutions are interchangeably constituted as agents vested with (intellectual) colonialising powers. Overwhelmingly, "American" (and sometimes "Anglo") concepts and theories are understood to originate in and travel from North America, get imported, imposed, or translated into different contexts which are often understood as "different"; or, their Anglo-American origins are disputed through insistence on their prior, "European" heritage; such as with post-structuralist or queer theory. At the same time, the arrival of "new" bodies into the region and the field, most notably migrant bodies, but also bodies that bring themes such as masculinity, queer, intersectionality, and/or race and ethnicity. Given the 2008 conference, they do not seem to easily "assimilate" or be understood to "belong" under the umbrella of Nordic.

While debates about what the "Nordic" might be take place in some locations, a critical intervention regarding the place and discussion about "race"/ethnicity sheds a different light and postcolonial "Nordic" scholars offer other stories about the development and translation of feminist theory. In an article that began as a conference paper entitled "'Race'/Ethnicity in a "Nordic" Context: A Reflection from the Swedish Borderlands," presented at a conference entitled *Svensk genusforskning i världen* [Swedish Gender Research in the World] in 2000, Diana Mulinari (2001, 11) draws attention to the contributions of postcolonial and critical race theory "in the centre" and their place within what she calls "new forms of transnational structures of cultural exchange." She too begins by noting "the subordinated position that Swedish and Nordic feminism have in relation to the powerful voices of US feminism" (Mulinari 2001, 10) including on a structural level in the context of conferences and so on. Importantly, she stresses that this "US hegemony" is a form of a broader "intellectual imperialism" that far exceeds feminist studies and is in fact a structural, not just a linguistic, problem (Mulinari 2001, 11). Mulinari shares the frustrations of scholars such as Widerberg, but strongly disagrees with Widerberg's (1998) contention that Nordic feminism has addressed the question of difference (Mulinari 2001, 12). Pointing to the history of *Kvinnovetenskaplig tidskrift*, the Swedish national journal of women's studies, she notes that, while a wide range of international political debates have been "translated," some significant ones have not.[13]

Mulinari (2001, 13) asserts that "there is a lot of ethnicity talk going on in the Swedish context" and she asks "who" is doing that talking and who should be?" If such debates were going on at this time, they are rarely reflected in publications, nor in discussions of "who" the Nordic feminist is. Mulinari questions the lack of internal debate and exemplifies this by drawing attention to two issues of *Kvinnovetenskaplig tidskrift* that had dealt with race/ethnicity. In the first one, researchers on immigration and discrimination Wuokko Knocke and Alexandra Åhlund call attention to the lack of attention given to "the centrality of racism shaping the daily life of minority groups" (Mulnari 2001, 14). Mulinari notes that, first of all this issue published in 1991 is almost ten years after the emergence of Black cultural studies in the international feminist press. This can be compared with the same journal publishing an article about queer theory and Butler's radical reworking of "identity" in *Gender Trouble* very shortly after its publication (Liljeström 1990) and to Widerberg's (un-cited) invocation of "norms." Mulinari (2001, 14) writes, "in the following numbers no response can be traced. No debate. No reactions." For her, this raises a number of key questions, including "is Swedish feminism passively ethnocentric or has Swedish feminism actively worked to privilege white women"(Mulnari 2001, 14). This study cannot answer that question, but it is clear that when Nordic women's and gender studies argues that it has close proximity to Anglo-American scholarship, in this time period, such affinities do not seem to extend to critical race theory or postcolonial theory.

---

[13] For a different discussion of Mulinari's critique, see further Manns' chapter.

In contrast to NIKK's 2008 conference in Karlstad discussed above, and, which highlighted the Nordic as cooperation, welfare, and everyday life, we might by way of comparison look at another conference which included the term "Nordic" in its title and where papers on gender were presented. For instance, in 2006 a conference entitled "Rethinking Nordic Colonialism," which included Iceland, Greenland, Faroe Islands, Finnish Sápmi, Denmark, Norway, Finland, and Sweden in their definition of Nordic, was organised in Iceland. Here the very question of "who is representable"[14] is presented on the website. Here the introductory text reads:

> The colonial history of the Nordic region is a dark chapter that seems to have slipped the memory of many of the Nordic populations. Although it continues to make itself very much felt in the region's former colonies, this history is alarmingly absent in the collective memory of the once-colonizing Nordic countries.

This conference, like many in women's and gender studies, drew artists, activists, and academics from all over the world for the aim of sharing experiences and examining "why this past has been forgotten and how it continues to reproduce itself as waves of intolerance, xenophobia, and nationalism." Director Cecilia Gelin of the Nordic Institute for Contemporary Art also invokes "our cultural heritage," but states that the aim of this conference was to explore "an unwritten part of our Nordic cultural heritage" and whether it was possible to "find the roots of the nationalistic and xenophobic tendencies today" in this heritage. Many of the participants had feminist or gender related themes in their papers, yet these researchers do not appear at Nordic gender or women's studies conferences at this time. These examples illuminate the fact that we are called to and organise knowledge formations by different narratives and questions.

In the accounts discussed in this chapter, the idea of cooperation based in similarity is at this point understood as a distinctly Nordic trait and tradition. The conception of a common "Nordic" imaginary as predicated on histories of social democratic welfare states, narratives of ethnic and cultural homogeneity, and distinct understandings of gender (equality) as well as conceptions of Europe as a global economic power and "old world," while often repeated, are all challenged in the years around the beginning of the new millennium by growing political, intellectual, and labour migration

---

[14] http://www.rethinking-nordic-colonialism.org.; last accessed 2016-05-05.

to and from these overlapping regions and by a heightened interest in the very question of (national) belonging. In her article, "A Phenomenology of Whiteness" Ahmed (2007) argues that by invoking ideas of "shared ancestry," race, and whiteness in particular, is often presented in familial forms. The discourse of being "like"others, she argues, works to secure that whiteness becomes "'like itself,' as a form of family resemblance" (Ahmed 2007, 154). Ahmed contends that what seems to be "like" might be better understood as being in near proximity. Ahmed further notes:

> [T]o suggest that we inherit proximities is also to point to how that past that is "behind" our arrival restricts as well as enables human action: if we are shaped by "what" we come into contact with, then we are also shaped by what we inherit, which de-limits the objects that we might come into contact with. (Ahmed 2007, 155)

Building on Ahmed, I argue that narratives of Nordic similarity and "we-ness" as a form of "like-ness" not only naturalise Nordicness as whiteness, cast as cultural and historical similarity, but also that we might re-read such Nordicness as the effect of proximity. If we are shaped by what we come into contact with, it matters what bodies of flesh and knowledge assemble under the name "Nordic" women's and gender studies. Indigeneity and histories of colonialism are thus erased in the main stories of what counts as Nordic. I propose that the effect of a geopolitical grammar is that Nordic-ness, presented as shared language, research questions and theoretical and methodological trajectories *and* as an effect of a shared space, or geopo-litical location as citizens of welfare states with long histories of collabora-tion, comparison and joint institutional support becomes alikeness. If we re-read such understandings not as essential primordial categories, or as racially constituted definitions of ethnicity, but as an effect of proximity and contact, we may better understand how both Nordicness and its proximity to some, and distance to other, Anglo-American theories takes the shape that it does in this time period.

While some actors and stories, especially those whose job it is to actively produce Nordicness continue to repeat shared features, others do not. Reflecting on what the Nordic has meant the first six years of *NORA*, in 1999 the incoming editors of the Nordic journal *NORA*, Marianne Lilje-ström and Harriet Silius ask:

> What is Nordic? Should the authors be of Nordic origin? Should *NORA* reflect Nordic debates? Is there a specific Nordic Feminism? Is a Nordic

reading audience enough? How can one be Nordic and internationally understandable at the same time? Should *NORA* "export" Nordic scholarship to an international audience or "import" international debates to the Nordic one? How should *NORA* meet the expectations of the large Nordic feminist community which conducts research on questions that do not have any Nordic aspects? What should such aspects consist of? (Liljeström and Silius 1999, 5)

Indeed, there are no simple answers to these questions, but this editorial offers a kind of orientation device to (Nordic) scientific feminist futures and an invitation to scholars to reflect on them. Yet, overall these questions are rarely addressed explicitly or answered. Instead, the Nordic seems to enable scholars to embrace, reflect, and contest geopolitical and territorialised notions of communities of practice. The 1990s are characterised by the growing influences of deconstructivist approaches to hitherto seemingly self-evident identity categories more broadly, as challenging declarative statements with regards to "any" identity characteristic and as producing ambivalences. At the same time, certain kinds of features, such as "tradition," "cooperation," "state feminism," and "close relationships between movements, academia, and the state," continue to be defined as distinctly Nordic. The Nordic is thus at once self-evident and under scrutiny, both pragmatically staked out and seemingly contested.

At the same time as certain stories are repeated, increasing reflexivity characterises the deployment of identity categories in this time. For instance, Lykke's (2001b) (Danish) contribution to the discussion of "is there a Nordic feminism/women's studies" in 2001 is more cautious. To her, invocations of the Nordic are problematic insofar as they tend to invoke essentialist, romanticised, and racialised meanings that have also been mobilised by problematic agendas, including Nazism. Lykke (2001b, 79) thus wonders whether it is necessary to use the Nordic at all, and argues that "although there is a strong feminist research tradition in the Nordic countries, perhaps when it comes down to it we really may not be doing so much Nordic, feminist research." Remaining rooted in geopolitics, Lykke instead argues for "a Northern European feminist research" and draws inspiration from Butler's (1990) deconstructive approach to gender and argues:

> [N]ational and regional identity is not something we have or don't have, rather it is something we do. Danishness, Swedishness, Nordicness, etc., are in that line of thought not essential phenomena, but rather identity categories that we culturally create and recreate. (Lykke 2001b, 79; my translation)

Lykke reframes the question and asks instead: *Should* we do Nordic feminist research? Her response is yes and no. "Yes," she argues,

> risks bringing too much focus to feminism and gender systems in the Nordic region, demarcated from the rest of the world and with too little attention to the interconnected international perspectives and a wider perspective on the self and "the other" that this implies. (Lykke 2001b, 80; my translation)

On the other hand, "No" for Lykke risks,

> too little focus on the meaning of difference in sociocultural contexts and in an abstract feminist theorizing that does not reflect its own situatedness in the local and regional contexts they emerge from. (Lykke 2001b, 80; my translation)

Lykke's reasoning echoes that of transnational feminism (cf. Mohanty 2006) and is quite unique in approaching the geopolitical imaginary of women's, gender, and feminist studies in this way, even if the sentiment of deconstruction of categories is not; rather it can be seen as the metanarrative of this era. Lykke draws on Rosenbeck's work in *Is There a Nordic Feminism?* (1998), where Rosenbeck is convinced that there is a future in the Nordic, in intra-Nordic comparisons, cooperation, and powerful international marketing. In an interesting way, Rosenbeck's historicised discussion of the "invention" of the Nordic offers possibilities for imagining multiple futures.

The deconstruction of the meaning of Nordicness and Lykke's intervention can be understood to reflect broader epistemological changes that take place in the 1990s. Both theoretically and demographically, Europe was changing and feminism and feminist theorising along with it. Another factor, I argue, is that the Nordic region also became increasingly concerned with presumed changes *within* the region itself, which coincided with a shift towards focusing on internal differences. What is striking however, is that to narrators of Nordic women's and gender studies, it is the arrival of *others* into the "Nordic" formation that calls the self-evidence of location, belonging, and tradition into question and both unsettle and demand a sense of a Nordic or European specificity in territorialised ways. In that process, particular ideas, concepts, and approaches are understood to be linked to some bodies, and not to others. Interestingly, the question of what particular kinds of theoretical traditions and epistemological frameworks can be understood as Nordic or European remains up for discussion. Put differently, it is the arrival of a new political order of knowledge and of belonging that demands scrutiny of what counts as Nordic and European in the first place.

So, what then, do we make of the Nordic as a geopolitical grammar? In a famous essay about the limits of sexual difference theory, Teresa de Lauretis (1987, 2) argued that gender is both a representation and a self-represen-tation, the product of various social technologies and of "institutionalized discourses, epistemologies, and critical practices as well as practices of daily life," and perhaps geopolitically defined bodies of flesh and knowledge work in similar ways. With de Lauretis' Foucaultian framework, we can see geopolitical entities such as Nordic or European as a set of effects, produced by political technologies such as funding regimes and governing practices. They are representations, and as such, they are effected by ongoing attempts at deconstruction as much as by their repeated narration and represen-tation. Geopolitical categories are thus not only manifested *in* and through bodies of both flesh and knowledge, they are material-semiotic actors (Haraway 1991) in stories about regionalisation.

Given the diverse ways in which people use and engage the idea of the Nordic, another way to understand how the geopolitical grammar works is as what Susan Leigh Star has called a boundary object. These are, as Adele Clarke (2010, 588) puts it, "objects that are loosely structured in common practice, and tailored for local usage by particular social worlds when and as specific needs arise." The usefulness of boundary objects is that "they afford the possibility of cooperation without consensus" (Clarke 2010, 588). For a knowledge formation such as women's and gender studies, deploying a geo-political grammar and making the Nordic a kind of boundary object, allows not only for the production of feminist knowledge, but for the making of a particular social world: that of feminist and/or gender research. Without a doubt, the mid and late nineties reflected a kind of institutional hay-day of women's and gender studies. At the same time, at the moment the full effects on notions of Nordicness as a kind of family resemblance engen-dered by the imagined arrivals of "new" bodies of flesh and knowledge that press upon Nordic women's and gender studies in particular ways remain to be seen and analysed by a different project.

Conferences as constitutive moments

Spirits are particularly high after the successful completion of the 4th European Feminist Research Conference in Bologna, an event to which ATHENA contributed both intellectually and materially. This conference demonstrated the high levels of scientific excellence, as well as the professional and political maturity reached by European Women's Studies programmes, at all levels of activity. We are proud of it. (Braidotti et al. 2000, 9)

As I have already alluded to in the above sections, invitations to conferences as well as to publications, can work to include or exclude members in an imagined "we." If texts that recount histories and legacies are central parts in the overall construction of a culture called Nordic women's and gender studies, conferences may be seen as another form of "constitutive moment." Conferences are simultaneously mundane professional academic events and affective community and knowledge-making practices. Successful conferences can, as in the above quote, be seen to "lift spirits," demonstrate "excellence" and "maturity," and even generate "pride," both for individual researchers and for an imagined "we." In short, they are centrally concerned with producing "we-ness" and belonging. A conference thus constitutes a kind of symbolic heart of a dispersed academic community and its contributors and proceedings give a knowledge formation content, shape, and feeling, such as in reports discussed in the previous section. To arrive at a conference is to arrive at the heart, to witness a world unfold from a moment in time when some bodies have gathered, as bodies in a room, orientated toward particular speakers and themes, in particular groups, around particular questions. To arrive at a conference and to belong to the formation that makes it a heart, is also to be positioned as having something to offer and to receive a welcome or an opening. To be able to do so also requires, as it were, what Adrienne Rich (1993) once called a common language. In the millennial decades, the question of whether English is "the feminist language" remains a sore point for Nordic and European women's and gender studies.

A conference, with all its institutional exclusions in terms of costs and travel obstacles, its required disciplinary conventions for the submission of abstracts and papers, and degrees of cultural competence when it comes to academic performance, marks a coming together around a particular set of presumed common interests with which its participants might have different "experiences" or to which they may have different "approaches." A geopolitical grammar works to assign both researchers and research themes belonging and frames an invitation in particular ways. The framing of a conference can be read as an invitation, and its invitation gives direction. A call may make some feel invited to and be part of a particular field, others not. While they insist on the openness of terms, invitations often include narratives of origin and cohesion and offer future orientations, such as with the NIKK 2008 conference discussed above.

While feminist conferences were certainly not invented in the 1990s – indeed feminists have been coming together for at least 100 years around a range of topics from suffrage to reproductive rights, from peace to unionising – for the field of women's and gender studies they certainly grew in numbers, frequencies, and scope, both under the rubric "Nordic" and "European." In this section, I analyse documentation from feminist research conferences around the turn of the millennium with an eye to how the grammar of Nordic and the European are used and thus given meaning. I also attend to how a narrative of origin and progress shapes stories about conferences and how some conferences rather than others become what King (1994) calls "moments," which constitute origins and engender cohesion.

Feminist research conferences: The Nordic in/and the European

Joint European feminist *research* conferences have been organised since 1991, and tellingly, the first conference in Aalborg, Denmark, was entitled "Women in a Changing Europe." Following this conference were three conferences with epistemological frames of organisation, such as the 'Women, Work and Ecology" theme of Graz, Austria, 1994; the more unsettling theme of "Shifting Bonds, Shifting Boundaries," in Coimbra, Portugal, 1997; and one on embodiment at the "Body Gender Subjectivity: Crossing Disciplinary and Institutional Borders," in Bologna, Italy, in 2000, before the European conference returned to the Nordic region in 2003 under the heading "Gender and Power in the New Europe," and taking place in Lund, Sweden. These titles point out to us that in twelve years, the idea of Europe went from changing to new and the subject from women to gender. That the sheer size and scope of this knowledge formation's conferences has grown from 300 participants in 1991 to over 700 in 2003, points both to the "success" of institutionalisation and growth of the field as well as to the effectiveness of a geopolitical grammar in academic professionalisation of women's and gender studies. In her work on feminist organising in the early

1990s, anthropologist Annelise Riles (2000, 1) argues that "networks" work as "both 'designs' and 'paths across territory,'" and following Riles, I argue that the geopolitically defined feminist conference is not only a significant "invention" and "tradition" in the 1990s, it also builds on a geopolitical grammar of "we-ness" that creates certain Nordic paths across a territory known as European women's studies.

Origins: Arriving in a changing Europe

According to informal stories and available accounts about the development of women's and gender studies as fields, as bodies of knowledge and communities, "Women in a Changing Europe" in 1991 marked the beginning of a *new* kind of European collaboration (Royer 1992). Differently put, it marks the arrival of a moment when this field began to take a particular shape. On an organisational and funding level, in terms of the material conditions of its production, this event was the result of the joining of funding forces of feminist research in Denmark and the European Network for Women's Studies. The date is important, and as one conference reporter writes in *Australian Feminist Studies*:

> [T]he reasons behind the conference lay in the sudden changes Europe is undergoing culturally, politically and economically since the *Perestroika*, the fall of the Berlin Wall and with the prospects of the development of the European Community. (Royer 1992, 99)

The conference thus also importantly involved the arrival of new bodies into the body of women's studies and the body of Europe, namely researchers and mostly women from former Communist countries. According to Michelle Royer's (1992, 101) report, "the dichotomy of East/West is indeed very schematic, but was nevertheless very real during the conference and discomfort persisted among the participants until the last day." In this account, the arrival, proximity and above all, theoretical and empirical presentations of "Eastern" feminists at this conference, left Royer (1992, 100) "with contradictory feelings of unity and diversity." Following Ahmed (2000), I argue that the "we" of this geopolitically defined epistemic community comes into being precisely in the moment of encountering and knowing strangers. In other words, it is with the expansion of Europe that "Western," including Nordic feminist theory and activism, can appear to be progressive and advanced. Royer's narrative reminds us of Allaine Cerwonka's argument that Anglo-American women's studies is constituted through a set of framing devices that result in a logic where,

> when new groups (be it Eastern European women or any other group) are accepted into the discipline in a gesture of inclusion or as a corrective to ethnocentrism, their inclusion in fact does not disrupt the centrality of American/Western women. (Cerwonka 2008, 820)

While Nordic and European women's and gender studies often situates itself in relation to that American tradition, a similar logic seems to play out with the arrival of the "East" in Europe; one that we have also seen with the Nordic conference in Turku in 1994 discussed above, which welcomed Baltic participation. For Royer, the conference and thus the report on it is also filled with emotion; a special song opens the conference, "the atmosphere was electric" (and the conference "carefully staged") and news of the on-going coup in the Soviet Union charged the event. In many ways then, what sets women's studies conferences apart, is the degree to which it builds on and produces emotion; particularly of political unity (and disunity).

Even as it is intentional, temporary, and laden with complex webs of emotion, power and status, a conference such as "Women in a Changing Europe," also has specific institution building and knowledge dissemination aspirations and effects. They may also, as at the 1997 European feminist research conference in Coimbra, result in the founding of new organisations, such as in that case the Association of Institutions of Feminist Education and Research in Europe (AOIFE) (cf NIKK Årsrapport 1997), or in Utrecht in 2009, the founding of AtGender, the European Association for Gender Research, Education and Documentation. For participants, conferences are embodied and often affective events, full of encounters and transmissions of all kinds, and as such, they are interesting ethnographic objects and settings (Dahl 2004). Memories of conferences live on in everyday storytelling, as the repeated comments on (my) readings of conferences – "You weren't there! You don't know how it felt!" – have often demonstrated. Here I can only analyse "Women in a Changing Europe" and other conferences, not as "experience" or "memory," but through the written accounts of those who were "there" and who have been authorised to give accounts. Many of these reports do work as archives of feeling (Cvetkovich 2003), and convey emotions, such as pride and joy (spirits lifted), or discomfort, or an "electric atmosphere" that often lives on in "memory," whereas the most common "output" of conferences, namely revised and published papers or organisational reports, rarely capture such complexities.

If the arrival of "new" European feminist subjects at the "Women in a Changing Europe" helped move a discussion of both geopolitics and difference in new directions, narratives about the arrival of a "new" generation also stands out in stories about Nordic and European women's and gender studies. According to *NIKK Magazine* (2000, 1), "one of the most thought provoking events" of the 4th European feminist research conference in Bologna in 2000, that drew more than 500 participants "from Europe and all over the world," was a multimedia performance by the "Utrecht fraction of the next genderation network" in cooperation with Italian feminist networks. Making front page news in the newsletter, their commentary on "multiple issues such as trafficking in women, exclusion of different groups on the background of race, sexual orientation and gender, the economic order etc." was described as an "untraditional conference presentation." Nine years after "Women in a Changing Europe" a new category had "arrived" in both European and Nordic women's and gender studies, namely a new generation. According to the interview conducted with members in the newsletter, NextGENDERation,[15] "was founded in Lund in June 1998, with the aim of constructing a European network for younger feminists both within and outside academia" (*NIKK Magazine* 2000, 3). One of the founders, Sarah Bracke, stated that an early point of discussion was "the Kosovo crisis and the NATO bombings in Serbia" (*NIKK Magazine* 2000, 2). Members also discuss and critique the structure and form of an academic conference, stating that "the dominant speakers were from the older generation and some of them are really starting to act like members of 'the old boy's network'" (*NIKK Magazine* 2000, 2), arguing for the use of new technologies, a critique of the idea of an "apolitical" and "postfeminist" generation and also stressing that there was no clear cut agenda or formal structure, and making "problematizing notions of 'generation', 'European', 'feminist', 'white' and other axes of differentiation between women" (*NIKK Magazine* 2000, 2) a central part of the project.[16]

---

[15] NextGENDERation was and remains primarily a e-mail discussion list, but the group has also authored several papers in publications made by the ATHENA network.

[16] Ahmed's (2007) discussion of family resemblances gains particular salience when we consider how the idea of "generations" gets used as a way to address different understandings of what might constitute both the Nordic/European and the field of gender and women's studies. Recent scholarship (van der Tuin 2008) suggests that stories about the development of both feminism and women's and gender studies are often cast in

Whether or not "Women in a Changing Europe" was in fact the first time "European" feminists came together, is of course, a matter of interpretation, but the notion of "first" is significant. Many conferences, workshops, and meetings have been called Nordic or European over the past decades. According to the report from the abovementioned 2001 conference called *Gråt gärna – men forska* [Do cry, but also do research],[17] that addressed "the women's movement and women's/gender research in Norden,"[18] held at Linköping University in Sweden, the motivation was that such a conference with an explicit interdisciplinary focus, had not been organised in the Nordic region before (Frangeur ed. 2001a, 5). Indeed, in order to motivate funding and gathering, conference calls often build on either a logic of discovery and newness (this is "the first") or of return (we need to "follow up" on what has happened to our questions).

The written accounts analysed here, however, suggest that "Women in a Changing Europe" worked as what King (1994, 2) calls a constitutive "moment" in the origin story of this knowledge formation and the (re)making of "Nordic" and "European" women's and gender studies. That is, such stories build their narrative with a geopolitical grammar and they also produce the cohesive sense of geopolitical "we-ness." It matters, I argue, to the subsequent position that the Nordic has had within the larger European imaginary, that this conference was held in the Nordic region and that its orientation was to a "new" Europe, which was deeply marked by both new and old cartographies of empire and capitalist expansion. These "changes"

terms of relationships between "generations" of scholars and their respective theoretical and methodological approaches. Kinship terms like "mother," "daughter," "sister" are frequently used both within feminist politics and scholarship. The time period under study here is not only marked by increased professionalisation or diversification but also by the presence of several generations of scholars – that is, scholars who have come of intellectual and political age in different historical moments and under different conditions of apprenticeship within the field. Becoming a scholar is in no small part becoming part of a particular genealogy. How are such genealogies rooted and routed? As all the students know, it matters who your teachers are, what stories they tell, who they put you in contact with, what courses you can take, and so on. Paying attention to kinship and how reproductive metaphors are both used and contested in telling stories about belonging in time and space and to considering the use of generational metaphors reveals, again, that some bodies more than others are understood as extending legacies and offering interesting new perspectives. Space limitations in this chapter prevents me from exploring this topic further (for a brief discussion of this theme, see Dahl 2014).

[17] The title itself alludes to a book edited by Karin Westman Berg and published in 1979 entitled *Gråt inte – forska!* [Don't cry – do research!]. For further discussion of this, see Manns' chapter in this book.

[18] In the original: "Kvinnorörelse och kvinno/genusforskning i Norden."

not only concerned the war-ridden Balkan region of the time or the *coup d'état* in the Soviet Union that occurred during the time of the conference, but also, as Royer's account shows, the redrawn lines between East and West and gradually between the growing numbers of members of an ever-expanding European Union and the rest. The conference was also centrally concerned with questions that this "changing Europe" posed for feminist activism and knowledge.

The timeliness of "Women in a Changing Europe" and the subsequent strengthening of "pre-existing" networks and making new collaborations point to how the field of women's and gender studies was quick to respond to and utilise new geopolitical imaginaries, socialities, and funding regimes. Following the conference and with the benefit of European funding, a particular *European* women's and gender studies gained its shape in the decades surrounding the beginning of the 21stcentury, clustered around networks of collaboration, funding, education and research. Riles (2001, 3) argues that the network, as "a set of institutions, knowledge practices, and artefacts thereof that internally generate the effects of their own reality by reflecting on themselves", was the greatest innovations of global women's movements of the 1980s and 1990s. As an organisational form, Riles contends that the network transforms personal relations into formal structures and is both a means to an end and an end in itself; and the goal, Riles argues, is often to produce more networks and "outcomes" in the forms of research, reports, and conferences. Understood this way, I argue that the field of women's and gender studies is not outside of, but rather simultaneously mirrors and creates, "the new Europe" that was emerging under the sign "the European Union" and thus also of the "enterprising up" of knowledge and politics within a neoliberal and late capitalist regime.

Under structural and intellectual (if ever informal) leadership, networks of key scholars have laboured to create a distinct "European" field of feminist and women's studies both in organisational and research terms – one that would simultaneously make its mark on a larger international community of feminist scholars and contribute to the increasing professionalisation of the field through the creation of organisations (of women's studies programs, scholars, and research), regular meetings and joint publications, from journals such as *European Journal of Women's Studies*, founded in 1994, and *NORA*, founded in 1993 to shared teaching materials like *Thinking Differently* (see also Lykke 2004a). Insisting on linguistic, cultural, and political differences from the dominant "Anglo-America," as well as within

Europe, the European thus emerges through a collection of comparable national units rather than along different epistemological trajectories.

The 1991 conference reflects how women's and gender studies departments had moved past their initial and marginalised place, one that in the Nordic context as Manns' shows in this book, is constituted through a feminist "we" set against a male-dominated academy. Over the next two decades, it took the shape of institutionalisation, complete with criteria of excellence for the production and publication of feminist research in new journals and strategies for degrees, joint courses, and large-scale, (comparative) research projects. Institutionalisation, understood as a process, has indeed also become a key theme in introspective studies of this field in recent years, and often focuses the complex interplay between educational and research regimes, political movements, and disciplinarisation (cf. Liinason 2011). In such stories, indicators of success are often concerned with the reproduction of the institution and the relationships it generates and thus include the securing of positions, autonomous departments, status of scholars, degree programs, and funding (Griffin ed. 2004; Liinason 2011); the very framework in which knowledge is understood to emerge. Understood in this way, institutionalisation is dependent on clear demarcations of inside and outside, boundaries that a larger institutional framework of global academic restructuring including indexes and standards of excellence, tuning, and standardisation of degree programmes and an increasing understanding of the added or use values of research to a larger society.

Many accounts are also concerned with the relationship between state, movement, and knowledge production and whether they are "successful or not," in an imagined comparative framework. I argue that the assumed need for a relationship between knowledge production and feminist movements, past and present, can be understood as, what Ahmed (2006) calls, an orientation device that directs research and reflects the "directions" of feminist activism through the question of the relationship between theory and practice. In that respect, a central feature is the meaning of the alleged "US distinction" of "sex/gender" in its multiple translations into European languages and the very naming of the field itself continue to generate both research and affect in so far as it often denotes the key marker of difference from such an imagined "norm." The *European* field is no different from a larger "international" imaginary in those respects and while it is also shaped by what is often seen as "inter-generational" conflicts around the state of the field. With Hemmings' (2011) popular terms, it is a debate about feminism's history as loss and/or progress and sometimes return) and who its appropriate subjects and objects of research might be. Following a similar yet more specific trajectory, what most concerns me in this chapter is the very (re)making of *European* women's and gender studies, and more importantly, the place that the "Nordic" plays within this field.

NORA: Making journals, making place

Surveying the entire scholarly production within Nordic women's and gender studies from 1990 to 2005 is a daunting task, given the growing numbers of dissertations, monographs, edited volumes, and reports within the field. As McDermott's (1994) study shows, the rise of academic journals in women's and gender studies not only reveals how what was initially a critique of the patriarchal knowledge structure of the university becomes institutionalised and professionalised, it also offers a unique site in which to study a knowledge formation. Lykke (2004a, 74) also notes that, in particular, journal editorials are significant sites of collective enunciations and community building. In this part of the chapter I conduct a close and detailed reading of editorials from one key journal, *NORA*, from its inception in 1993 to 2005, in order to give *one* picture of the (re)making of Nordic women's and gender studies[19] and pay particular attention to how the geopolitical grammar works in the introduction of new theoretical frames and research themes "into" this field. In order to place the journal in a context, however, I begin by considering how the "European" arrives in the "international" in the early 1990s.

[19] The choice to focus on these journals relates to the overall aim of the study as such, namely, the construction and place of the "Nordic" in relation to that of the "European" in 1990 to 2005. While there are other and more specialized journals such as *lambda nordica: Nordic Journal of GLBTQ Studies* (founded in 1989), and *NORMA: Nordic Journal for Masculinity Studies* (founded in 2006) that explicitly use a geopolitical grammar in their names and thus presumably engage and orient themselves towards and with the Nordic, they have been omitted here for different reasons. While *lambda nordica* was central in creating an imagined community of Nordic gay and lesbian studies in this time period and among other things published conference proceedings and the first special issue on queer theory in 1996, edited by Don Kulick, editorials from this time do not engage a geopolitical grammar and do not seek to outline the characteristics of the Nordic – aside from publishing in "Scandinavian" (that is Swedish, Norwegian, and Danish but not Finnish or Icelandic). *NORMA*, would provide an excellent source for analysis of the Nordic, insofar as it seeks to establish the field of Nordic masculinity studies and not only explicitly theorises gender equality, men's movements, homosexuality and, also what might constitute Nordic masculinity theory. But since it was founded in 2006 it falls outside of the scope of this project.

A selection of papers from the conference "Women in a Changing Europe" in 1990 discussed above, was published in a special issue of the US-based international journal *Women's Studies International Forum*[20] in 1994. Prior to this publication, edited by Nina Lykke, Anna-Birte Ravn, and Birte Siim, *Women's Studies International Forum* had published very little on Nordic and European scholarship[21] and this was the first collective "report" on the state of women('s studies) in Europe in this time. While the idea of feminism and women's studies as an international imagined community was not new, the importance of publishing scholarly work in English gained increasing salience. The editorial, entitled "Images from Women in a Changing Europe," reported on the "outcomes" of the conference, organised into three thematic sections entitled differences and commonalities, feminisms in context, and women in East and Central Europe. The language of measurable outcomes can itself be seen as an outcome of the institutionalisation of this knowledge formation. Given its editors and place of location, "Women in a Changing Europe" and the special issue(s) indicate what themes characterised women's and gender studies in both the Nordic context and in Europe in the 1990s; an increasing orientation towards "differences between women" that is also tied to a debate about the epistemological effects of translation and invocations of terms such as sex and gender; an emphasis on feminisms in the plural (as opposed to "the" women's movement) and their relations to shifting meanings of the state and the organisation of private and public (labour)relations, and an on-going focus on the national and cultural as variables of differential comparison.

The publication of collections of "European" articles in an international scholarly journal points to the context in which the "European" and its internal national units are imagined and to the heightened importance placed on international recognition of individual and collective theoretical achievements and conversation. The first focus, the editors explain, was,

---

[20] As McDermott (1994) notes, *Women's Studies International Forum* is one of the earliest established journals in the field, founded in 1978 in London.

[21] Prior publications in the time period under study here were a special issue in 1992 on "A Continent in Transition: Issues for Women in Europe in the 1990s," edited by Claire Duchen, and a special issue on "Women's Studies at the University of Utrecht," edited by Rosi Braidotti in 1993. These were followed by a special issue on women's studies in Poland in 1995, edited by Elzbieta Oleksy. The conclusion from this is that *Women's Studies International Forum* tends to organise its knowledge geopolitically, that Europe received relatively little attention, and that Braidotti's department successfully established itself as a singular successful department and example of "Europe" in this era.

chosen because one of the important *outcomes* of the conference has been to make us aware of the increasing importance of *differences* among women as a basis for developing feminist theory and feminist politics (Lykke et al. 1994, 112; emphasis mine)

Here the very idea of difference is in fact an effect of Europeanness and more specifically of European expansion and differentiation. The second theme was concerned with "context," which in the "context" of the conference and its outcomes primarily referred to the national, cultural, political, and historical dimensions that make up difference on the level of the relationship between theory and practice; a power-laden spatialisation of knowledge which has continued to shape women's and gender studies. The third focus pointed to a recent "arrival" in the "European" field: an awareness of issues surrounding its new members and issues related to the new cartography of Europe. While in retrospect it appears that much was seemingly in flux in 1991 – including the very meaning of Europeanness and the significance of geopolitics more broadly – *women* remained the proper subjects and little of the coming "arrivals" of other others (such as queers, genders, or masculinities, among other objects and subjects) can be traced in *Women's Studies International Forum* at that time.

It was a collective desire to reach audiences beyond those considered "local" as in "national" that motivated the establishment of the English language journal *NORA, Nordic Journal for Feminist and Gender Research* in 1993, on behalf of the Nordic Association of Gender Research (Liljeström and Silius 1999; Halsaa 2001, 72).[22] Liljeström and Silius (1999, 4) retrospectively describe *NORA* as "a dream of a common journal,"[23] as both a "bold move" and "the result of years of Nordic cooperation in the field of women's studies." They point to the work of the Nordic women's studies coordinator (Solveig Bergman) and the "pioneering work" of the founding editors who established scientific practices such as peer-review processes. The

---

[22] "Nordisk förening för kvinno- och könsforskning" was founded at a Nordic forum in Turku, Finland in 1994, for the purpose of ownership of *NORA*; and to "gather the force and interest of women's research in the form of conferences" (New from NIKK 1996).
[23] This is a clear reference to American poet and feminist Adrienne Rich's famous formulation "the dream of a common language," from her first collection of poetry by the same name in 1978; also famously rewritten as an "ironic" dream by Donna Haraway in her often cited text "Situated Knowledges" in 1988. Here it suggests that the imagined Nordic feminist "we" that Manns outlines in her chapter also works as a kind of inheritance for the founding of *NORA*.

first issue invokes discussions at the "Women in a Changing Europe" conference, again pointing to the significance of this conference and of debates over English as the common language. Here the (feminist) time of *NORA*'s inception is described as "overwhelming, causing intensive debates." However, to point to debate is not always to engage in debate, and we see little of these debates *in NORA*, even if we might suspect that they are concerned with language. According to the editors, "feminist research from the Nordic countries is certainly not well known in an outside world" and authors seem to choose *NORA* in order to reach out, rather than to engage in "Nordic" debate. A sister journal, *European Journal of Women's Studies* founded in the same time period,

> emerged out of a growing dissatisfaction among European feminist scholars with what was perceived as the hegemony of US feminist theory and scholarship within the field of women's studies and the conviction that it was necessary to provide a platform for European feminist scholarship, a forum from which feminists could address specifically European concerns from European feminist perspectives. (Evans and Davis eds. 2010, 1)

In contrast, *NORA*'s aspirations were not only to discuss "Nordic" concerns, but also to disseminate "Nordic" research.

First issues are always hopeful and ambitious; *NORA* is presented as a "new voice in the international community of women's studies" that "aims to find a room of her own" (Bjerrum Nielsen and Steinfeld 1993, 1). Calling *NORA* a she, a reference to the famous main character in Henrik Ibsen's drama *A Doll's House*, is not only a feminist feminisation of scientific production; the makers and writers of *NORA* are quite literally, and not very surprisingly, female in this time and beyond. Less than a handful of articles by male scholars were published, despite the inaugural editors' insistence that "the gendering of men is certainly also a neglected field of research. *NORA* therefore welcomes papers which focus on gender relations or which discuss men in a gender perspective" (Nielsen and Steinfeld 1993, 2). The inaugural passage points to the scoping and scaling of the making of feminist community and to how the place of (Nordic) difference is constituted within a larger territorialised community. This room of her own, as Manns points out in her chapter, is thus literally a territorialised idea. Ambitions for *NORA* are high; editors insist that it will not limit itself to "Nordic" research – but rather seek contributions from other countries and the journal "acknowledges the need to transcend borders and to challenge linguistic, national and cultural boundaries as well as the traditional stratified world of the academy" (Bjerrum Nielsen and Steinfeld 1993, 1). While sisterhood in its academic form is understood as both global and regional, most non-Nordic writers publishing in *NORA* are "Anglo-American" scholars.

NORA is described as "an interdisciplinary journal of gender and women's studies and a channel for high-quality research from all disciplines," which is a point that subsequent editors also take up. Most articles tend to be either concerned with broader feminist theoretical issues or focused on very specific disciplinary issues, such as sociological perspectives on gender equality, education, or literature. *NORA*, Halsaa argues, aims to,

> give a Nordic profile to feminist research, with regard to both contents and theoretical and methodological approaches. *NORA* aims to discuss and examine the realities and myths of women's and men's lives in the Nordic countries, historically and today. (Halsaa 2001, 72)

The geopolitical grammar and territorialised understandings of knowledge are here thus both the starting point and the end result. The formation of this field is therefore predicated on two kinds of narratives of place: one where the regional (Nordic) is either generalised or rendered specific in relation to the global or the European, and another where the national (Swedish, Danish, etcetera) is either exemplary of the regional or contrasted within the regional (Nordic).

Origins and declarations can become orientations. Taking over editorship, as the journal's "home" moved from Norway to Finland, Liljeström and Silius note:

> [T]he scope of *NORA* has been established during these first three years, we will continue the "old line." *NORA* is a channel for feminist research in all disciplines. Our aim is to provide Nordic perspectives on topics of both theoretical and methodological relevance to women's studies. We encourage interdisciplinarity and critical approaches. (Liljeström and Silius 1996, 1)

This declaration declares that first, *NORA* is simultaneously multi- and interdisciplinary, secondly that it stresses the Nordic (even though the Nordic is not explicitly defined), and thirdly, that it names the field as women's studies.

Again, the dilemma of what is meant by the Nordic (authors' origins, topics, audiences) or what its aims are (international circulation of ideas, meeting the demands of academia) is never quite resolved, even if the ambitions of the editors are high (Liljeström and Silius 1999, 5). While critical questions are repeatedly asked (see also Lykke 2004a) they are rarely explicitly answered. On some level, we could say that the same is true for a range of journals that claim to be "international" – what this really means is rarely resolved. The difference, I would argue, is that Nordic refers to a specific geopolitical location and, at the same time, it is a kind of identity. In practice, scholars continue to embrace, reflect, and contest geopolitical and territorialised notions of communities of practice. Perhaps we can under-stand the 1990s and the growing influences of deconstructivist approaches to hitherto seemingly self-evident identity categories, as challenging de-clarative statements with regards to "any" identity characteristic and as pro-ducing ambivalences. Again and again, certain kinds of seemingly inherited traits such as "tradition," "cooperation," "state feminism," and "close re-lationships between movements, academia, and the state" continue to be defined as distinctly Nordic.

The first three years and six issues of *NORA* largely present national empirical examples, and focus on women. Even if attention is given to sexuality and variations of femininity in the second issue, it takes until 1996 before an explicit topic is queer or lesbian.[24] Only one article in the first three years is explicitly concerned with the EU and none addresses race, ethnicity, or migration. Since these issues are raised in special issues of *Women's Studies International Forum*, their absence in *NORA* suggests that they are not (yet) understood as "Nordic." Several articles are concerned with feminist epistemologies and the development of women's studies (most notably on the rhetoric of positioning by Sara Heinämaa 1994). In 1998 there is a notable shift in approach on multiple levels. Outgoing editors Liljeström and Silius ask:

> How should we – or can we – select articles in a situation of ongoing diversification among writers as well as among readers? One of our aims – although not the only one – has been to choose topics, which have not been extensively discussed in the Nordic countries. Another aim has been to introduce unknown coming feminist scholars rather than estab-lished ones. (Liljeström and Silius 1998, 75).

---

[24] Ellen Mortensen (1996) discusses the work of Butler and Braidotti, and Julie Wuthnow (1996) a New Zealand-based scholar discusses Hawai'ian lesbians, colonialism, and nationalism.

The reader of *NORA* is often implicitly assumed to be familiar with both institutional politics and theoretical developments, and is thus not told what has been missing or what this might include. Rather, the narrative tactics of invoking declarations such as "ongoing diversification" (involving a range of dimensions) and "established scholars" (which suggests that the canon tends to be a canon because it is narrated as such) become declarative statements. Referring to Elina Oksinas' article "The sexy Woman and the smart girl: Embodied gender identity and middle-class adolescence" in that issue, the editors also define "two theoretically important questions of Nordic feminist thought" (Liljeström and Silius 1998, 75) the assumption about relatively small class differences and the naturalisation of middle-classness and the "the discussion about heterosexuality among Nordic scholars." Furthermore, they write,

> the increasing ethnic and cultural heterogeneity of the population in the Nordic countries has resulted in a growing interest among feminists in research on the gendered character of the reproduction of hierarchic racial, ethnic and cultural differences. (Liljeström and Silius 1998, 75),

Again, a story of the recent arrival of cultural heterogeneity to the Nordic region is invoked as the reason for an interest in difference, which also suggests that Nordic feminists are, intentionally or unintentionally, largely driven by local concerns.[25]

The first issue dedicated to "gender and ethnicity" came in 2003 (no. 2). Before that, a total of three articles that explicitly focus on this question in the Nordic context have been published and only one of these is on issues beyond the Nordic.[26] The editors subsequently declare that they wish to present "*a relatively recent debate* and a *young* research field in the Nordic countries*" (Knudsen and Meyer 2003, 66; emphasis mine) and go on to offer two sentences about the growing immigration to Nordic countries "since the sixties" stating that "in the Nordic media, immigrants and refugees are very often positioned as a homogeneous group and their presence has provoked much debate, both racial and anti-racial." The use of

[25] Åsa Eldén's (1998) article about "honour killings" is the second article, after Knocke's (1997) critique of multiculturalism (echoing, perhaps the keynote presented by Aleksandra Åhlund at the Nordic research conference "*Frö och Frukter*"), to explicitly take up ethnicity.
[26] Knocke (1997) on multiculturalism, Eldén (1998) on "honour killings," and Mehrdad Darvishpour (1999) on divorce rates among Iranians in Sweden.

the terms "racial and anti-racial" to refer to this debate is notable and suggests a "we" to whom the topic is presumed to be new; "multiculturalism and multicultural settings have been eye-openers" (Knudsen and Meyer 2003, 66). For the first time, editors and special editors note that "articles are written by researchers with a *Nordic ethnic* background," which differs from previous uses of "background," which referred to disciplinary training and nationality. Here we get a story of development rather than arrival:

> [D]uring the past 30 years the Nordic countries have developed into more multicultural and diverse settings and in recent years gender has become one of the key issues in both everyday life and in the discussions of how these multicultural processes work. (Mørck and Staunæs 2003, 67)

They contend that "articles reflect the diversity that exists both in society and in academia by presenting five articles written in different national settings" but then add that the issue reflects "a lack of categorical diversity" and that "all the writers can be categorized as (female) members of the ethnic majorities in Sweden, Denmark and Norway respectively" (Mørck and Staunæs 2003, 68). They conclude, "the study of multicultural issues, gendered multiculturalisms and ethnicized masculinities and femininities is relatively *new* in the Nordic countries" (Mørck and Staunæs 2003, 68). By such narrative, and without any reference to previous work, editors confirm a story of newness and establish themselves as introducing a new topic to *NORA*'s readers.

As we have already seen, editorials can be read as seeking an orientation and presenting a hope or an aspiration. In 1999, editors announce that at least one issue a year will be a special issue. Among suggested themes are "Nordic women inside and outside the European Union (EU)," a "focus on Nordic feminist theory in relation to its international influences and sources of inspiration," and the question "is there a Nordic feminism" (Borgström and Mósesdóttir 1999, 3). None of these questions is, however, addressed under this editorship. In contrast to the previous editorship, editorials after 1999 say little regarding the politics of the journal itself, with one notable exception; a short editorial commentary that Taylor and Francis has taken over managing the journal. This is presented as an "intermediate solution," in line with the times and in order to reach a larger readership; even as nearly twelve years later, Taylor and Francis still publishes *NORA*. This editorial has a gloomy tone, expressing frustration with the vision to offer a diversity of approaches because "academia is increasingly pressuring scholars to adhere to ever narrower channels of disciplines, careers and publications." According to editors, the institutionalisation of the field, which had recently been discussed at a Swedish conference, leads to a "narrower and narrower focus" and *NORA* has an important role in "counteracting this repressive current towards narrow disciplinarity" (Borgström and Mósesdóttir 2000, 3).

In 1999, the diversification of the field begins to be reflected in *NORA* with special issues on "new" themes. Special issue editorials produce distinct narratives of what constitutes the Nordic in this time. For instance, Susanne Knudsen, Bente Meyer, Mette Kunøe, and Kirsten Gomard (2001, 76) introduce a "Nordic" field of language and gender and explain that "the extensive collaboration that exists between Nordic researchers is a result of similar political, social and cultural conditions, and has proved fruitful also in the present area – gender research." The medium for such collaboration, the editors contend, is in fact language, and thus the linguistic history of the "Nordic" languages that has led to their close proximity is outlined, while Finnish here presented as an Indo-European language is "different." However, they contend:

> Swedish, although spoken by only a minority (6%), is a national language in Finland (and Aaland) and taught in school besides Finnish, which is the majority language (94%). Therefore, in academic settings across the Nordic countries, scholars use and understand Danish, Norwegian and Swedish – or they use the modern lingua franca English. (Knudsen et al. 2001, 76)

Neither historical reasons (colonialism), nor the existence of other languages in the "Nordic" region (due to colonialism and immigration) in 2001 are mentioned in this narrative that focuses on language and power. Following a discussion about the words for sex and gender in the various languages and how this relates to discussions of key concepts, the subfield is defined by its biannual conferences and networks of scientific collaboration and conversation.

As we have seen, in the first decade *NORA* is a journal largely concerned with "women." While editorials never explicitly comment on a broader transition from "women's" to "gender" studies, the 2002 special issue on men and masculinity, guestedited by Jeff Hearn and Emmi Lattu symbolically recognises this topic as a part of the larger knowledge formation:

[R]ecent, expanding interest in gender studies and in "doing gender" has definitely highlighted the need for scholarly discussions of how men are gendered, not least in the Nordic context, where the "man" issue has always been part of the more publicly pronounced "woman" issue. (Meyer and Knudsen 2002, 2)

In 1998, introducing the publication of Widerberg's article "Translating Gender" editors point to a debate on what they call "the problem of the so-called 'import of theoretical concepts,' above all from the Anglo-American context to the Nordic 'environment'" (Liljeström and Silius 1998, 77) and they welcome further contributions to this debate. However, this "problem" had not been addressed before and such a debate never happens in *NORA*. While the term gender is increasingly used, now "man" has "always" been part of the woman issue and yet,

the number of women writing in this special issue only adds to the impression that critical studies of men are a *natural* continuation of what is often called women's studies, but might sometimes more accurately be called critical gender research. (Liljeström and Silius 1998, 77; emphasis mine)

A quite striking observation here is that this public and symbolic declaration of politeness and invitation differs notably from those that introduce other others into the field of women's studies:

[W]e welcome these Nordic critical studies of men and masculinities, which in significant ways both take up and challenge aspects brought up by Nordic women's studies in the past thirty years. (Liljeström and Silius 1998, 77)

With such a welcoming gesture, the field of masculinity studies has "arrived," not as a stranger, but as something that has "always belonged" and is now an established part of the field of women's and gender studies. Subsequently, "men's studies" slips in as a self-evident part of gender and feminist research and the editors seem to imply that that the journal will continue to orient itself toward an international community of gender researchers. In what follows, very few articles by non-Nordic based scholars or on materials not related to the region are published, however. Jeff Hearn (Hearn and Lattu 2002) is the only guest editor who has migrated to the region and has been given this opportunity; yet, masculinity is never seen as a migrated concept.

In contrast, guest editor Dorthe Staunæs (2003, 102) presents inter-sectionality as a "theoretical but empirical based reworking of the concept," described as "often used to grasp the interconnections between the tradi-tional background categories of gender, ethnicity, race, age, sexuality and class," a definition that became increasingly common in the latter part of the first decade of the 2000s. Staunæs' article, "Where Have All the Subjects Gone" makes claims on introducing the concept of intersectionality in the "Nordic" context, which makes it of central interest to the questions raised in this chapter. According to Staunæs (2003, 102), it is particularly in the "American" context that the concept of intersectionality has been used and the debate has flourished in "recent decades," referencing mid-1990s pub-lications by authors working in the USA and the UK (Patricia Hill Collins, Kimberlé Crenshaw, Audre Lorde, Floya Anthias, and Iris Marion Young). Staunæs notes that it is through critical race theory that feminist theory's discussion of intersectionality has been most fruitfully developed, and here the main reference is the "African-American Feminist" Patricia Hill Collins (1998) whose idea of a "matrix of domination" is outlined in brief to point to a society dominated by white, middle-class, Christian males. Staunæs (2003, 103) contends that such a structural approach raises a lot of ques-tions and that her interest lies less in large theories than in exceptions, moves, ruptures, and gaps. Her main argument is that categories do not only carry relevance for those belonging to minorities, but also shape all subject formations. Rather than wholeheartedly embracing large theories, she contends, "we" must "wait" and see what actually matters in empirical work and continue to attend to the formation of subjects in a complex sense. While certainly a scientifically sound argument, it is noteworthy that, in the context of "Nordic" feminist debate and NORA, in the journal's ten years of existence, there has not been a single article dedicated to ques-tioning whether gender or sex are relevant categories or whether their use-fulness is fused with relations of power. Thus, it seems that the "arrival" of intersectionality, as presented by a researcher of self-defined "Nordic ethni-city," is coupled with the critique of that very concept as well as the critique it offers. Put differently, the reader is asked to refrain from immediately embracing an analysis of relations of power as constituted through eth-nicity, race, age and so on, on a structural level. Furthermore, the article draws attention to a particular form of debate around intersectionality in the Nordic context, which is its tendency to primarily discuss whether the concept itself is useful, and what, in fact, it "is" and "does."

While the debate about the concept of intersectionality that has since become central to discussions in women's and gender studies had barely started at this point, the lack of citation of, for instance, the work done by postcolonial scholars in Sweden (see de los Reyes et al. eds. 2002, for further discussion of this), suggests that there is little circulation of work and conversations among scholars *in* the Nordic context; or at least among the particular authors who participate in this special issue. A brief survey of references used in articles in *NORA*'s first issue on gender and ethnicity is thus instructive. In terms of theories of race and ethnicity (stated to be of relevance for the emergence of this part of the field by guest editor Staunæs), Hanne Haavind's (2003) article on boyhood and masculinity only makes reference to Ann Phoenix aside from Norwegian authors. Randi Gressgård and Christine Jacobsen's (2003) discussion of Susan Moller Okin's article "Is Multiculturalism Bad for Women" and its relevance for debates about immigration in Norway make reference to bell hooks and Edward Said. Co-guest editor Yvonne Mørck (2003), who also discusses masculinity, references Paul Gilroy and Norwegian sources. Only one of the articles, by Anna Bredström (2003), attends to questions of racism; the rest are largely concerned with issues of gender in relation to "multiculturalism." Bredström references a feminist tradition of research on racism in Sweden and a dozen other sources from feminist and critical race theory, which is unique. From this we might infer that the presumed "Anglo-Americanisation" of Nordic women's and gender studies discussed above has either changed or does not include the tradition of intersectional, postcolonial or critical race theory.

The last issue of 2003 thematises gender and new media. Editors point to "the social constructions of gender and new media," "the problems of access and representation in 'technological' spaces" and contend that in "the Nordic countries people of all ages, ethnicities and genders generally have access to new media through home computers, work environments or public services" (Meyer and Knudsen 2003, 123). While "ethnicity" is presented as "new" and "young" and is given a short introduction, this is several pages longer. Here the Nordic region is characterised by a high level of technology and new media use. Less a question of transformation and troubling change, as with immigration and multiculturalism, this is cast in a positive and self-evident light. As with the special issues on gender and language, masculinities, and several other special issues, guest editors offer an account of a vibrant subfield, summarise research done in different national contexts and intra-regional collaboration, including researchers from the Baltic states and North-West Russia, and state that "research on gender and new media is a well-established research field in the Nordic countries" (Holm Sørensen and Meyer 2003, 127).

How then is the Nordic region's relationship to Europe accounted for in *NORA*? The 2004 special issue "Gender and Power in Europe: Intersections of Ethnicity, Class, Disability, Sexualities and Generations," continues the practice of communicating findings from European feminist research conferences with a broader international community that began with the Lykke et al. (1994) issue of *Women's Studies International Forum*. It marks a symbolic larger shift of institutionalisation and collaboration within both Nordic and European women's and gender studies that is evident in the editors' statement that the scope of *NORA* will shift to "from time to time" even if "as the profile is extending to the New Europe, there is in most of the articles a connection to gender studies in the Nordic countries" (Meyer and Knudsen 2004, 66).[27]

The editorial, like those of other conference paper themed editorials, tells a story about the succession of European feminist research conferences, summarises key themes of the recent one and, for the purposes of *NORA*'s particular readership, discusses the role of the "Nordic" within this context. In so doing, it also stresses the role of NIKK, in both fostering and funding Nordic collaboration, and now, importantly, in collaborations with both "adjacent and other areas" of Europe. Echoing the agenda set up at the first conference, "Women in a Changing Europe," guest editors note that collaboration between the Baltic region, former Eastern Europe, and Western Europe is not only a matter of formal politics but also a central research area for the field itself. The first issue includes the conference key note by Nina Lykke (2004a) that addresses how the universal and the particular has been deployed in three different feminist journals, and also an article by Philomena Essed (2004) that shifts the approach from multiculturalism and diversity to a focus on hegemony and normativity by analysing academia's practices of "cloning" in particular white men. The second issue hones in on questions of identity (not new in the journal), nationalism, and post-nationalism (not previously thematised) and contends that "these questions

---

[27] It is worth noting that editors of the two conference issues are Susanne Knudsen (also a senior editor) and Lotta Strandberg, both researchers affiliated with NIKK, which funded both the conference and the journal.

open for discussion the Nordic profile in *NORA* not only as it extends into the New Europe, but also in connection with a multicultural Europe" (Knudsen and Strandberg 2004 126). The editorial shows that questions such as "What is Europe? What does 'Europe' entail as a space where various identities are negotiated?" (Strandberg and Knudson 2004, 127), are now asked and that there are "new locations from which to contest *Eurocentrism* and look upon history, politics and culture" as well an "aim at showing some of the diversity of European cultural expressions." The concept of "Eurocentrism" is new to *NORA*. Strikingly, Europe and the EU go from being absent to being an entity worth addressing in complex ways. It is also notable that the second issue consists largely of papers by scholars who do not work, address, or originate in what has hitherto been defined as the Nordic region.

The first issue of *NORA* solely dedicated to the question of gender and sexualities came in 2005. Guest editor Jan Wickman (2005) begins his introduction with the declarative statement:

> [A]s we all know [...] the past 15 years has been characterized by the prominence of post- structuralist analytical approaches that challenge the biology-based naturalness of genders and sexualities, and emphasize, in different ways, the socio-cultural and discursive construction of sexual categories and identities. (Wickman 2005, 3)

Wickman (2005, 4) states that "queer theory" has been influential in Nordic gay and lesbian studies since the early 1990s; suggesting the existence of a field hitherto not reflected in *NORA* and referring to a 2003 debate in *NIKK Magazine*, a popular science publication founded in 2000.[28] He also notes that the concept of intersectionality "has been up for discussion" but not related to sexuality until recently. Like others, Wickman comments on how Nordic scholars, as representatives of "smaller countries," can never take their "context" for granted in addressing an international audience. At the same time, he stresses the dangers of homogenising both regional and

---

[28] Space limitations prevent me from including a longer discussion of the themes presented in *NIKK Magazine*, which was founded in 2000 for the purpose of "popularising" women's and gender research. In many ways, this magazine showcases a greater diversity of research themes and debates than *NORA* does in this time. There we learn that queer theory is contested by radical feminists, that pornography is a central concern, that the field of masculinity studies was heavily dominated by women in its early years, among other things.

national settings, especially with regards to gender and sexual politics (Wickman 2005, 5) and suggests that one of the contributions instead stresses heterogeneity. Wickman (2005, 5) warns against "uncritical employment of Anglo-American concepts" and describes another article as "without the Butlerian jargon" (6), suggesting that such a jargon exists. Wickman's editorial is interesting insofar as it again suggests that *NORA*'s readers are familiar with debates that have not taken place in the journal itself. Needless to say, authors and readers of a given journal do not simply engage in debates in that very journal, but what is interesting here is that something called "Butlerian jargon" is presumed to exist among those who engage in "uncritical employment of Anglo-American concepts." I would argue that here Wickman participates in a larger narrative in which the "Anglo-American" is presumed to be dominant, jargony, and not always relevant. Importantly for those who wish to understand *NORA* as a journal that reflects a broader women's and gender studies imaginary, it also suggests that there exists a field of gay and lesbian studies in the Nordic context, again something not mentioned before in *NORA*. While the Nordic journal of gay and lesbian studies, *lambda nordica*, has existed since 1989, and published its first issue on queer theory in 1996, this Scandinavian language journal has very little debate on queer theory as such in this time period.

The year 2005 ends with an issue on "Critical Studies of Nordic Discourses of Gender and Gender Equality," guest edited by Anne Maria Holli, Eva Magnusson, and Malin Rönnblom (2005). By this time, the phenomena of gender equality has emerged as one of the key sites in which ideas of both a joint Nordic, and a productive intra-regional comparison is most strikingly produced. The guest editors stated that critical analysis of gender equality have been developing for "decades" and have subsequently become intensified in the 1990s. They question the very consensus around gender equality as a distinctly Nordic feature and instead propose a hitherto unexplored approach to the issue, namely "a livelier dialogue between critical discursive analyses on gender equality and theoretical and normative approaches would also be a productive area of study for the future" (Holli et al. 2005, 150–151). As is often the case in *NORA*, however, the "Nordic" here consists of national examples, with one key exception, namely Magnusson's comparison of discussions of gender equality among couples in three different Nordic countries.

This close reading of the editorials of *NORA* offers one story that sheds light on how theories, concepts, and themes become "Nordic" and "at home" in women's and gender studies. The journal repeatedly assumes that its readership is familiar with both international and Nordic discussions, even if those are rarely directly referenced. Interestingly, some concepts and theories are presented as already part of the debate, whereas others are understood to be new arrivals. Most striking is that, whereas men and masculinities are immediately welcomed, technology is already a tradition, language is nationalised, gender equality is a key feature of the Nordic, and sexuality studies centrally engage with Butler's work, questions of race and ethnicity are treated as new bodies of both flesh and knowledge. Their inherent newness, the lack of citation of existing work and the small, but growing reflexivity of "ethnic Nordicness" points to how Nordic women's and gender studies repeatedly presumes and reproduces an understanding of Nordicness as "ethnic" and by extension as white, secular/Lutheran, and homogeneous. An analysis of *NORA* editorials thus offers one story of how the field of "Nordic" women's and gender studies has "developed." The gradual institutionalisation and thematisation of issues show an increasingly professionalised and diversified field, with a rotating editorship, connection to a large international publishing house, and an increasing focus on questions of how belonging in the Nordic is constructed. While the appointment of editors, selection of themes, and referee processes that underline the production are rarely revealed in this material, by attending to the transitions between editors and the common practice of thanking referees we gain a sense of key actors and of who is considered trustworthy for evaluating the claims made by and scientific validity of individual authors. Judging by the acknowledgments of reviewers, this is a community of peers, largely located within the Nordic context. Less than a handful of listed referees have institutional belonging outside of the region, and even fewer could be considered non-Nordic according to the journal's own definition of "Nordic ethnicity." If journals are central to the architecture of feminist knowledge, this also tells us something about the reproduction of Nordicness as a body of flesh and knowledge.

Conclusion: Geopolitics inside out

As we arrive at the conclusion of this chapter, it is possible that you, the reader, do not recognise yourself in the story that I have told. It is possible that you expected a different story or that you find my analysis and its focus on the geopolitical grammar used in the production of stories about Nordic and European women's and gender studies "unfair," reductive, or that you think that there are other, more important stories to be told about theoretical trajectories, epistemic "turns" and central debates. Recall that this chapter has been concerned with stories that describe Nordic and European women's and gender studies around the turn of the millennium presented in journal editorials, conference calls and reports and reports from institutions that produce and promote research and above all that I have been concerned with what I have called the workings of a geopolitical grammar. In so doing, this analysis has dealt with the same geopolitical space/region and contains some empirical overlaps with the first chapter in this book. However, Manns' chapter does not convey a taken-for-granted "Nordicness" as the origin of (academic) feminism, and mine has neither presumed or detailed an inevitable "development" or outlined an easily identifiable and clearly demarcated field's increasing institutional success or theoretical complexity.

Instead, I have been deeply inspired by Hemmings' (2011) argument that stories of feminism's recent past are easily cast as stories of either progress, loss or return. Moreover, I have taken my cue from her argument that it is the amenability of these stories, that is, the way they are always inevitably "partial and motivated, speak directly and indirectly to each other, and seek to displace one another" (Hemmings 2011, 132) that points us to the underlying grammar and also that offer us hope if we are dissatisfied. Hemmings argues that there is,

> a feminist desire to distance ourselves from uses of gender or feminism within which we do not recognise ourselves [especially as it often] over-relies on the capacities of a feminist subject to carry the burden of that difference, and in so doing is likely to miss important points of overlap that link a range of narratives about the feminist past and present. (Hemmings 2011, 132)

It seems to me that moments of mis-recognition can be insightful points of departure for analysis, but also that we always run the risk of overlooking moments of overlap. As Haraway (1997, 39 argues, an ethnographic attitude can be adopted even within textual analysis, as "a mode of practical and theoretical attention, a way of remaining mindful and accountable," which in my case means in relation to the very Nordic women's and gender studies that I both study and am a part of. As she contends, "it is not about 'taking sides' in a predetermined way. But it is about risks, purposes and hopes – one's own and others' – embedded in knowledge projects" (Haraway 1997, 39).

Why, then, should we care about the geopolitical grammar of women's and gender studies? Indeed, to many academics, using such a grammar to demarcate and describe a field might seem self-evident, even necessary for the architecture of knowledge itself and certainly for the stories we tell about its origin and development. Given that our work is generally produced within national tax-funded institutions and research projects, that we belong to nationally and regionally organised associations and attend their conferences, a certain kind of intellectual nationalism might seem inevitable and required; while we often stress the need to "situate ourselves" both theoretically and spatiotemporally, we also cannot, it seems, participate in institutional and professional practices without doing precisely that. Furthermore, the comparative imperative of knowledge production and a whole range of knowledge-producing practices, such as conferences and journals, not to mention formal and informal analyses of both research and conditions of this presume, reproduce ideas of geopolitical difference – even as their specific content is repeatedly questioned[29]. In feminist research, it is almost taken for granted that how we come to care about certain questions in women's and gender studies and affirm certain positions is linked to or can be explained by our own (political) stakes in specific locations, even as the grain of detail or specificity of our presumed locations seem to come into view when we move, change or come into contact with others.

In a sense, this chapter's questions and methodology turn such an understanding of geopolitics inside out (cf. Riles 2000). It was through close reading of the source materials (outlined further below) that it became clear that taking (comparable and yet, discernible) differences for granted, has become part of what Riles (Riles 2000, 1–2) has described as features "endemic to the 'inside' of modern institutional and academic analysis." From a methodological standpoint, it seemed to me that an attempt to carry out the initial objective of this research: namely to describe the making of Nordic and European women's and gender studies would simply invoke the very same geopolitical grammar and assign geopolitical characteristics to bodies of flesh and knowledge. My conclusion was that I could not use such

---

[29] For instance, the Baltic Sea Foundation that has funded my research is predicated on the principle of geopolitical and comparable difference. As I outline in the chapter, the Nordic Council of Ministers and the EU, governing bodies that support the institutionalisation and professionalisation of Nordic and European feminist research are also predicated on and insist on similarities and differences based in geopolitics when they encourage and support efforts to create networks of scholars in gender studies.

a technology of analysis for studying or describing the forming of a territorialised epistemic community, because the materials I have studied, in the words of Riles (2000, 1) "share with our interpretive tools a singular aesthetic and a set of practices of representation." To that end, I argue that it is not enough to propose that communities of Nordic and European women's and gender studies are "imagined" rather than existing *a priori* (Anderson 2006). Indeed, as this chapter has proposed, to do so would be to use the same "point of departure" that the past two decades' theoretical insistence on the social constructedness of identities, the material effects of discursive regimes of power and knowledge, and the deconstructive impulse, have used as its central epistemological framework and orientation device. This too is more or less common sense.

Turning this logic inside out, then, I have aimed to unsettle the familiar story of what counts as Nordic, or to defamiliarise the familiar (Dahl 2004). The point in so doing is not simply to argue that stories about the development of feminist theory are untrue or that geopolitical categories are "socially constructed." Nor is the point to suggest that they are not universal, and that geopolitical specificity matters. To stop there would still be part of a familiar story, one that also, in the context of Nordic and European women's and gender studies often tends to set itself up in comparison, or even opposition, to a perceived "Anglo-American"/English-speaking norm; in fact, as I have shown here, that is precisely what the geopolitical logic reproduces. Instead, I have sought to show that stories of the making of Nordic and European women's and gender studies produce belonging around some (nomadic) bodies of flesh and knowledge and not others, and that they are orientated to particular audiences in ways that reveal larger institutional and analytic patterns in (feminist) knowledge/epistemology. What Hemmings (2011) usefully identifies as stories of progress, loss and return with regards to the subject of women's and gender studies, are here thus not simply complemented with stories of geopolitical specificity, but rather, the method is to pay attention to the workings of a geopolitical logic within such stories.

My approach both builds on and challenges previous work on Nordic and European women's and gender studies and in that sense, I am conducting my analysis "from the inside," as a participant observer. I take part of my cue from Lykke (2004a, 74), who has contributed significantly to both the building and the study of Nordic women's and gender studies, and who argues that while feminisms and feminists are often assigned geopolitical belonging, these "have too rarely been accompanied by in-depth reflections on their epistemological and analytical implications." Lykke notes that it is postcolonial feminist thinkers who have most prominently stressed the importance of a more complex politics of location, one that goes beyond categories tied to national origin or belonging and done so in complex ways by stressing movement, diaspora, displacement, and so on. Lykke (2004a, 75) describes herself as "Danish-Swedish-Nordic" and insists that this is a unique position from which to reflect on the field, and yet she does not spell out what this location, or an arrival there, does for her, nor does she give any analysis other than to suggest difference and particularity, while at the same time claiming a certain "at-homeness" in Nordic settings that, as we shall see here, is rarely extended to postcolonial scholars.

In Lykke's, as in many others', accounts, assigned geopolitical belonging, such as national or regional identification, often erases or renders invisible other dimensions, ranging from race, class, gender, age, and sexuality to epistemological or disciplinary training. As the chapter has shown, in the Nordic context, the very idea of a more complex politics of location than one that stresses regionality/nationality and gender is itself presented as one of several "other" and "new" approaches that are set in contrast to a more "stable" notion of familiarity and at-homeness meant by the national or regional. In so doing, postcolonial arguments, unlike those that stress gender and class, as addressed in Manns' chapter, are placed as late arrivals, and as outsiders whose location is always already *elsewhere*, outside the Nordic. If feminist theory in recent years has begun to question any static politics of location for an idea or a theorist and instead stress interconnectedness, travel, translation, and context, in the time period from 1990 to 2005 and in the sources considered here, the content of the geopolitical, if ever contested, was central to the story of women's and gender studies. As Caren Kaplan (1994) has argued, the idea of "a politics of location," often attributed to poet and theorist Adrienne Rich in the 1980s, emerged in a specific location; namely the North American feminist (academic) context, at a time when questions of racism and homophobia had become intensely fraught within "the white feminist mainstream." The very idea of a politics of location, Kaplan (1994, 140) argues, specifically called into question "the position, identity and privilege of whiteness" at a time when tensions were so high that white feminism was "forced to turn its attention away from such assertions of similarity and homogeneity to examinations of difference."[30] Yet, as Kaplan (1994 139) contends, "a politics of location is not useful when it is construed to be the reflection of authentic, primordial identities that are to be re-established and reaffirmed."

As US anthropologist Anna Tsing (1997, 254) has argued, the scholarly understanding that feminism is intrinsically Western dominates most understandings of and stories about translation and indeed, she writes, "funding, conference siting, publishing, training – and certainly many basic frameworks and assumptions" do have a tendency to "come out of Europe and North America." Tsing (1997, 254) suggests that we need to "acknowledge the power of this flow without identifying it as the only history we know" and proposes that we instead attend to "the heterogeneous encounters, interactions, and developments in which particular discursive resources [...] are forged." Some of those encounters and interactions are accounted for in the materials analysed here, and yet the logic of regionality and representation, the geopolitical grammar of knowledge formation, often reduces such encounters to a logic of difference. Inspired by Tsing's mode of attending to alternate stories, I argue that the European and Nordic preoccupation with an Anglo-American norm, and a scepticism towards "importing concepts" have served to produce homogeneity and obscure differences *within* these formations that far exceed those of nation-based ethnic, religious, and cultural difference.

As Hemmings (2011) has argued, how feminists tell stories of our recent (theoretical) past matters for how we orient ourselves and are oriented by those stories. Her account quite explicitly concerns itself with "Western" theory and we might say that it is even more specific; predominantly concerned with what those actors that I have discussed here would call"Anglo-American" theory. Clearly, those who have invested much of their scholarship in promoting and ensuring institutionalisation of this field under the rubric of "Nordic" and/or "European" have made important interventions in arguing for specificity, by contesting the power inequalities inherent in making English the *lingua franca* and so on. However, my concern with the territorialisation of bodies of flesh and knowledge and the effects of a geopolitical grammar is that it repeats a story about a Nordic homogeneity that then gets interrupted by the arrival of "others" that unfortunately tends to follow a logic that at certain moments comes dangerously close to that of

---

[30] It is worth noting that the question of whiteness becomes a thematic theme in the by then renamed *Tidskrift för genusvetenskap* [Journal for Gender Studies] in 2010.

the growing wave of right-wing, fascist, and anti-immigration politics in the Nordic region and Europe. While feminist politics have long served as an antidote to such projects, it seems to me that an undesired and unintended effect of the geopolitical grammar of storytelling has not. My aim in analysing and denaturalising the geopolitical grammar and showing the work it does to assign ideas, theories and theorists geopolitical belonging, contributes to discussions of translations and transitions and to a feminist politics of knowledge production that seeks to radically rethink how belonging is produced through the stories we tell. It also reflects a desire to make space for other stories and understandings of knowledge-making as a meaningful feminist political intervention. What, we might ask ourselves, would be the political grammar of such stories? And if we are to hold on to "our ways of thinking," namely those steeped in an agreed upon importance of historicising, contextualising, comparing, and contrasting, with what building blocks and units are we to make feminist stories that make room for more subjects, trajectories, and imaginaries?

Constructing the West/Nordic: The Rise of Gender Studies in Russia

Marianne Liljeström

This book is about geographical regions, nations, and, above all, about institutional feminist knowledge production. It is also about translations across borders, about travelling theories, ideas, people and practices, and about being situated, mentally and materially in a region or location. Borders are never purely local institutions, but are always already "global" places; they are, therefore, also constitutive for people's relations to or being in the world. We also know that borders are always intrinsically ambivalent, since they are both external, in terms of (state) control and regulation, and internalised as identifications and assumptions (Mignolo and Tlostanova 2006, 206–207). In this sense, borders, and border activities – drawing up borders, enforcing them, interpreting and negotiating them – mark peoples, languages, and genealogies. In this chapter, I look at the travelling and recycling of feminist ideas and theories across the border between East and West, between Russia and Eastern Europe, on the one hand, and the Nordic countries, particularly Finland, on the other. The American philosopher Nanette Funk (2004) underlines the need to address how different, historically specific local political theories within which East and West operate. Criticising Susan Gal and Gail Kligman's (2000) argument that gender issues of the period of East European transformation can be incorporated into categories and analyses of Western feminist discourse, she demands sharp attention both to the complexity of travelling feminist theory, and to the local specificities, which, in her view, will continue to differ and affect feminist categories and analyses (Funk 2004). Such emphasis on the particularity of sites in feminist theories clearly valorises the local, often as the locus of political and cultural resistance. However, reference to the local is not transformative in and of itself. In fact, as Olga

Zubkovskaya, Gender Studies at the Central European University in Budapest, (2009) has shown, by questioning if Western postcolonial theory is adaptable to the analysis of postsocialist feminism, specifying location is a standard gesture in the West, part of the production of nationalist value and knowledge that creates races, genders, and a host of other marked categories. Here, I refer to location first and foremost in the meaning of scholarly, theoretical, and methodological position, and by local and locality I mean geographical, regional, national areas, and geopolitical spaces.

The global feminist community is anything but uniform – in spite of worldwide oppressive practices directed against women, in spite of the call for justice as a joint goal, and in spite of an ethics as the shared mode of relating across differences. My interest in this global community, with its need for temporary and changing alliances of feminist solidarity, lies not only in problematising and re-evaluating locality, but in the obvious contradiction between, on the one hand, the merging, in spite of their differences, of feminists into a new "universalism" and, on the other hand, the constant reproductions of feminist localities, especially along the East/West divide of the global feminist community. Furthermore, I am interested in thinking about alternative ways to problematise the divide as a binary between the categories of universal and local, and, perhaps, to surpass this divide. The binary with its Western hegemonic know-it-all-ness rests on the view and conviction that feminism is ultimately monocultural with a unilateral historiography, which narrates the emergence of feminism as a linear march from premodernity to modernity and postmodernity (Wiegman 2000). The narrative suggests that postmodernity (unaided by any critical thought "outside" of the imaginary space of the West) has created a space for diverse others. However, the narrative also insists that, in the world of experience an enormous range of very distinct events is in fact, when fully revealed, the same. In accordance to this narrative, then, feminists in the West always know where the latecomers are heading because we have already been there. This attitude creates a stringent hierarchy between feminist knowledge producers, where those in the East have a hard time attaining the position of *proper* feminist knowing subjects.

In this chapter, I ask how, in the contemporary circumstances of post-socialism and the ongoing remoulding of the dichotomy between East and West, we are to imagine new communities of knowledge and different feminist genealogies connected to the varieties of "we-ness" of transnational feminism.[1] The question is fundamentally linked to the wide-ranging and extensive discussion on hegemony and otherness in the postsocialist era, and my main concern is the dismantling of hierarchies, exclusions, and inclusions in feminist knowledge production. More specifically, I analyse the topical debate among Russian feminists about the implementation of Gender Studies in Russian academia. I investigate this question situated in a Finnish-Nordic context with its specificities concerning the institutionalisation of gender studies.[2] In this setting – where I easily become a "Nordic feminist scholar" – it is intriguing to examine how the concept of West/Nordic is constructed in the process of establishing gender studies as a legitimate Russian academic field. In this specific transnational context, the topic is dealt with as a part of the growing and lively examination of the content and history of academic feminism, and styles of feminist theorising (cf. Hemmings 2011; Wiegman 2012). In order to contrast the "North-West Russian/East European" and "Western/Nordic" regional settings and contexts, I think it can be illuminating to look at the implementation of the feminist research field in an academic context known for its strong anti-feminism, so vividly expressed in the recent verdicts on the feminist protest conducted by the members of Pussy Riot.

Methodologically I discuss two important circumstances: *firstly*, a contrastive approach based on the situatedness of thinking and writing, requires that the concepts of geopolitics and politics of location are scrutinised, and seen as both a strategy and a method in knowledge production. With these notions, I refer to politically informed cartographies of the position of researchers. In my case, this means taking into account my location as researcher in the context of feminist Russian studies in Finland. *Secondly*, taking the multiplicity of transnational feminisms seriously, I reflect upon the conditions of postsocialism with the purpose of problematising both the taken-for-granted genealogies of feminist thinking and the strong tendency of integrationism within this thinking. Along with a critical deconstruction of the binary East/West bloc-thinking, such issues might outline interesting new challenges for feminist communication and the dismantling of hierarchies within transnational feminist communities.

In this chapter, I concentrate on two broad issues: on the one hand, I focus on the "travelling feminist theory" and the question of "borrowing"

---

[1] About the notion of transnational feminism, see the discussion in the last section of this chapter.
[2] See Manns and Dahl's chapters in this book.

key concepts, examining the interrelationship between "specificity" (locality) and "generic" (global). On the other hand, I ask what in my research context could potentially be considered to be subversive thinking within canonised feminist theory. In dealing with these issues, I ask how we can envision feminist communication between non-identically positioned communities. How can we create intellectual dialogues that bypass the firmly existing institutional settings and scenarios? How can we loosen old dichotomies, geopolitical bloc-thinking, and easy identifications, which continually allow thinking about others as "something," as a generalised figure, or as "not-really-proper" feminist subjects? How can we understand that the coherence of the "we-ness" of knowledge-producing or epistemic communities is always imaginary, and, thus, that this "we" does not eliminate differences, but emerges through them?

My primary material in dealing with these questions consists of Russian feminists' writings published in various journals, such as the only gender studies journal published in Russia, *Gendernye issledovaniya* [Gender Research] (circulation 1,000), *NLO: Novoe literaturnoe obozreniye* [New Literary Review] (circulation 448,000). *Russkii Zhurnal* [Russian Journal], internet-based journal with an enormous circulation), and *Obshestvennye nauki i sovremennost'* [Social Sciences and Present Times]. I also study textbooks, such as *Gender dlya 'chainikov'* [Gender for Tearooms] (2006) and *Gendernyi kaleidoskop* [Gender Kaleidoscope] (2002), and anthologies on gender research, such as *Gendernye issledovaniya v sovremennoi Rossii: Issledovaniya 1990-kh godov* [Gender Research in Contemporary Russia: Research from the 1990s] (2003); and the excellent web sites *Tsentralno-Aziatskaya Set' po gendernym issledovaniyam* [Central-Asian Network on Gender Studies], founded in 2002[3], and the information portal Open Women Line[4]. The material also consists of articles, commentaries, and critiques written by both Western and East European feminists and researchers. My purpose is to utilise this material in order to present discussions on definitions of feminism and gender studies, about "foreignness" and "familiarity," among certain prominent Russian academic feminists, and to review their voices and opinions in my reading and interpretation.

---

[3] See further: www.eldis.org/go/home&id=7780&type=Organisation#.VqCTZ0ZMb9s; last accessed 2016-05-02.
[4] See further: www.owl.ru/; last accessed 2016-05-02.

The emergence of Russian gender studies

The temporal-spatial dimension and the historical contexts linked to feminist theory are of utmost importance when looking at the implementation of Gender Studies into Russian academia. In 2000 (when gender studies had been conducted in Russia for about ten years), Zoya Khotkina, Moscow Centre for Gender Studies, writes about the emergence of gender studies, connecting this emergence with both social changes in Russian society and with the development of Russian academic life, especially in the humanities. She differentiates between four stages in this development: *first*, the introduction of a new paradigm, from the end of the 1980s to 1992, is a period in which, in her view, enthusiasm among feminists was greater than theoretical knowledge and practical experience, and the main tasks were organisational and informational (Khotkina 2000, 22). *Second*, the stage of institutionalisation occurred between 1993 and 1995, when scholarly collectives and organisations were founded. She links the preparations for the 4th World Conference on Women, organised by the UN in Beijing as important to the establishment of gender studies in Russia. During this time a new discipline, feminology,[5] also emerged (Khotkina 2000, 23). At this stage, there was not yet cooperation among the different centres, and most publications generated in Russia were printed abroad. *Third*, a stage of consolidation can be observed in 1996 to 1998; in Khotkina's (2000, 24) view, this is a very important stage at which a type of gender studies particular to Russian and referred to as *sobstvennye* [our own] emerged. *Fourth*, Khotkina considers the temporal stage lasting until 2000, where she finds the implementation successful but the "gender scholarly segment" as being still small (ibid). Of course, analysed from the present perspective, her stages would be somewhat different today. Nevertheless, subsequent observations and comments by prominent feminists, as we will see, indicate similar stages but longer timelines.

However, Olga Voronina, Director of the Centre for Gender Studies in Moscow, (2007) takes quite a different view of the results of the implementation of gender studies. She thinks that there are reasons for the lack of success, such as feminist unwillingness to analyse concrete problems in contemporary Russia and the problem of self-isolation from thinking and working with questions of power. According to Voronina, there are (in

---

[5] Interestingly enough, this concept was introduced in Denmark in the late 1970s as an alternative to the more affect-loaded notion of feminism (Koch 1975).

2007) no prospects of serious gender studies institutionalisation in the post-Soviet space, as well as no perspectives of positive dialogue with the regime, that is, no perspectives for having an impact on the political situation. Serious problems on these fronts hinder the development of a women's movement and of a specifically Russian feminist theory (Voronina 2007, 174). Therefore, Voronina (2007, 176) is quite pessimistic about the current situation: she does not find any of the earlier optimism and euphoria from the 1990s concerning "the drive" or the energetic activism of feminists.

Compared to the diametrically opposed views of Khotkina and Voronina, several gender scholars express certain modified observations. For example, though more in line with Voronina, Olga Zdravomyslova, Director for the Gorbachev Foundation, (2010) comes to the conclusion that, if the beginning of the 2000s was still characterised by great possibilities for the development of gender studies (and also the independent women's movement "on the basis of them"), then at the end of this first decade of the new millennium, gender researchers have faced a much stronger division between, on the one hand, the official, state-defined gender discourse and, on the other hand, the everyday discourse with numerous rhetorical exclamations on "gender themes." These themes are simultaneously belittled and considered taboo (O. Zdravomyslova, 2010, 124–127).

The current stage, according to Voronina (2007, 174), is distinguished by three gender studies schools: the sociological orientation,[6] led by the sociology professors at the European University in St. Petersburg, Elena Zdravomyslova and Anna Temkina; the humanist orientation, dominated by the Kharkov Centre of Gender Studies; and the course directed by the Moscow Centre of Gender Studies with its analysis of social, political, and economic gender problems in Russia. In the article "Systematic Outlines of the Gender Studies in Russia: From fragments to Critical Rethinking of Political Strategies" (2007), Elena Kochkina, Moscow Centre for Gender Studies, presents an optimistic account of the institutional development of these studies, as the title of her article clearly indicates. She brings forth certain facts in order to underscore the success of institutionalisation. For example, in 2005–2006 there were more than one hundred *vuzy* [institutions of higher education] that taught courses in gender studies, and course clusters as programmes of gender studies were implemented in forty *vuzy*. Further-

---

[6] Elena Kochkina (2008, 291) calls this orientation the Russian school of gender constructivists.

more, nine academic institutes of the Russian Science Academy (RAN) had laboratories and groups on gender studies, and, lastly, fifteen gender studies centres carried out their activities as NGOs (Kochkina 2007, 96). These quantitative measures demonstrate, in her opinion, the successful integration of gender studies into the academic and educational system in Russia (Kochkina 2007, 96).

Gender studies teaching and training

The views quoted above tend to regard the implementation and academic institutionalisation of gender studies as either a success or a disappointment. However, in order to evaluate the slippery notion of success, the authors emphasise the need for various qualitative approaches, for example, mapping what courses were taught within gender studies. A roundtable discussion held in October 2009 within the realm of the 13th International Summer School of Gender Studies is an interesting example of intense debates about the definition of the gender category, as well as about the question of what should be considered "proper" gender research. One of the young discussants noted that, although the discipline had already existed for about twenty years and the Summer School of gender studies was meeting for the thirteenth time, the discussion still nevertheless evolved around the issue of what gender is (*Gendernye issledovaniya*, 2010, 114). Indeed, many of the participants in the discussion (mostly younger students) were worried that the category was being used in the "wrong way," that is, in a non-feminist way and/or limiting the term to "gender-role thinking" (*Gendernye issledovaniya* 2010, 71). The discussion moderator Dimitri Vorontsov, offers three usages of the term: gender understood as naturalised/essentialist characteristics; as some partial aspects of reality, and as a category with universal meaning. He thinks that such different definitions should be included – and allowed – within gender studies, and considers methodological reflections about one's own place within the discipline as decisive (ibid, 75). The moderator's opinions depart here from those of many others participating in the heated discussion: compared to them he does not ascribe himself the role of gatekeeper to some sort of disciplinary purity, which makes him less strict and more inclusive than others. The content of the gender studies courses taught at different gender studies centres, universities and institutes of higher education, *vuzy*, is manifold and diverse. The teaching organised by the gender studies centres[7] varies significantly. For example, the Moscow Centre offers a programme called "Bases of Gender Studies," consisting of six modules set up in accordance with larger disciplinary fields (economics, law, sociology, social policy, and humanities) and one module on the theoretical and methodological bases of gender studies. At the Minsk Centre (relocated to Vilnius), themes vary considerably ranging from the sociology of gender and gender history to gendered representations in the visual arts. More specifically, these overall clusters include courses on gender and capitalism, trauma, memory and narrative, masculinity, the culture of childhood, technology of gender in the post-Soviet mass media, and political theory of feminism, theory of postfeminism, and courses on methodological issues. The modules of gender studies offered at the Kharkov Centre have a noticeably stronger profile in the field of humanities than many other centres. The head of the Centre, Professor Irina Zherebkina (2003), writes that the specificity of Russian gender studies lies in the emergence of the discipline from within a thinking around social statuses and not gender attributes (a heritage already from the Soviet times), a consequence of which was that Russian gender studies, taking form in the 1990s, did not have to deal with the types of questions that had faced women's studies in the West, such as the content and character of female subjectivity. Therefore, she explains, the new post-Soviet gender discourse has not been particularly interested in for ˥ a été cpsychoanalysis, literature, philosophy, psychology, cultural studies, dies, or even history. Research within these areas was initiated much later (Zherebkina 2003, 227–228). The Centre in Kharkov is one of the few places were the gender studies modules consist of research areas in literature, psychology, and cultural studies as well. There are courses in "Gender and mass communication," "Gender and identity," "Gender and presentation of women's images on TV and the internet," "Gender, language, and globalisation," "Contemporary women's movement in Ukraine," and so on. The Kharkov Centre for Gender Studies has also created the very successful

---

[7] The oldest and quite firmly established centres include the Moscow Centre for Women's and Gender Studies (founded in 1990), the Women's Studies Centre at Khazan University (1991), the Kharkov Centre for Gender Studies (1994), the Ivanovo Centre for Gender Studies (1996), the Centre for Gender Studies at the European Humanities University in Minsk (founded in 1997 and today after it was closed by the Belorussian authorities, located in Vilnius), and the Tver Centre for Women's and Gender Studies (1998).

institution of Summer Schools (the abovementioned debate about gender took place precisely at the 13th Summer School in 2009). This annual, three-week school has been run since 1997. Sponsored by the John D. and Catherine T. MacArthur Foundation, the Summer School has developed into a most important network resource for the institutionalisation of gender studies in the countries of the former Soviet Union. Thematically the schools have been organised around such issues as feminist methodology, East/West dialogue, women's studies, globalisation, distance learning, nationalism, post-Soviet feminism, women in politics, love and art, and new political challenges (Phillips 2008, 78).

The disciplinary prominence of sociology within gender studies

One of the discussions that took place at the 13th Summer School in 2009 was entitled, "Why Is Sociology the 'Favourite' Discourse on the Development of Gender Studies in the Former USSR?" According to the moderator Natal'ya Zagurskaya, Centre for Gender Studies in Kharkov, this question, together with the continuing debates on the content of gender research today, has become strongly connected to specific disciplines (*Gendernye issledovaniya*, no. 19/2010, 93). Those feminist analyses that examine the content and character of Russian gender studies, and taking into account both research and teaching, deal almost exclusively with the discipline of sociology. One of the participants in the debate noticed that the place of sociology is prominent because sociology seems to have "the gender approach" built into its disciplinary boundaries (ibid). Indeed, at the Faculty of Political Science and Sociology at the European University in St. Petersburg, the basic programme includes since 1997 a specific programme on gender studies encompassing the entire academic year: the students are taught social theory from a gender perspective, qualitative methods, feminist theory, and gender relations in Russia.[8] In her comparison of teaching gender sociology in Germany and Ukraine, Tat'yana Khavlin, Kharkov Centre for Gender Studies, (2010) shows that, in spite of the quantitative imbalance of courses – 250 special courses arranged in Germany at thirteen *vusy* against thirty-seven in Ukraine during the period 2000 to 2009 – the field faces the same kind of problems and challenges in both countries: the relation between educational functions and social activities, and the relation

[8] https://eu.spb.ru/en/gender-studies/courses

between various methodological teaching paradigms, such as structuralism and functionalism, symbolic interactionism, ethnomethodology and others. Furthermore, both countries currently contend with topical issues such as integrating gender into curriculum courses in sociology; the impact of gender critiques on the traditional academy; and the influence of feminist theories and their integration into the theoretical canon of the discipline (Khavlin 2010, 254, 252).

However, the question posed, that is, why should gender studies research and teaching be most successful precisely within sociology, begs some sort of answer. On the one hand, I think that the earlier presented explanation by Zherebkina (2003) is quite accurate: both the former "woman's question" of Soviet times and the starting point of gender problematisation during glasnost, were carried out as a problem of social statuses. This also means that both strands have contributed to certain homologising ways of thinking of equality. On the other hand, I want to underscore in this connection that it is important to take into account that all the valuable work done is a result of the efforts of dedicated feminist teachers and researchers to make their case and to bring decisive pressure to bear on institutions. As all feminists working within gender studies know, it takes considerable persuasiveness and serious credibility to incorporate a gender studies programme into the general academic curriculum.

Nuances of success

Olga Plakhotnik, Kharkov Centre for Gender Studies, (2010) problematises the question of the success of the discipline in an article on the institutionalisation of gender studies in Ukraine. She pays attention to what she refers to as "some nuances" amidst all the talk about success, examining both what is commonly considered a "gender studies course" and its content. In Ukraine, the Ministry of Family, Youth, and Sport is responsible for the implementation of gender politics (which ironically releases the Ministry of Education from this task). The Ministry in question annually gathers information on the implementation from all the institutes of higher education within the Kharkov area. When Plakhotnik (2010, 158) looked more closely at this information, she discovered quite "interesting" courses categorised as gender studies, for example, "Spiritual health" (Kharkiv Humanist Pedagogical University), "The basics of sexology and sexual pathology" (National Aerospace University, named after N.E. Zhukovsky), and "The everyday family culture and domestic economy" (Kharkiv State Zooveterinary Academy). Furthermore, she mentions some other courses, which she thinks are ingeniously included as dealing with the gender problematic, for instance, "Latin-American ball room dance and methods of teaching" (Kharkov State Academy of Culture), "Conflictology (gender differences)" (the Kharkiv State Zooveterinary Academy), "Chinese language: The specificity of using the grapheme 'woman' and 'man, human being'" (Kharkiv National Pedagogical University after G.S. Skovoroda) and so on (Plakhotnik 2010, 158). If anything – apart from humorous curiosa – the names of the courses point to quite a lot of confusion concerning the notion of gender and its invocation in teaching.

In "nuancing" the question of success, it is of special interest to examine student participation in, and understanding of, gender studies. A sociological survey among students of Kharkov in 2009 shows that two-thirds of the students asked had never dealt with any gender problematic in their studies.[9] Of the remaining one third, 10 percent had taken courses that had in some way dealt with some sort of problematic or theme about gender, but only 3 percent had taken "real" gender studies courses (Plakhotnik 2010, 159). The survey also included the question, "How understandable is the meaning of gender for you in such word combinations as gender politics and gender equality?" The students' answers were grouped in "thirds" in the following way: 32 percent answered that they know and can explain the meaning of gender, 38 percent said that they knew the words but could not give strict definitions, and 30 percent said that they did not know what gender meant. Plakhotnik (2010, 159) observes that the 38 percent mentioned could also include so-called masked or hidden ignorance, meaning that the respondents may not wish to acknowledge their lack of knowledge. Interestingly, the survey also showed that the role of the university training concerning the basic sources of information about gender questions was less than expected: various kinds of electronic forms of communication (especially the internet) turned out to be very important (Plakhotnik 2010, 160).

---

[9] The survey is part of a research project "Male and Female Students about Gender Equality" in which 900 students participated. They studied at course levels 1–5 within 22 faculties of 15 *vuzy* in Kharkov (cf. Plakhotnik 2010, 164).

Implementation of gender studies and Russian higher education

The circumstances examined above make it clear that gender studies is tenuously integrated into the educational system of the former Soviet states. There are no departments of gender studies because the discipline is not yet included in the state educational standard and it is not acknowledged as an independent scientific field of research, study, and expertise. The general organisation of the university and educational system supports and reproduces this lack of recognition: almost all post-Soviet university systems are built in accordance with the strict conventional disciplinary division characteristic to Humboltian ideals of higher education, where all disciplines have their place and the boundaries between them are stringently drawn. This organisation effectively works against the development of all kind of interdisciplinarity, and, hence, gender studies.

When engaging with the question of why gender studies has been difficult to institutionalise, Zherebkina (2003, 233) discusses teaching practices "from below," which, in her view, tend to be seen as representing something "from the West". In her opinion, this means that the development of gender studies has an ecstatic character and is hard to institutionalise, not only because of its interdisciplinarity, but because of the personal, embodied, what she calls "obscene addition" it makes to the university (Zherebkina 2003, 233–234). In general, gender studies is exercised more inside disciplines than in the form of independent basic courses. According to Zherebkina (2003, 237–238), the reason for this situation lies above all in the disciplinary structure of Russian higher education, but also in the change of teaching methodology and the accentuated problematic of female subjectivity as linked to different disciplines, that is, precisely the reason why such courses emerge as "women's history," "women's literature," "feminist theory," or "feminist anthropology," "women's rights," etcetera. Here the following regularity is observed: as long as the gender thematic is taught within different disciplines, the methodology of that one is used.

Plakhotnik (2010) mentions two additional factors that negatively influence the institutionalisation of gender studies in the academic system of Russia, Ukraine, and other postsocialist states. The first factor is the emphasis on applied research and knowledge in teaching, what she calls the "re-translation" of knowledge. This emphasis gives a secondary status to gender studies, with its stress on the production and implementation of new and critical knowledge. Second, she underlines the fact that research and educational policies are always part of "big politics," and, therefore, are linked to the formation of general gender discourse (Plakhotnik 2010, 163). In Khavlin's earlier mentioned comparison between gender sociology in Germany and Ukraine, the specificities of the university and educational systems in "West" and "East" also point clearly to the differences between the contexts. In Ukraine, a majority of courses are standardised programmes, while in Germany the students have much greater freedom to choose various courses (known as *Forschungskurse*) (Khavlin 2010, 255). When it comes to the question of mandatory gender studies courses versus elective courses in academic programmes, Plakhotnik (2010) is in favour of the latter. She draws parallels to the stages of implementation of gender studies in the North American academy, where the programmes are built on elective courses, and where gender studies are well integrated and popular among students. Being fully aware of the discrepancy and differences in the development of the discipline in the USA and in postsocialism, she nevertheless makes the comparison by emphasising "the West" as an example and concludes that it would only be detrimental to gender studies in Russia and other post-Soviet countries if the compulsory courses were integrated in study programmes (Plakhotnik 2010, 161–162).

In her discussion of the "national specificity" of feminist research, Irina Savkina, Russian Language and Literature at the University of Tampere, (2007) stresses that (Western) feminist literary criticism can operate only on the general level because "the details are beyond its zone of focus." However, she thinks that, in spite of problems and contradictions, feminist literary criticism provides general methodological approaches which make it possible not only to see practices that are hidden from conventional scholarship, but also to enrich such research areas and questions that are considered already fully examined (Savkina 2007). Hence, Savkina belongs to those who construct a clear division between theory and methods, where feminism can be used as some sort of theoretical tool, as an eye-opener for new research questions, but where methods are still determined and categorised in accordance with disciplinary specificity. This point of view works against the promotion of interdisciplinarity and does not take into account the fact that methodology is a theoretical field where the criteria for research objects, theories, methods of analysis and interpretations, and writing styles are debated.

Aid from the West

With the fall of the Soviet Union, it became possible for universities and research centres to become independent. It is commonly agreed that almost all post-Soviet independent scholarly structures, with some sort of new "liberal direction" have emerged as a result of Western financial help. With her localisation in both east and west, Elena Gapova, Director of the Centre for Gender Studies, European Humanities University, Vilnius/Minsk and affiliated with the University of Western Michigan, underlines that a new category of intellectual workers has appeared, who gains special status because of their contacts with the West. In other words, a new class has emerged, which is professionally linked to Western academia (Gapova 2007, 152). In her view, this state of affairs also pertains to gender studies in Russia, which is formulated as a part of Western knowledge. More importantly, without the support from the West, gender studies would lack disciplinary legitimacy (Gapova 2007, 153–154).

In her overview of the history of founding centres of gender research, Natal'ya Pushkareva (2007a), a well-known and distinguished feminist anthropologist working at the Russian Academy of Science in Moscow, continues Gapova's line of thought. She emphasises, on the one hand, that many centres for the study of, for example, women's history, such as the Ivanovo Centre for Gender Research, were established already in the early days of perestroika, and, on the other hand, that the majority of them were set up in the 1990s, when there was a push for it – "not from the bottom but from above" – meaning as part of "Western feminism," not of "ours," as she expresses it. Pushkareva (2007a, 167) emphasises that the intellectual and financial support from Western foundations had an enormous influence in this connection. Pushkareva's evaluation of the results and consequences of what she terms "the golden rain" echoes Gapova's views: the aim of the financial aid was to spread the ideals of "liberal society" in accordance with a Western model to make possible a "Western style" gender equality in Russia. Pushkareva considers the results after the ten to fifteen years of financial support from the West, to be strongly negative: those groups that were founded with foreign aid work only in accordance with "foreign needs," not domestic, and, therefore, a phenomenon of "false activism" corresponding with the event of "false civil society" emerged. Because the language used is English, ordinary Russian people do not know about these groups and centres, and, thus, a new elite, and some hierarchic women's organisations have appeared as the result of the financial aid (Pushkareva

2007a, 168–169). Pushkareva (2007b, 400) also notes that, when the financial aid has been radically reduced, the work of the centres has been seriously affected. Today, financial aid is for them often necessary for survival.

Gender research of our own: Russian specificity

The notions of "feminology" and "genderistics" have been introduced as specifically Russian, and thus as important to resisting the imposition of "foreign" frameworks for gender studies. As I mentioned earlier, Khotkina, Moscow Centre for Gender Studies, (2000) believes that Russian gender studies of *sobstvennye* [our own] emerged in 1996–1998. However, I find it noteworthy that those feminists who mention these *sobstvennye* studies approach them very critically. Thus, according to Gapova (2007), this scholarly tradition emerged already in the late 1960s and represents above all a discursive return to traditional femininity, that is, it stands in opposition to gender constructionist theories and critical social theory in general. This tradition is based on and clings to an opposition between male and female, examining "roles" and "stereotypes" on the basis of biologisation or naturalisation of the social and cultural. In Gapova's (2007, 156) view, the category of gender turns in this perspective from that which *requires* explanation (why are men and women different?) to an *explanation* of differences (women and men are different, therefore they also behave differently). In this way, for example, "gender history" becomes traditional history of prominent women or a glorification of maternal origins, "gender linguistics" becomes the science of men's and women's different speech. According to Pushkareva (2007a, 167), there are two types of simultaneous gender discourses striving for definitional dominance: first, the discourse of traditional gender roles – which Voronina, for example, has named "the false theory of gender" – which legitimates female characteristics as complementary to male roles, and second, the critique of the naturalisation of gender roles, that is, what she calls an antiessentialist discourse.

Zherebkina's (2003) curious and distinctive thesis concerning the institutional practice of gender studies in Russia is that it can only be performative. As I noted earlier, for her, Russian "specificity" means that gender studies emerged within the logics of social statuses, that is, the basic form of

these studies is data collecting[10] (a tradition which builds upon the publication of the many articles on Soviet women's situation in earlier times),
they do not deal with the content of femaleness, but with the criteria of its
performative existence (Zherebkina 2003, 227–228). Zherebkina draws interesting conclusions. In her opinion, gender discourse in the former Soviet
Union is a specifically postmodern discourse, and this defines the particular
forms of institutionalisation of Russian gender studies (Zherebkina 2003,
230–231). This means, in her view, that post-Soviet gender studies finds
itself in conflict with the emerging female practices of becoming subjects
(referring not only to practices of female literature and art, but also to the
appearance of feminist movements) (Zherebkina 2003, 237). The reason for
this is above all the generally very low status attributed or alluded to the
concept of "female" in the pre-Soviet, Soviet, and post-Soviet cultures.

Evaluating the success of post-Soviet gender studies

In my reading, some processes of forming academic gender studies communities are interpreted quite unanimously among Russian feminist
scholars. For example, many agree that to "catch up" after the many years of
isolation, researchers had to be extremely receptive and open-minded to the
new thinking in its compressed and overwhelming form. Thus, Tat'yana
Barchunova, Novosibirsk State University, (2003, 4, 10) emphasises that, by
the time the Russian scientific and philosophical community gained access
to the discussions that had taken place elsewhere, many of these debates had
already receded into history. For the post-Soviet gender community, all the
temporal layers of gender and feminist discourses turned out to be simultaneous intellectual endeavours. In her view, and in accordance with the
firmly established, but criticised chronology of "Western" feminist waves,
these included liberal feminism and the concept of sex-roles, the criticism of
liberal feminism, the essentialist (universalistic) approach to women, and
the notion of gender as a social construction. Therefore, Barchunova believes that it is not an exaggeration to claim that post-Soviet gender studies
and feminist academic practices have found themselves in a multitemporal,
multiparadigmatic, multicultural intellectual environment. She reminds us
that Simone de Beauvoir's *Le Deuxième Sexe* (1949) was translated into Rus-

---

[10] According to Kochkina (2007, 97, n. 37) the main bulk of research consists of empirical work (about 3,000 pieces).

sian in 1994, at the same time as Adrienne Rich's texts became available to Russian readers. It is easy to agree with Barchunova that those debates, which, in the West, were connected to the emergence of gender as a construction, did not take place in Russia. As examples of such theoretical-methodological debates, Barchunova mentions those concerning ethno-methodology, symbolic interactionism, existentialism, and psychoanalysis.

While Barchunova emphasises the eclectic theoretical base of Russian Gender Studies as characteristic for circumstances in Russia, Zdravomyslova and Temkina (2003) underline the specificity of the historical context on a wider societal level. They describe this context, which can easily be seen as generally hostile to feminism as it is represented in Russian public discourse, in terms of the reaction to the legacy of the Soviet etacratic (state socialist) gender order. This legacy includes the so-called "resolution of the women's question" in the Soviet period, as well as the "working mother"-gender contract, the strong position of women in society, "failed masculinity" or the "crisis of masculinity" (Zdravomyslova and Temkina 2003, 53).

Nevertheless, Almira Ousmanova, European Humanities University in Vilnius/Minsk, (2003) along with many other feminist scholars, characterises the development of gender studies as a success story. "In less than a decade it has 'conquered' the whole of Eastern Europe and the ex-Soviet Union," she writes (Ousmanova 2003, 42). With an ironic remark about the lack of interest among Western scholars in the reasons for this achievement, she connects – quite differently from Barchunova – the success story to the context of epistemological discussion in post-Soviet humanities: the breakdown of Soviet ideology created a special "free" space, which was occupied by feminism and gender studies. Besides forming a remedy for the methodology of class and economic reductionism, gender studies also offers interdisciplinarity, new perspectives and concepts, and the possibility of combining social activism and academic interests. Here Ousmanova joins Zherebkina (2003, 239), who emphasises that the gender discourse with its gender constructed position is the only post-Soviet critical discourse, which goes beyond the discursive limits of gender manipulation, as defined by the state. In contrast to these scholars, Zdravomyslova and Temkina (2003, 51) argue for a different and very controversial basis for the success, Russian gender studies "began to develop as a whole thanks to the application of Western concepts and theories." The Russian-American researcher Sergei Oushakine (2005, 197) provides support for this view by characterising gender studies in Russia as a "translation project." However, Zdravomyslova and Temkina (2003, 51) underline in the same breath that gender studies, "[h]ave come to be recognized both as a new field of research and a space in which open discourse is possible."

In evaluating the success of gender studies teaching and implementation in academia, both the critical and the celebratory views are in one way or another contrasted to the West, to some specific country (mainly the USA), or to some established, widely agreed upon (Western) criteria. This contrast is understandable because of the empirical and historical differences between the regions concerning the institutionalisation of gender studies. More difficult to accept is the originality and distinctiveness of the Russian feminist theory and Russian "feminizm," eagerly proposed by the British scholar Carol Adlam, (who replaces the "s" in feminism with a "z" in order to emphasise difference):

> Today it is understood that Russian feminism emerges from *totally* other philosophical foundations than the Western (not from the denial of the "biological" in favour of "the social," for example), and that its tasks to-day are *totally* different, that is, continue to confirm feminism in the conditions of new forms of masculinism and social exclusion. Today Russian feminist theory, together with its Western partner, tries to demonstrate that Russian feminizm – which did not emerge from the West – but is shaped in the process of its repeated redoing (*peresechenie*, "re-cutting") emerged on the basis of its own conditions and history and moved according to a trajectory which was oppositional enough in relation to the trajectory of the development of Western feminism. (Adlam 2010, 224; my translation and emphasis)

The remainder of my chapter deals with, and deconstructs in many ways, the issues touched upon in this long quotation. Hence, to sum up the first part of this chapter: the discussions concerning the emergence and develop-ment of Russian gender studies focus both on evaluating achievements, and on examining (past) stages of development. The (relative) success of gender studies – a discussion I will also return to later – is predominantly due to various kinds of private initiatives of enthusiastic teachers and activists. At the same time, the question of the integrity of Russian gender studies remains both topical and ambivalent.

Travelling and borrowing concepts: The question of the "foreign"

Among Russian feminist scholars, it has become commonplace to complain about the uncritical borrowing of the language and questions of Western feminism for the analysis of local cultural and social reality (see, for example, Savkina 2007; Kashina 2012; Oushakine 2012). The irritation is noticeably connected to the linguistic discrepancies caused by what is characterised as imported terminology. This is the reason why many scholars, who underline the local perspective and reproduce the gap between some sort of taken-for-granted, unchangeable feminist theory as "general" and national distinctiveness as unique and "real," tend to understand key categories as empty signifiers. These scholars are paradoxically simultaneously worried about sidestepping and overlooking the national specificities and about "incorrect" usage of feminist terminology. Some are worried about "the faithfulness to the original," about *dilemma vernosti* (Zdravomyslova and Temkina 2007, 82), especially as connected to the translation of Western texts to Russian. These scholars point out the double effects of translations. On the one hand, we change our own language in order to retain the meanings of the original texts, on the other hand, we simultaneously change the original with the purpose of fitting it into the flow of our native language. They point out that translation generates not only problems with grammatical structure, but also of discursive resistance. Therefore, they conclude by observing that problems with translations of feminist texts are always political (Zdravomyslova and Temkina 2007, 83). This problematic and anxiety derives from the acknowledgment that all well-established concepts have their own history within different theoretical traditions, and, hence, drag along a special baggage of definitions and meanings.

Among those debating this topic, Galina Zvereva, Russian State University for the Humanities in Moscow, (2005) has dealt with different approaches to the concept of "foreign" in an interesting article about the usage of feminist and gender concepts within the current Russian gender studies community. In her view, understandings of these concepts have been shaped in the process of adapting to "global" intellectual knowledge and experience – that which in post-Soviet society is interpreted as "Western." Zvereva distinguishes between three "forms" of "foreign," as alien, as ours, and as different/other. In the first case, there is a strict hierarchy constructed between us and them, between "foreign" intellectual fashions and "our" realities and concerns. A mechanism of strongly negative identification is present here, and Russia is often elevated in relation to the West, with Russia viewed as "spiritual" and the West as "soulless" and "technological" (Zvereva 2005). The second approach, supported by many Russian feminists and intellectuals already at the turn of the 1990s, underlines the possibility of forming a mixture between the "ordinary" (ours) and the new (foreign) by domesticating the foreign. As a result, many hybrids of cognition and representation have emerged, for example, there is an ongoing process of semantic refashioning of basic words (ibid). The third case, foreign as other, acknowledges the complexity of assimilating another or "difference." According to Zvereva, this approach has been/is the most laborious for Russian intellectuals to grasp. Besides the insight of qualitative changes in knowledge regimes worldwide, this third approach also includes the realisation of the non-existence of pure knowledge. Zvereva underlines the difficulties linked to this approach by pointing to the necessity of thinking about the process where concepts from other contexts are used in one's own work, a common enough challenge to all of us.

Zvereva acknowledges here the difficulty of creating new terminological ground in a situation which Temkina and Zdravomyslova (2003) has characterised as "discursive chaos," where fragments of modernist and post-modernist theories participate simultaneously and equally in the shaping of a new gender discourse. Oushakine (2002, 16–17) has a distinct standpoint on the Russian use of the notion of gender: he believes that the terminological imitation (the adaptation of the word "gender" itself in Russian) is a symptom of colonial consciousness exposing a lack of belief in the language and history of Russia. He also pays attention to the presence of "conceptual homonyms," that is, terms, which are spelled and pronounced in the same way, but refer to different realities. In line with these thoughts, but expressed more critically and in a quite pessimistic tone, Oushakine (2012, 7) says in an interview that he finds the word "gender" very problematical, artificial, and useless in Russian: "For me 'Russian gender' is an academic variety of 'cover-versions' of Western songs."

Savkina (2007) takes the example of the private/public division, calling attention to the central and principal character of this question in both Russian and Western feminist thinking. Like many before her,[11] she questions whether the (post-)Soviet "private" and the "private" of western liberal societies actually refer to the same phenomenon (Savkina 2007). Savkina states that the question of Western methodologies concerns above all the ethnography of methodological practices, that is, the question of those con-

---

[11] See Gal and Kligman (2000), and much earlier Shlapentokh (1989). The way, for example, Savkina picks examples and arguments, tells about a firm and monolithic understanding of feminist genealogy: the use of certain notions and terms, for example, the private/public division, are stubbornly described as belonging to the canonised feminism/gender studies.

texts where the "new theories" strike or where they are inscribed. However, she also notes that a straight adaptation of Western theories to "Russian reality" results too often in a problematical use of the concepts in the hope that they are universal enough and therefore can explain everything (Savkina 2007). Zdravomyslova and Temkina (2000) in their turn have noticed that creating a new terminological ground for feminist scholarship in Russia requires translated texts in order to investigate what in these texts can be said to reflect transcultural processes, what in them can be said to be meaningful for the Russian experience, and, conversely, what can Russian experience and language challenge in the translated texts? "Through the opposition of the foreign, its adaptation and remodelling a new feminist discursiveness is created," they write (Zdravomyslova and Temkina 2000, 7). Fourteen years later, these feminist researchers underline that Western discussions on the content of feminist research do not reach Russia because of the specific antifeminist character of Russian academic and social life (Zdravomyslova and Temkina 2014, 86). Thus, the process of constituting a "new feminist discursiveness" remains obscure.

Hence, Zdravomyslova and Temkina deal with the "one-way" movement of feminist concepts travelling from the West to the East. The common view holds that it is then for Russian feminists to decide what suits the Russian national specificity and to adopt a selective range of concepts and theories. Here it can be useful to recall Edward Said's (1991) definition of the stages common to the way that any theory or idea travels: first is the point of origin or what seems like one. Second is the distance transversed, a passage through the pressure of various contexts as the idea moves from one point to another time and place where it will come to a new prominence. Third is a set of conditions informing acceptance and resistance, making possible its introduction or toleration, however alien it might appear to be. Fourth, the accommodated idea is to some extent transformed by its new uses, its new position in a new time and place (Said 1991, 226–227). This is, I think, what Zdravomyslova and Temkina mean by the appearance of a new feminist discursiveness. Said (1991, 230) believes that looking at how theories travel can tell us a lot about the theory itself, its limits and possibilities. However, it can also suggest quite a lot about the relationship between theory and criticism, on the one hand, and society and culture, on the other. Importantly Said (1991, 241) emphasises that we must borrow theory if we are to elude the constraints of our immediate intellectual environment. No reading is neutral or innocent, and by the same token every text and every reader is to some extent the product of a theoretical standpoint.

153

Travelling theory as "borrowing" can also be seen as travesty or ironic imitation. The Bulgarian feminist researcher Ralitsa Muharska (2006) has observed that, when Russian and East European feminists are always conceived of as speaking something translated, something that "must come" as related to the Western "is," there is always the possibility of speaking inadequately, always the risk of unsuccessful imitation, of unintended caricature. This is, in my opinion, a promising thought of (maybe) filling old notions with new meaning (Muharska 2006, 8). In the situation where Western and Nordic feminism is for Russian feminists the Lacanian Other, only two alternatives for identification exist for Russian feminists. As Marina Nosova (2004) has emphasised, they must either develop the concept of uniqueness concerning their subjective experiences via oppositional logics, or use the resources of the periphery's distance and construct themselves as the subjects of critique. Thus, the "marginalised position" and situatedness of Russian feminism and feminists within feminist theory and research, is interestingly also discussed in terms of potential subversiveness, understood as a contribution to productive developments in feminism. Here the distancing resources of the periphery are used in the feminists' construction of themselves as influential critical subjects (Nosova 2004, 239). Hence, the space of articulation consisting of celebratory imitation or creative counter-discourses in "secondary," peripheral, or "colonial" situations also means a movement from temporal toward spatial conceptualisations.

The key question here then, is in my opinion the so-called transfer of meaning. Being aware of the extreme importance of taking into account both the historical and the contemporary contexts, one may wonder why the ambition of Russian and East European feminists would be to incorporate Western meanings "as correctly as possible" into their usage of key concepts. Why would the quintessence of travelling concepts be that the transfer of meaning should be granted? And, what would that mean in practice anyhow: who is the gatekeeper or authority to decide when the transfer of meaning has been successfully completed? However, some sort of competition for authority can be noticed here (as elsewhere), which builds on a "more learned," "more correct" (and therefore "deeper") internalisation and adaptation of "Western" feminist theory.

Analysis of social processes and identities particular to Russia and East Europe can certainly challenge current theoretical paradigms. This is so, not because feminists are theorising from a position outside Western feminist theory, or because they articulate an authentic and distinct "national" gender experience or identity. Rather, it might be so because feminists offer analyses of phenomena specific to the region that prompt us to see complications and new dimensions of existing theoretical concepts. Furthermore, the way Russian and East European feminist scholars use some "Western" feminist theorists to represent the hegemony of Western feminism, while at the same time using others to support their critique of that hegemony, is a perfect illustration of the way in which people engage in a selective use of feminist ideas as a consequence of specific historical circumstances and aims (Cerwonka 2008, 822). Therefore, it is less accurate to say that the East is "lacking" in connection to specific "Western" or Nordic characteristics of feminist movements and thinking than just to admit that there are different feminist genealogies. It is important to deconstruct the "neat" divisions between these feminist genealogies, and perhaps, besides deconstructing the East/West divide, assist thinking in more courageously decentralised feminist paths.

Russian feminism: Western waves or "totalitarian feminism"?

An excellent example of differing genealogies is the on-going discussion of the temporality of Russian feminism, of the time(s) of feminism in Russian history. Partially this concerns the existence of feminism's so-called second wave, involving a re-evaluation of the strict East/West bloc-thinking binary, according to which this wave never entered the country. For example, the American historian Maria Bucur (2008, 1380) examines some of the reasons why, in the postcommunist disarray after 1989, feminism appeared as a foreign import rather than a homegrown product, in denial of the vibrant legacy that had been curtailed and ultimately suppressed in the Soviet Union after 1945. Adlam (2010), in her examination of the "westernised" feminist discourse in Russia at the beginning of the 1990s, also emphasises that the problematic situation for Russian feminism is strongly dependent on the understanding of it as an ideological and theoretical import from the West, a view that does not take into account the long and complicated history of gender questions in Russia. The situation of Russian feminism in the early 1990s was interpreted simultaneously as an import and as copying some methodological postulates of Soviet ideology, a situation where accounts about feminism were combined with the emphasis on formal political rights of civil society (Adlam 2010, 207).

In the view of Irina Zherebkina (2007a), the genealogy of post-Soviet feminism, which she calls "totalitarian feminism," started in the Stalin era with all its political characteristics. The nodal point in this genealogy is the late Soviet times (late 1980s – early 1990s) when both the official discourse of freedom, and the first non-official feminism is born (Zherebkina 2007a, 219). The signifying cultural practices of freedom, involving poetic creativity, existential film directing, collective activity of the theatres Taganka, Sovremennika, and Lenkoma, the first dissidents, the creativity of poet and musician Bulat Okudzhava, are all very well known (Zherebkina 2007a, 220). Precisely during Brezhnev's administration, the practice of "personal needs" was made legitimate for the first time, and such needs were considered more important than the abstract "needs of the society" (Zherebkina 2007a, 221). At the same time, the theoretical creativity of the late Soviet era (Yuri Lotman, Mikhail Gasparov, and Merab Mamardashvili) extended into the post-Soviet scholarly discourse and, in Zherebkina's (2007a, 222) opinion, did not emerge in terms of dependence on Western postmodernist theories.

Emerging in 1979 from those late-Soviet "Brezhnevia" conditions where the borders between the blocs were both repressively closed and strangely open were the non-official late-Soviet feminism, the group around the annual publication, *Woman and Russia*. The women who wrote in this almanac had been actively involved in the dissident movement from the late 1960s and on. However, they became deeply disappointed in the male-centred character of dissidentism, in the same way that many of their Western sisters were disappointed in the androcentric traits of the Leftist movements. The annual publication was confiscated and the group was silenced, and the leader of the group, Tat'yana Mamonova, was interrogated and warned by the KGB. She declared that she intended to pursue "my feminist activities, because I consider that feminism is progressive and that a women's movement is an essential part of the world democratic movement" (quoted in Holt 1985, 241). The policy of intimidation was un-successful, because within a couple of months two new feminist journals were published, *Rossiyanka* and *Maria*, which also meant a split in the small feminist movement, basically because of different attitudes towards religion and politics (Holt 1985, 248). In the next year, 1980, all activists were forced to leave the country. Once in the West, the activists became more accessible to the media and gained quite a lot of publicity.[12] These women also looked

---

[12] I myself participated in July 1980 in the UN's Mid-Decade Conference on Women in Copenhagen, in the Forum for non-governmental organisations held simultaneously.

to the Western feminist movement for support and defence, and the coverage of their activities was descriptive and supportive (Holt 1985, 257).

A re-evaluation of the activities of Soviet-era feminists should, in Push-kareva's (2007a) view, also include the valuable work on women's studies and gender studies done during Soviet times. She believes that contem-porary feminist research is based on that earlier work. It is, in her opinion, hard to overestimate the research, which was done during the Brezhnev years and even earlier by those who started to collect empirical material on women's history and ethnography of gender and family. Though the questions were examined within conceptual frameworks of gendered di-morphism, and though they represented "the false gender theory," the important circumstance, according to her, was that they were asked in the first place (Pushkareva 2007a, 166).

Thus, Pushkareva (2007a) constructs the picture of a small, dedicated group of scholars, who heroically did their "women's studies" in the context of dogmatic scholarly history. Pushkareva's (2007a, 166) conclusion is importantly that "we should not deny that women's studies emerged in our country simultaneously with the appearance of the interest in them in the West." However, Zvereva (2005) argues that Pushkareva in fact avoids discussing the problem of the general and special in the contemporary theory and practice of knowledge production. Zvereva names Pushkareva's approach to women's studies in the Soviet Union "formalist-institutional." Here then qualitative contextual differences resulted in different views of methods of knowing, on science, and on disciplinary and interdisciplinary knowledge (Zvereva 2005). I tend to agree with Pushkareva on what comes to determine the temporality of Russian feminists' interest in academic research of gender issues and phenomena. Having myself studied in Moscow in the 1970s, I can testify to an interest among female scholars in gender equality and the position of women in the areas of work and family. This interest did not temporally lag behind that which emerged in Finland. Interestingly enough, the same can be noted about the time for the appea-rance in my country of academic feminism in a broad understanding of the term: in both countries, the Soviet Union and Finland, and differing from other Nordic countries, above all Sweden, Norway and Denmark, this con-cern was shaped in the late 1980s, and institutionalised only in the 1990s.

4 000 attended the Forum and the participants greeted warmly and with loud ovations the Russian feminists who, now in exile, attended the Forum.

Most Russian feminists agree that feminism as theory, ideology and political movement is considered by both the hegemonic discourse, the Russian political reality and probably also by the majority of "ordinary people" as hateful and most foreign, that is, alien according to Zvereva's definition. Savkina (2007) summarises some of the (scattered and populist) reasons for this hatred: because it is "imported," because it is not orthodox (or not Christian), because it is a manifestation of "neo-globalism," which is assumed to eliminate all national specificities, because feminism accentuates embodiment and not the spiritual, and because it is too abstract, theoretical, and detached from real life in general, and especially from the problems of Russian women. Nosova's (2004, 239) argument is convergent with Savkina's: feminism in the post-Soviet space is possible, according to her, only in the academic world. Therefore, it did not manifest itself as a protest ideology or as a liberal practice in the form of a struggle for gender equality.

The main reason for the antifeminist sentiments in Russia is, in Voronina's (2007, 176) view, the archaic character of the Russian culture, where the ground for women's self-identification is *pol* [(biological) sex], with motherhood as its most vivid expression. On the other hand, Voronina considers it impossible to completely deny feminism: this is why it is marked by the discourse of the "most famous" Russian media feminist of the 1990s, the writer Masha Arbatova (*Russian Journal* 1999), who emphasises both gender equality and so-called feminine values. Arbatova's feminism is not an exclusive banner to be raised by women only; it is more of a social philosophy, a platform for the changes she thinks would make for healthier individuals and happier marriages.

Taking into account the complexity of post-Soviet feminism as practice, Zherebkina (2007a; 2007b) names a number of paradoxes linked to it. The first of these is the belief that feminism was "born from nothing" and emerged from nowhere. She notes that this way of thinking led to enthusiastic hopes in the beginning of the 1990s for a simultaneous realisation of the heterogeneous processes of "democratic individuation" and a feminism of "our own." Second, there is no division between discourse and practice "so typical for the West," by which she means the conflict between "academic feminism" and the "women's movement." Instead, she proposes that the opposite is the case in Russia: there is an unusual desire or passion, *strast*, for movement, for "activity." In her view, it looks as if there is no other logical ground for gender studies discourse under post-Soviet conditions except the argument of "the women's movement" (Zherebkina 2007a, 214; 2007b, 306).

This seems to me an old problematic in the history of Russian social movements: a genuine movement can and should be initiated only from "below"; it must emerge from the activity of enthusiastic masses thirsting for profound change. Thus, Pushkareva (2007b) answers her own question about *whose* feminism formed the basis for gender studies centres and institutes, that the push for them did not come from below but from above – "as always in Russian history," she states. Therefore, this feminism was not "Russian," but Western (Pushkareva 2007b, 58). To the same line of thinking belongs the declaration of the existence of a gender studies select, an academic elite formed on the basis of Western/foreign funding, which does not speak the language of "ordinary" people. "[I]f we admit that we have this elite, we have to think about how to eliminate the gap between us and the people," Pushkareva demands (2007b, 63–64). The hierarchy connected to the appearance of a new (gender studies) academic elitist class is disturbing for many Russian feminists. For me, it seems as if feminists would have wholeheartedly adapted an entire range of old "Leninist" rhetorical postulates. These include firstly a justification for political movements generally, that is, the slogan "to the masses", secondly, the requirement of a correct revolutionary, political vocabulary, that is, consisting of a politics orientated tirelessly to changing people's/women's lives, eliminating discrimination, etcetera, thirdly, the old revolutionary role prescribed for the Russian intelligentsia, that is, only and exclusively to "serve the people," and lastly, as the sole purpose of gender studies to produce "emancipating" knowledge serving "the people." It may be that these types of claims also provide a rationale for the huge and serious treatment and processing of the troublesome influence from the "Western" gender studies and feminism, that is, that these are not considered to emanate "from below." This makes them not only historically suspect, but also politically non-legitimate.

The global-local binary...

It is common practice today that the local, what is known as the specific, has to present itself "outward" to the "global," which is considered "more general," perhaps even "universal." The specific and local cannot make generalisations. From this follows that the (feminist) East/West dialogue needs to be about the Russian (and East European) experience, something that is different and important. Therefore, when Russian and East European feminists speak "outward," that is, to the West, they assume a representative function, and in many cases they speak or produce texts in a narrative mode with the purpose of presenting, informing, showing, and filling information gaps about the "specifics" of Russian and East European feminism. Hence, within the discourse of the East-West divide in feminism, the most commonly proposed solution has been a call for "Eastern" women and feminists to articulate the difference of their experience. Western feminists ask East European feminists to raise their voice, which among Eastern feminists has resulted in an understandable sense of ownership of authority and knowledge about the Eastern European region (Cerwonka 2008, 816–818).

A renewed emphasis on the local, regional, or particular sites and positions in Euro-American feminist theories of subjectivity valorise the local as the practice of political and cultural resistance. The local, and in the Nordic context, the regional, appears as this kind of primary site through the construction of temporalised narratives of identity (new histories, rediscovered genealogies, imagined geographies, etcetera), yet that very site prepares the ground for appropriation, nativism, and exclusion, as Caren Kaplan (2000, 146) has shown. How, then, should the politics of any location be articulated with that of another in a situation of "unsutured global reality," one can ask, as does Rajagopalan Radhakrishnan (1996, 136–137). What is the nature of "location": is it autochthonous or movable? And, how should theory help in translations among and across different and uneven political terrains? These questions become even more urgent when we consider that the purpose of theory can be seen as "making us see" connections, homologies, similarities, and isomorphisms among disconnected and disparate realities, an understanding that easily emphasises the predisposition of convergence among feminists.

The emphasis of one of the other axes in the global-local binary strongly affects how the implementation of gender studies is understood and explained, and, in the case of Russia, how the question of "foreign" theories (in connection to local specificities and historical specific contexts) is tackled. Those feminists who participate in the discussions of the character and development of Russian gender studies usually have quite a clear-cut position in relation to the axes of the binary.

For example, Zdravomyslova and Temkina (2007), in line with Gal and Kligman (2000), claim that, because knowledge under contemporary conditions has a transnational character, gender researchers in both Eastern and Western Europe ask the same kind of questions, such as the perspectives of feminism, marginalisation, ghettoisation, generational differences, demobilisation within the women's movement, and the splitting of the political subject of the postmodern paradigm (Zdravomyslova and Temkina 2007, 76). They do not consider it a problem that Western feminists in very different contexts have been asking these questions for more than forty years. Using the problematic notion of "international feminist discourse," they believe that Russian feminists apply the discourse selectively, approaching the West as a heterogeneous entity and orienting themselves at developing such connections that are based on methodological and thematic similarities, on the experience of joint research and even on individual sympathies (Zdravomyslova and Temkina 2007, 77). Their views are in accordance with those of Zherebkina (2007a), who regards all association and alignment with the West as doubtlessly healthy. Russian feminism should have a conscious theoretical orientation to the West, and continue the tradition of Russian "feminism before feminism" as an attempt to solve the utopian antinomy between that which "is" ("West"), and that, which "must be" ("East") (Zherebkina 2007a, 218).

By underlining the fact that it is common knowledge that gender studies came to Russia from the West, that ideas "grew" through books, and that there was some sort of readiness – albeit a limited one – for gender themes, Voronina (2007) constructs huge differences between Russia and the West. Admiring strongly Western feminism and gender studies, she represents quite a common view that Russia is backward, and that the West is, and should be, the ideal. For example, when comparing attitudes to human rights, she states that, whereas people in the West know when their rights have been overstepped, nobody in Russia believes in these rights; they are empty sounds (Voronina 2007, 174). She also believes that, while it is characteristic of the development of Western scholarship to reflect upon the content of science as a form of knowledge, as well as upon the mission of science, ethical norms, and the clash of theory with other approaches, Russian scholarship has different characteristics, due to its earlier violent isolation from the rest of the world, the established legitimacy of only one theory, and the limitation of free development of ideas. Russian feminism emerges from a very different context. In answering her own question about the "foreignness" of gender theory and methodology in Russia, Voronina (2007, 174) underlines that politically the context is certainly different, but concerning methods, the "use of Western methodology" in order to analyse social processes in Russia is not dangerous. In accordance with Savkina and others, she argues that all belief about the necessity to "adapt" gender methodology to the "Russian soil" is ideologically motivated (Voronina 2007, 174). Thus, if we follow Voronina's line of thinking, one can notice that the "West" and "Western" models have turned into another important cultural and economic authority against which the Russian, post-Soviet culture places itself in general, and its academic-intellectual discourse, in particular (see also Lerner 2008, 6).

Gapova's (2007) thinking is in line with Voronina's, especially when it comes to the extremely critical stance on the so-called conservatism and backwardness of Russia. She considers the lack of a gender studies canon in Russia to be genuinely problematic, because this circumstance makes it impossible to show that the Russian thinking, "is not *that* gender," referring to some taken-for-granted, hegemonic definition of gender (Gapova 2007, 157; emphasis mine). This means that, besides understanding the West as a very homogenous notion, Gapova divides the existence of the canon of feminist thinking along the East/West binary. Because she thinks that there is a canon in the West ("that gender"), but not in the East, she assigns herself the position of a knower of what the "correct" definition of gender is about. The task of the (Western) canon is precisely to show what the "correct" understanding of gender involves. Her unambiguous statement is: "'Gender' in our space stops being that for which this concept was developed: as a means for critical thinking, deconstruction and *changing* of the world" (Gapova 2007, 157; emphasis in original). In a review of the anthology *Praktiki i identitnosti: Gendernoe ustroistvo*, Gapova (2012) continues underlining the differences between Russia and the West concerning the emergence of gender studies: while the studies in the West from the 1970s onwards formed a part of an epistemological transformation, a contrary process took place in the post-Soviet space creating new forms of inequality, among others also gender inequality. She thinks that the post-Soviet "woman's question" has not hitherto even been formulated (Gapova 2012, 153–155). However, instead of placing Western and domestic/Russian in open opposition to each other, Gapova importantly emphasises the need for Russian researchers to think about the usefulness of the deconstructed "Western gaze." In other words, Russian researchers should reflect upon their own research position and situatedness (Gapova 2012, 152).

The assertions about common, global feminist issues examined above converge with the accounts of the American scholar Breny Mendoza (2002) in her discussion of the differences between the notions of transnational and global feminism. She observes that, with the destabilisation of the nation-state, an opposition between the local and the global is created whereby the global seems to gain precedence over the local (Mendoza 2002, 299). In her view, what happens at the local level lacks in substance unless it hits the cyberspace or is hypermediatised and becomes a global demonstration. Consequently, it is not place per se, but the non-place of networks, flows, circuits – the transcendence of geographical, social, economic, cultural and political locations – that builds transnational politics and history (Mendoza 2002, 300).

On the other hand, when Russian feminists underline the importance of the local and of contextualisation, in opposition to those who emphasise the importance of the global, their statements consider the import of Western gender theories to be very problematic. Besides intense talk of differences and hierarchies, the "local" feminists put a strong emphasis on the taxonomy of experience. The views of Funk (2004), who underscores the meaning of differences concerning contexts and who thinks that feminist arguments should be tailored to local contexts, are parallel with Kochkina's (2007), who strongly stresses the differences between Russia and the West. In the opinion of the latter, the ideological boundaries between different strands in the Western feminist theory are strict, a circumstance not typical for Russia. It is important for Kochkina (2007, 104) to emphasise that no other feminist "paths" are suitable for Russia, "not the British, the Scandinavian, the American, or the French paths."

The juggling in emphasising either the global or the local, either the meaning of common, joint feminist/gender studies issues or of specific contexts, seems to be a consequence of the enormous power of East/West bloc-thinking. Simultaneously, discussions strengthen the binary, which thus takes a firm grip on our geopolitical imaginary and thinking. By thus structuring the genealogy of feminist theory, bloc-thinking is a serious obstacle to grasping new challenges of knowledge production within transnational feminist contexts. As the feminist scholar Allaine Cerwonka (2008) noted, within the discourse about the East/West divide people comment on the challenge of trying to identify and theorise gender issues important to post-state socialist societies *in the shadow* of an already well-established feminist heritage from the USA and Western Europe (Cerwonka 2008, 811). Furthermore, the women's studies and gender studies discipline itself shares some characteristics of, for example, area studies, that is, disciplines developed in the shadow of the Cold War. Importantly this shadow concerns the nationalist biases in the discipline. These complexities illustrate the problems of taking East and West as stable identities or analytical categories out of which to generate a feminist epistemology. Simultaneously these complexities illustrate how there are in fact multiple both "Western" and "Eastern" feminisms that contradict or contest each other.

...and deconstruction of the East/West bloc-thinking

In an interesting article from 1995, Vida Penezic deals with the loss of belief in the givenness, the clear-cutness, the descriptive accuracy of the East/West bloc division. By using the term "fircond" for the joining of what used to be two ostensibly different worlds (the first and the second) into a larger and more complex political and discursive space, she emphasises that negotiating the space of this "fircond" world, theoretically at least, means re-defining *both* of its constitutive discourses (Penezic 1995, 58). However, she also shows how the fall of communism, which could have been seen as a creation of an entirely new political and discursive space, was considered in practice as a confirmation of the Cold War paradigm's legitimacy, that is, communism lost, and the "Free World" won (Penezic 1995, 62). In accordance with bloc- and Cold War-thinking, all the disorder, wars, nationalisms, and economic crises following the big changes were blamed on the former communist regimes (Penezic 1995, 63). Therefore, the Eastern bloc is still considered different from "us" and homogenous within itself in particular because of its past (Penezic 1995, 66). She writes:

> And it is, perhaps, precisely because we still think of it as somewhat different (in that unclearly negative sense) that we feel we need to acknowledge it, to give it prominence and visibility. (Penezic 1995, 66–67)

However – as discussed – there are also other formations of "we" produced in accordance with geopolitical regions; the "Nordic" is such a geopolitical entity constructed as part of our identities and situatedness. With differing discursive fetters, "we" are, at least for the moment, depending on spatial and temporal circumstances, expected to manifest our belonging to this region.

Hence, binary thinking assumes, both in the East and in the West/Nordic, that the two blocs are/were completely ideologically different, and that the acceptance of that difference should be the starting point of any communication. As long as the contacts between the blocs persist as external, meaning that the blocs only communicate with each other as separate entities, the difference and separateness explain every phenomenon within the bloc, as well as every perception of all phenomena from the other bloc (see Penezic 1995, 70). Deconstruction and a conscious critical stand on these distance-creating, dualistic assumptions show, on the one hand, that the blocs were perhaps not that ideologically different as popularly thought.

Their propaganda techniques against each other were quite similar, and, although there were genuine ideological differences, similarities existed, for example, in their educational canons. They were also both part of Euro/Western/Nordic civilisation and subscribed to some of the same cultural and economic goals and ideals, mainly industrialisation, urbanisation, and logocentrism.

On the other hand, the strictness of the boundaries separating the blocs has been exaggerated; the borders were not impermeable but porous: popular and other cultural products, people, political and financial interests, constantly seeped through, ensuring the presence of the other on each side of the boundary. The contemporary common sense idea about the impermeability of the two blocs overgeneralises and misrepresents the multifaceted ways in which ideas circulated well before the present era of globalisation (Cerwonka 2008, 820). The constant leakage has worked together with other globalising trends towards forming (or, rather, maintaining) a common cultural space, which frequently went unrecognised. Therefore, within the Cold War-paradigm's assumptions of across-the-board difference between the blocs may not be accurate, and in a descriptive way they postulate a difference, which is then imposed on the actual variety existing inside the blocs. This is done in such a way that only certain characteristics – those that are different – are considered accurate, while others are ignored as uncertain (Penezic 1995, 71). "Nordic gender equality" is often constructed and treated as such a difference: it is presented as in some way "self-evident," something inherently typical for both the Nordic mentality and politics (Liljeström 2009).

In her interesting article about "the seminar," the Bulgarian scholar Miglena Nikolchina (2002) looks at how the regime was bound to produce its subversion through the intellectual in order to sustain itself. The "seminar" was an event or phenomenon that emerged in the late 1970s as a major feature of the last decade of the communist regime in Bulgaria that was produced as the dominant trajectory of the crumbling of totalitarian power (Deyanova 2014, 445). Nikolchina (2002, 103) asserts that the discursive disintegration of communism happened from within, and her main issue consists of the relationship between the seminar's highly theoretical, interdisciplinary functioning, on the one hand, and its actual role in the ensuing of political events, on the other hand. In order to dismantle the sharp division and disparity between Eastern and Western intellectual experience, she avoids the term dissident and looks instead into ways that systems structured as total discursive control might be challenged from within. Therefore, her discussion leaves aside the role that the West as an "outside" played in bringing about the fall of communism (Nikolchina 2002, 106). Nikolchina (2002, 114) discusses the seminar at the background of the private/public distinction, so important in the East/West/Nordic debate about feminism, or as she puts it, rather, about the Eastern resistance to feminism, where feminism in her opinion is for the most part wrongly perceived as a monolithic doctrine of one sort or another rather than a field of contention that cuts across any problem and debate. She shows how ambiguous both the division and the characterisation of each sphere is, but also how the private sphere was gendered (conservative roles) in contrast to the "genderlessness" (or "maleness") of the public one (Nikolchina 2002, 111), a trait often attached also to "Finnish Nordicness."

In thinking about feminist bloc-crossing communication, the Croatian feminist scholar Biljana Kašić (2004) states that there is an ongoing production of a feminist imaginary across the East/West divide. This imaginary transmits validity and acknowledgement or, alternatively, a sense of cultural otherness and the seductiveness of the exotic (Kašić 2004, 476). She emphasises how, from an Eastern European perspective, feminist cross-mainstreaming is challenged by a double constraint. On the one hand, it must deal with the West as a sort of "mainstream" within the present "historical/spatial compression," which includes "invasions" (of authority, institutionalisations, theoretical canons, etcetera) as well as "disruptions" (including the problem of whether Western feminism(s) is itself "mainstream" for the Eastern feminist imaginary). On the other hand, it must deal with diverse hidden demands and hindrances concerning "mainstreaming" around such questions as power and marginality, commodification and opposition, integration and obstruction (Kašić 2004, 477).

Mainstreaming is closely linked to the feminist human rights agenda and its way of constructing conceptual monoliths. For example, in the volume *Is Multiculturalism Bad for Women?* (Okin et al. 1999), these are, according to Alys Weinbaum (2005), the following: first, "women" is seen as an incontestable, universally recognisable political category and the protection of human rights is the proper terrain of global feminism. Second, "special interest politics" and "multiculturalism" are one and the same, and other sections or differences fragment the unity of the world's women. Third, liberalism is global feminism's natural political idiom (Weinbaum 2005, 215). Differing from this human rights feminism, "global/local" feminism strives to understand the gendering of "global culture" in a diverse array of local situations. However, globalisation is here often posited as a homogenising force that brings women together because of a perceived common plight, resistance to which is then construed as expressive of a shared "global" political agenda. According to Weinbaum (2005, 215), both these feminisms, human rights and glocal, fail to produce a robust politics of difference in the context of globalisation. Because of the strong impact of the integrationist, globalising forces in "standardising" gender policy agendas, there is a great risk of creating the illusion of familiarity with a variety of local feminisms. Weinbaum writes:

> It is *as if*, taken together, the individual causes could be viewed *as if* they were common, *as if* the juxtaposition of disparate images and the shared articulation of a political agenda are one and the same. (Weinbaum 2005, 217)

This is avoided by taking the multiplicity of feminisms seriously, and by dismantling a clear-cut distinction between feminist and non-feminist mobilisations of gender discourse.

In contrast, within transnational feminist approaches, the local is produced in its multitude as an object of study. Because localism emerged as a "pluri-versal" response and confrontation with universal Eurocentrism, Walter Mignolo (2010) points out (in the context of decolonisation, but also in the context of postsocialism, I would add) that localism is global, or cosmopolitical. He reasons that we can make the paradoxical conclusion that if cosmopolitanism is to be preserved in visions for the future, it should be "cosmopolitan localism," an oxymoron no doubt. For him it is, however, just another expression of "pluri-versality as a global project" (Mignolo 2010, 126–127). Thus, while the localities and local movements, be it Russian, East European, or Nordic, certainly run the risk of being read as local symptoms of homogenising global, transnational forces, the emphasis should rest on differences and dispersions as well as solidarities and coalitions (see Mignolo 2010, 121, and also Friedman 1998, 5; Mohanty 2006, 242). Therefore, while transnational feminism offers "scattered" geopolitical locations, incomplete geopolitical coverage, and interrupted genealogies, it should simultaneously be more attentive to achieving vivid communication and temporal allies across political and theoretical splits and divisions. In the context of "scattered" geopolitical locations and non-linear feminist genealogies, Russian academic feminists, as also other feminists of transnational localities, have possibilities to creatively form their "own" gender studies in dialogue with both mobile concepts and other feminist communities.

Conclusion: Re-thinking communication and the politics of location

The British scholar Richard Sakwa (1999, 713) notes that in many ways, "we are all postcommunist now." I read this statement as a critique of East/West bloc-thinking, of the East/West division, in which the East is always lagging behind the West, and also of the by now widely circulated historicist perspective that reduces geographical diversity to a lagging temporality. This association represents a form of othering, which is a "particular type of allochronisation" in which spatial difference is used, not to assert diversity and "coevalness," but to fix temporal differences (Glæser 2000, 325). The East is the past and the West represents the (already-known) future of the East. Furthermore, the East often remains the feminised "other" to the West's masculinised "self." Thus, when Russian feminists study the post-socialist world "in the same terms" as the "Western world" and benchmark it against "the Western feminism," they position their "own," overtly homo-genous world as much further behind, which also reveals a modernist strand in their approach. If "we are all postcommunist now," the chal-lenging question is what pondering over the current East/West problematic and glocal situation can teach us; how might the conditions of postsocialism reshape our feminist theorising more widely? At least more attention should be paid to how existing debates can be re-invigorated and developed by seriously grasping issues raised by the postcommunist condition (see Outhwaite and Ray 2005, vii).

Many post-Soviet scholars only problematise the relations between the First and the Second Worlds and still do not, in our postsocialist but also postcolonial world, take any notice of the Third World. Carl Pletsch pointed out already in 1981 the epistemological consequences of the socio-economic division of the three worlds. The division builds on an under-standing of the first world as "purely modern," the second as modern but authoritarian (or totalitarian), and the third as the world of tradition, culture, and irrationality. This division was paralleled by an epistemological one, according to which the first produced knowledge, while the second created ideology, and the third "culture" (Pletsch 1981, 574, 588). Because of First World supremacy and its epistemic privilege, the impression that knowledge-making has no geopolitical location and that its location is an ethereal place, or what the Colombian philosopher Santiago Castro-Gomez has described as "the hubris of the zero point," has been successfully naturalised (see Mignolo 2009, 166–167).

A new and exciting direction in "thinking between the blocs" in post-socialist studies investigates similarities and differences between post-colonialism and postsocialism, inviting us to think between the "posts." Postsocialism began as a temporal designation: it referred to whatever would follow once the means of production were privatised and the Party's political monopoly was disestablished, and only later did it come to signify a multiple critical standpoint. Postcolonial studies, on the other hand, had a different trajectory being established as a critical way of thinking in the 1980s. Despite differences in timing, both "posts" continue to reflect on consequences of periods of heightened political change. In contrast to these "posts," the West/Nordic seems strangely untouched, developmentally superior, and hegemonic. However, within the "Pletschian" line of thinking, Sharad Chari and Katherine Verdery (2009), for example, ask how Cold War representations of space and time have shaped knowledge and practice everywhere and continue to shape theory and politics. In doing this they propose to jettison the two posts in favour of a single overarching one, the post-Cold War (Chari and Verdery 2009, 18, 29). Nevertheless, this ambition, the geopolitical "post-regions" and divides carry on their existence and we need to continue to pay attention and problematise the constant flow and recycling of ideas and theories, and the changes between them.

Penezic (1995) isolates three understandings of that in-between space of communication that transcends the blocs, calling it transcultural. First, this space is seen as a complex and heterogeneous space in which all other cultural categories are immersed and out of which they are sometimes moulded. Second, this space is regarded as an aspect of everybody's culture, and third, it functions as a mode of interaction, which works fine where people are attentive of cultural differences and accept them rather than allowing them to divide them (Penezic, 1995, 73). She suggests that the transcultural space, being part of everybody's experience today, corresponds with Mike Featherstone's "global culture" and Marshall McLuhan's "global village," and that it is also outlined by global feminism (ibid, 74). Etienne Balibar (2004) in turn thinks that we should abandon the illusion that different regions, systems of representations, and ideals are complementary elements of one single "human culture" or "civilisation," but should not accept the idea that they clash by nature, since they have no nature. Regions and systems, Nordic or East European or other, have a history, and it is the unending process of translation that reflects and allows this history to be transformed (Balibar 2004, 22). This transformational process is precisely what we want this book to participate in, by tracing moves and movements within travelling feminist theories and institutionalisations of gender studies.

In his article "Europe as Borderland" (2004), Balibar pays central attention to the question of translation and linguistic difference, so importantly present in the discussions among Russian feminists, and today also one of the most sensitive marks of "collective identity." By referring to Zygmunt Baumann, Balibar (2004, 18) notes that translation was never an egalitarian practice, but the property common to all of us; it is a necessary aspect of being-in-the-world in the "information society." Translation should, then, be conceived as a basic instrument to create the European public space in a democratic sense, that is, ideas and projects should also be debated by the citizens themselves across linguistic and administrative borders. Discussing both Umberto Eco's remark that translation is the common language of Europe and Rosi Braidotti's thoughts on nomadism, which he sees as rooted in educational institutions, translation becomes for Balibar (2004, 19–20) a form of virtual de-territorialisation. This makes it possible to forestall and control political processes where borders are moved and the meaning of borders is transformed. Balibar underlines that languages are constantly translated, but they also remain untranslatable, by which he means that they do not express the same ideas or contents, but different and conflicting ideas. He argues that this conflictual model of the process of translation, the philological model, at the same time provides a tool and features a regulating ideal for the political handling of the issues of "multiculturalism" (Balibar 2004, 21). Balibar stresses that the issue of idioms and translations crosses the issue of borders. As in the binary East/West bloc-thinking, history can be used either to "essentialise" the contradictory narratives, enfolding them within "cultural borderlines," or it can be used to focus "subaltern" narratives to the "dominant" ones, or it can be used to set up a dialectical change of the regime of discourses (Balibar 2004, 22). It is only when we have made productive use of this internal diversity, instead of reducing it to national or civilisational stereotypes, such as "the West," the "Nordic," or the Russian, or subjecting it to "common politics," that we may prove able to work through our internal and external relationship to "others," from neighbours to strangers (Balibar 2004, 23).

Another way of problematising the in-between space of the blocs and of the nation states is done within "critical border thinking" introduced above all by Walter Mignolo and Madina Tlostanova. Already in 1995, in his important work on theorising colonial histories, Mignolo (1995, 173–174) underlined a new configuration of places, the increasing relevance of borders, boundaries and borderlines in dislocating national ontologies of geo-cultural location and reinscribing, in a transnational world, the spaces-in-between. He connects this with a politics of geocultural location, which recognises that one is always *from* and *at*, whether or not these locations happen to be the same place. He thinks, therefore, that it is the process of constructing identification rather than the description of identity that should be our concern. He sees this as a change of cognitive terrain, a shift from the analysis of representation to the analysis of the interactions that engender representation (Mignolo 1995, 175–176, see also Mignolo 2000). Critical border thinking involves incorporating Western contributions in different domains of life and knowledge into an epistemic and political project that affirms the colonial and/or imperial difference to which most of the population of the world has been subjected throughout at least five hundred years (Mignolo and Tlostanova 2006, 212). According to Mignolo and Tlostanova (2006, 214), it is not so much a question of studying the life and deeds of the borders, but of thinking from the borders themselves, that is, "rewriting geographic frontiers, imperial/colonial subjectivities and territorial epistemologies." They think that the problem of the 21st century – succeeding that the "colour (and gender and sexuality) line" – is the "epistemic line." Border thinking or border epistemology, which I find highly inspiring for transnational feminism, emerges in the crack between the lines and as an epistemic shift, a shift from the theo- and ego-, to geo- and body-politics of knowledge (Mignolo and Tlostanova 2006, 214).

The aim of critical border thinking is to acknowledge internal diversity, rather than to reduce or integrate differences into some sort of similarity. The integrationist feminism of many Russian and Western feminists seems capable of applying general and similar explanatory patterns to very different places and times. This creates problems and ethical dilemmas concerning priorities in feminist agendas, hierarchical constellations of centre and (semi)periphery, insider/outsider roles, and potential colonisation. These dilemmas involve responsibility for the rhetoric used in addressing the geopolitical differences among feminists.

Susan Stanford Friedman (1998) takes a clear step away from the strict and "total" integrationist feminism by advocating a locational approach to feminism, a locational epistemology, based on the assumption of changing historical and geographical specificities that produce different feminist theories, agendas, and political practices. In her view then, locational feminism encourages the study of difference in all its manifestations and requires a geopolitical literacy that acknowledges the interlocking dimen-

171

sion of global cultures, the way in which the local is always informed by the global and the global by the local (Friedman 1998, 5). However, by using the notion of "pseudolocality," Julia Lerner (2008) reminds us of the complexity of glocality: glocal forms are mostly understood as patterns that have been imported from the outside and that take on a local flavour. This pseudo-locality she writes, is the local instantiation of global mimesis (Lerner 2008, 15). In the light of these arguments, the talk about how feminists from the East could engage with feminists from the West "on their own theoretical terms" is filled with both challenges and dead-ends.

In writing about the politics of knowledge, Chandra Mohanty (2006) proposes a model of feminist solidarity or comparative feminist studies as the most useful approach in bridging the "local" and the "global" in feminist studies. The model presumes that local and global are not defined in terms of physical geography, but exist simultaneously and constitute each other. It is then the relationships between the local and the global that are fore-grounded, and these links that are understood as conceptual, material, tem-poral, and contextual. This framework assumes both distance and proximity as its analytical category. Mohanty (2006, 242) emphasises relations of mutuality, co-responsibility, and common interest, thus anchoring the idea of feminist solidarity.

In this framework, in light of the process of deconstructing the East/West bloc-thinking, we should also rethink how we look upon the catchphrase of "the politics of location." As Braidotti (2007) has noted, a "location" is a collectively shared and constructed, jointly occupied, spatio-temporal territory, which, because of its familiarity, escapes self-scrutiny. It is relational and outside-directed, a cartography of power, attained through a critical, genealogical self-narrative (Braidotti 2007, 27). Therefore, it is decisive for the politics of location that the power dynamic structuring the circulation and reception of feminist texts is foregrounded and made into a central object of analysis. To think that feminist scholars situated in the West can apprehend the impact of globalisation on the cultural formations and movements of women around the world without intimate knowledge of the languages and social conditions in which such are articulated, is to eliminate the potential insight that comes from becoming conscious of the place from which we speak (see Weinbaum 2005, 216). Only in this way can the politics of location make it necessary to imagine and implement feminist political alliances across lines of differences rather than through some shared identity, such as women (cf. Davies 2007, 9).

However, there is no easy interaction between feminists from East and West, but numerous dilemmas, old hierarchies, empty rhetoric and – certainly – an honest and interested search for different types of cooperation and acknowledgement. As Biljana Kašić (2004, 478) expresses it, in dealing with issues of the East/West divide, "it may be necessary to engage simultaneously in processes of mirroring and creating distance, fostering 'feminist' intimacy and staging marginality." Though I have focused here on the East/West divide, feminist interaction is geopolitically hierarchic also within the West/West divisions. For example, in Finland and the other Nordic countries, there have been recurring, fairly heated discussions about the "import" of "foreign" feminist terminology. According to Sara Ahmed (2000, 155), communication always involves working with "that which fails to get across," or that, which is necessarily a secret. Iris Marion Young (1997), in turn, suggests that communicative ethics must begin with recognition of the asymmetry of self and other. Young develops the notion of asymmetry by proposing that a "condition of our communication is that we acknowledge difference, interval, that others drag behind them shadows and histories, scars and traumas, that do not become present in our communication" (Young 1997, 354, see also Liljeström 2005).

It is not enough to change the content of conversation and communication; what is needed is to change the terms of communication. Enacting this change implies thinking critically at the borders, going beyond both disciplinary and interdisciplinary controversies and conflicts of interpretation. As far as controversies and understandings keep to the same rules or terms of exchange and debate, the control of knowledge is not called into question. And, in order to question the rules and terms, it is necessary to focus on the knower rather than the known (cf. Mignolo 2009, 163).

Therefore, communication must recognise the implication of the self in the encounter, and the responsibility the self has for the other to whom one is listening. This communication as affectivity is about a certain way of holding proximity and distance together, as Ahmed claims. The communication is, however, also dependent on a certain "structure of feeling" (Raymond Williams), which is not possessed in the same way by the many members of the "worldwide feminist community" (cf. Ahmed 2000, 157; 2004, 48). How should "we" form an epistemic community, though always imaginary, changing, and dynamic? This sensation of community and dialogue emerges through differences that are necessarily shaping feminism as complex and multifaceted for understanding and change.

Epilogue

There is always a story, sometimes several, behind our particular research interests, notes Sara Ahmed. To account for such a story, Ahmed (2006; 2012) proposes, is also to give an "account of an arrival" to that place or topic. If every project begins with an arrival, we could tell several stories with regards to our arrival "here" in this project, with an interest in and, perhaps more importantly, at times a disidentification from, the making of the field of women's/gender studies in the Nordic region and Russia as we have outlined them here. One obvious story line could be pragmatic (there was an opportunity for funding); another might be called passionate (a concern for the making of a "we" and solidarity). Accounts of arrivals often involve memories, incidents that have affected us, oriented us in particular directions and have made us ask some questions and not others. Arrivals are, therefore, also never just anywhere; rather they are in a particular place from which some "bodies of flesh and knowledge" (Sullivan 2006) might appear more than others. Arriving somewhere can also result in a dwelling there and yet, our dwellings "here" in a research material that is also a home, inside rather than outside, are situated and partial ones (Haraway 1991; Ahmed 2012).

Instead of telling an evolutionary story about the formation of the field of women's and gender studies, in this book we have sought to show how different arrivals of new bodies into the epistemic community have diverse consequences and effects: we want particularly to illuminate how such bodies never quite succeed to call into question the "we" that is understood to know the recent past, as well as the geopolitical boundaries of a community. Thus, the geopolitical grammar of assigning territorial belonging to both scholars and their ideas, like, for example, within the nationalist and regionalist realms of West/Nordic/Russian/Swedish/etcetera, and repeatedly locating certain ideas as "arrivals," is used to underline the authenticity of such belongings. There are many political reasons to find such a discursive approach alarming, including the growing presence in the Nordic region of nationalist, regionalist, and racist movements and political parties. While we might argue that the geopolitical grammar is so deeply naturalised that it appears self-evident and innocent, we would like to think that feminists could organise our epistemological claims and stories of the recent past in other, differing and challenging ways.

To that end, our own arrivals in and embodied experiences of being placed as belonging to an imagined Nordic field, while simultaneously feeling as if we did not always quite recognise or fit into what was presented *as* the Nordic, have provided paradoxical experiences that have often also worked as orientation moves and kept us unpretentious and alert to shifting objects and subjects of inquiry. At the same time, reflecting on how memories, incidents, and events themselves are methodologically central to the accounts of the making of our field and often serve to endorse some accounts and dismiss others ("You weren't there!"), is also to call into question how certain accounts become authorised and not others. If to tell a story about an epistemic community in which one claims belonging, as we have done here, is to open oneself up to objection, and if objections take the shape of authority through, what anthropologists call, the power of "being there," objections and endorsements always point to affective investments in particular versions of the past.

Any academic research project necessarily involves a declaration of intent in the shape of a proposal. Such a proposal is a map and an orientation manoeuvre, a generalising device with its promise of a certain, specific direction. Through the research process, even the ground upon which one stands in examining the very meaning of those grounds inevitably shifts. As we noted in the introduction, the last decade has witnessed a growing production of (post)disciplinary introspection and historiographic reflection on those very processes we are examining. What appeared as an unmapped terrain when this project started almost ten years ago, a virtually unwritten story of where we have been and the implications of directions to come, has thus in a short scope of time increasingly become a matter of methodological, political, and theoretical discussion, the subject of repeated thematic issues of journals and editorials and a concern steeped in the work that the grammars of storytelling and the politics of narrative and citation practices do. Subsequently, what is offered here claims to be neither a discovery, nor a comprehensive authority on matters of what has happened, or about the unfolding of a field, its successes, losses, and offspring.

Being ourselves immersed in the very processes we study in this book, supervising students, PhD projects and other research, and attending conferences on these topics, has contributed to our wish to think about origin and development stories, institutional formation and reproduction, and how the politics of why and how we tell stories the way we do, shape the imagined community of feminist research. It seems to us that the recent interest in the development of feminist theory and the institutionalisation of gender studies as an autonomous discipline both reflects a certain moment in the establishment of a knowledge formation and a form of passing on and accounting for an inheritance on the part of both "seniors" and "juniors" of academic research hierarchies. As situating oneself in relation to a theoretical genealogy is a common academic practice and orientation device, it is also not a surprising approach given the exponential growth of research and degree programs that now fall under the rubric of women's and gender studies. Orienting our own bodies of work as feminist researchers of knowledge to a conversation about these themes, we join the growing number of scholars who have become concerned with *how* stories of feminist and gender theory are told by bringing a focus on the ways that territorialisation and geopolitics figure in these conversations, especially on how, through migration and cultural translation – the very premise for intellectual exchange – ideas acquire geopolitical belonging.

Employing a geopolitical grammar on women's and gender research as body of flesh and knowledge, and we have argued that it is the *Nordic* body (in our period of investigation almost always unmarked white, yet differentiated by class and at times by location, and certainly by nationality and citizenship) that *feels* various things as it encounters collective and individual others and as it demarcates who belongs and who does not. When Karin Widerberg presented her polemic around the translation of the "Anglo-American" term gender, she recalled how "we," meaning the unmarked category of Nordic feminists in the 1980s, "were criticised for not highlighting the differences among women." This formed a critique that did not have a name; nor did it come from anywhere in particular. For Widerberg (1998, 135), "the US feminist critique has been read as *the* feminist critique" and "we took that to heart" (135). The seemingly singular "US feminist critique" allegedly cast against a Nordic "we," according to Widerberg (1998, 134), created a regional unity through shame and the idea that "we all sing the American tune, so familiar to us all," created a sense of inferiority. Widerberg (1998, 135) proposed an alternative: "[I]f we instead had looked inward and scrutinized our own research, we could have seen that this was simply not true for Scandinavian research." Looking inward to the Nordic rather than outward, was the solution and indirectly it seems that on Widerberg's inside, we are all the same. In this book, we have also looked inward, but we have found a different, more complex, conflicted and heterogeneous "we."

As we were completing this book, *NORA: Nordic Journal of Feminist and Gender Research* planned a special issue on "postcolonial Nordic spaces" (*NORA* 2015). The call for contributions seemed timely, indeed. Even if recent years has seen a growing interest in post- and decolonial, indigenous, and postsocialist theorising in the field, as the special issue editors note, following Rauna Kuokkonen, in the production of "Nordic" journal articles in the past ten years, Nordic feminism *still* "appear to be overwhelmingly white, even if this whiteness is intermittently pointed out in contributions written from a postcolonial point of view" (Andersen et al. 2015, 239). Indeed, and akin to how the editors of the special issue on lesbians in *Kvinnovetenskaplig tidskrift* in 1985 reflected on the absence of interest in non-heterosexuality and as Diana Mulinari (2001) noted regarding the lack of interest in race and ethnicity in 2000, the editors of this special issue of *NORA* stress the "plain ignorance" of, among others, Sami perspectives on feminism in the Nordic context (Kuokkonen *in* Andersen et al. 2015, 239). Hopefully this special issue of *NORA* and other coming publications will not be met with the same lack of response and debate that the critique of whiteness and heteronormativity have done in the time period of study in this book. Furthermore, we notice an increasing interest in transgender theorisation, especially its implications for re-conceptualising gender binaries. Finishing this book in 2016, amidst intense debates about migration and with our borders closing down due to a widespread media-induced panic about the end of the Nordic welfare states, we note that the long-lived tendency – a tendency that in fact can be described as a kind of theoretical performative tradition that has fed and reinforced feminist scholarly ideas of Norden as an imagined community – to understand "women" as a monolithic category, is increasingly scrutinised. We look forward to further discussion about Norden as a postcolonial space, about Norden as in fact comprising postcolonial spaces and heterotopias, and about Norden as an increasingly conflict ridden xenophobic and violent space.

In a reflection on the state of feminist studies in the USA in the early 2000s and its relation to feminist practice and to a range of feminisms, Robyn Wiegman notes:

> [T]here is an incommensurability between feminism's historicity and our necessary use of it, which means that there is a distinction to be drawn between what feminism is – as a historical force, social entity, revolutionary theory, body of critical thought, or agenda for change – and our attachments to it. (Wiegman 2010, 82)

According to Wiegman (2010, 82), the failure, much more than the success of feminism in obtaining its own objectives "is the constitutive condition of feminism's futurity." While in the Nordic case, success in terms of both institutionalisation and political impact seems to be the stronger, over-arching story, there is disagreement about whether such institutional success has meant a loss of a certain feminist political edge. Indeed, as Wiegman suggests, the successes of gender studies are often cast as a kind of failure, a break from the "political" visions of feminism, even among those who have contributed to its success. This tendency can be found, especially in some of the person-centred narratives of the field that have emerged in recent years. Hopefully, we have succeeded in telling different stories in this book; stories that attend to the geopolitical grammar of women's/gender studies. With Wiegman we observe that it is rare that any kind of feminist achievement engenders the kind of success that it hopes for when it is merely imagined. With Wiegman (2010, 82) we ask: "Might we take a different affective direction, such that the loss it imagines becomes the formative ground of feminism's renewal, a pedagogy of failure that generates not endings but optimism?"

References

Adlam, Carol. 2010. "Feminism ne perevoditsya: Rossiskie gendernye issle-dovaniya i mezhkul'turnyi perenos v 90-e i dale." *Gendernye issledovaniya* 19: 203–230.

Ahmed, Sara. 2000. *Strange Encounters: Embodied Others in Post-Coloniality.* London: Routledge.

Ahmed, Sara. 2004. *The Cultural Politics of Emotion.* Edinburgh: Edinburgh University Press.

Ahmed, Sara. 2006. *Queer Phenomenology: Orientations, Objects, Others.* Durham: Duke University Press.

Ahmed, Sara. 2007. "A Phenomenology of Whiteness." *Feminist Theory* 8.2: 149–168.

Ahmed, Sara. 2011. "Orienten, hemma." In Sara Ahmed, *Vithetens hegemoni*, 151–172. Stockholm: Tankekraft.

Ahmed, Sara. 2012. *On Being Included: Racism and Diversity in Institutional Life.* Durham: Duke University Press.

Alnebratt, Kerstin. 2009. *Meningen med genusforskning så som den framträder i forskningspolitiska texter 1970–2000.* Acta Universitatis Gothenburgensis: Göteborgs universitet.

Amos, Valerie and Pratibha Parmar. 1984. "Challenging Imperial Feminism." *Feminist Review*, 17: 3–19.

Andersen, Astrid, Kirsten Hvenegård, and Ina Knobblock. 2015. "Editorial." *NORA* 23.4: 239–245.

Anderson, Benedict. 2006. *Imagined Communities: Reflections on the Origin and Spread of Nationalism* [1983]. London: Verso.

Aniansson, Eva (ed.). 1983. *Rapport från Kvinnouniversitetet: Vetenskap, patriarkat och makt.* Stockholm: Akademilitteratur.

Arnfred, Signe, and Karen Syberg. 1974. "Inledning." In *Kvindesituation og kvindebevægelse under kapitalismen*, edited by Signe Arnfred and Karen Syberg, 5–23. Copenhagen: Nordisk Sommeruniversitet.

Arnfred, Signe, and Karen Syberg (eds.). 1974. *Kvindesituation og kvinde-bevægelse under kapitalismen.* Copenhagen: Nordisk Sommeruniversitet.

Aronsson, Peter. 1998. "En lomhörd dialog? Den historievetenskapliga debatten på 1990-talet." *Historisk tidskrift* 118: 53–76.

Aronsson, Peter, and Lizette Gradén. 2013. "Performing Nordic Heritage: Institutional Preservation and Popular Practices." In *Performing Nordic Heritage: Everyday Practices and Institutional Culture*, edited by Peter Aronsson and Lizette Gradén, 1–26. Farnham: Ashgate.

Bahovec, Eva D., and Clare Hemmings. 2004. "Teaching Travelling Concepts in Europe." *Feminist Theory* 5.3: 333–342.

Barchunova, Tat'yana. 2003. "The Selfish Gender, or the Reproduction of Gender Asymmetry in Gender Studies." *Studies in East European Thought* 55.1: 3–25.

Berg, Martin, and Jan Wickman. 2010. *Queer*. Malmö: Liber.

Bergman, Solveig. 1994. "Solveig's Corner." *NORA* 2.1: 62–63.

Bergman, Solveig. 2000a. "Organisering av kvinno- och könsforskning i Norden." In *Satsningar och samarbete: Nordisk kvinno- och könsforskning under 20 år*, edited by Solveig Bergman, 27–37. Oslo: NIKK småskrifter, 5.

Bergman, Solveig. 2000b. "Women's Studies in the Nordic Countries: Organisation, Resources, Strategies." In *The Making of European Women's Studies: A Work in Progress Report on Curriculum Development and Related Issues in Gender Education and Research*, Vol. 2, edited by Rosi Braidotti, Esther Vonk and Sonja van Wichelen, 51–66. Utrecht: ATHENA.

Bergman, Solveig. 2001. "Finns det en nordisk feminism och en nordisk kvinno/genusforskning? Det finska svaret." In *Gråt gärna – men forska: Rapport från konferensen 6–7 mars 2001 om kvinnorörelse och kvinno/genusforskning*, edited by Renée Frangeur, 65–68. Linköping: Forums skriftserie.

Bergman, Solveig. 2002a. *The Politics of Feminism: Autonomous Feminist Movements in Finland and West Germany from the 1960s to the 1980s*. Turku: Åbo Akademis Förlag.

Bergman, Solveig. 2002b. *Women's Studies and Gender Research in Finland. Evaluation Report*. Academy of Finland, no 08.

Bergman, Solveig (ed.). 1991. *Women's Studies and Research on Women in the Nordic Countries*. Turku: Åbo Akademi University.

Bergman, Solveig (ed.) 2000. *Satsningar och samarbete: Nordisk kvinno- och könsforskning under 20 år*. Oslo: NIKK småskrifter, 5.

Bergqvist, Christina. 2001. "Finns det en nordisk feminism och en nordisk kvinno/genusforskning? Det svenska svaret." In *Gråt gärna – men forska: Rapport från konferensen 6–7 mars 2001 om kvinnorörelse och kvinno/genusforskning*, edited by Renée Frangeur, 69–70. Linköping: Forums skriftserie.

Bjerrum Nielsen, Harriet. 2000. "Kvinne- og kjønnsforskning i Norden." In *Satsningar och samarbete: Nordisk kvinno- och könsforskning under 20 år*, edited by Solveig Bergman, 19–26. Oslo: NIKK småskrifter, 5.

Bjerrum Nielsen, Harriet, and Torild Steinfeld. 1993. "Editorial." *NORA* 1.1: 1–3.

Blažević, Dunja. 2015. *Jakten på et fagfelt: Den skandinaviske kvinne- og kjønns-historiens fremvekst i skjæringsfeltet mellom historieforskning og kvinne- og kjønnsforskning.* Bergen: University of Bergen.

Borgström, Eva, and Lilja Mósesdóttir. 1999. "Editorial." *NORA* 7.1: 3–4.

Borgström, Eva, and Lilje Mósesdóttir. 2000. "Editorial." *NORA* 8.1: 3–4.

Bornemann, John, and Nick Fowler. 1997. "Europeanization." *Annual Review of Anthropology* 26: 487–514.

Braidotti, Rosi. 1993. "Women's Studies at the University of Utrecht: Special Issue." *Women's Studies International Forum* 16.4: 311–324.

Braidotti, Rosi. 2002. "The Uses and Abuses of the Sex/Gender Distinction in European Feminist Practices." In *Thinking Differently: A Reader in European Women's Studies*, edited by Gabriele Griffin and Rosi Braidotti, 295–311. London: Zed.

Braidotti, Rosi. 2007. "On Becoming Europeans." In *Women Migrants from East to West: Gender, Mobility and Belonging in Contemporary Europe*, edited by Luisa Passerini, Dawn Lyon, Enrica Capussotti and Ioanna Laliotou, 23–44. Oxford: Berghahn.

Braidotti, Rosi, and Judith Butler. 1994. "Feminism By Any Other Name: Interview." *differences* 6.2–3: 27–61.

Braidotti, Rosi, Esther Vonk, and Sonja van Wichelen. 2000. *The Making of European Women's Studies: A Work in Progress Report on Curriculum Development and Related Issues in Gender Education and Research*, Vol. 2. Utrecht: ATHENA.

Bredström, Anna. 2003. "Gendered Racism and the Production of Cultural Difference: Media Representations and Identity Work among 'Immigrant Youth' in Contemporary Sweden." *NORA* 11.2: 78–88.

Brown, Wendy. 2002. "Feminism Unbound: Revolution, Mourning, Politics." In Wendy Brown, *Edgework: Critical Essays on Knowledge and Politics*. Princeton: Princeton University Press.

Bryld, Mette, and Nina Lykke. 1985. "Redaktionel indledning." In *Kvindespor i videnskaben: Rapport fra et tværfagligt, nordisk seminar om kvindeviden-skab*, edited by Mette Bryld and Nina Lykke. Odense: Odense Universitets-forlag.

Bryld, Mette, and Nina Lykke. (eds.). 1985. *Kvindespor i videnskaben: Rapport fra et tværfagligt, nordisk seminar om kvindevidenskab.* Odense: Odense universitetsforlag.

Bucur, Maria. 2008. "An Archipelago of Stories: Gender History in Eastern Europe." *American Historical Review* 113.5: 1375–1389.

Butler, Judith. 1990. *Gender Trouble: Feminism and the Subversion of Identity.* New York: Routledge.

Carlsson, Christina, Joke Esseveld, Sara Goodman, and Karin Widerberg. 1983. "Om patriarkatet: En kritisk granskning." *Kvinnovetenskaplig tidskrift* 4.1: 55–69.

Carlsson Wetterberg, Christina. 1992. "Från patriarkat till genussystem – och vad kommer sedan?" *Kvinnovetenskaplig tidskrift* 13.3: 34–48.

Cerwonka, Allaine. 2008. "Traveling Feminist Thought: Difference and Trans-culturation in Central and Eastern European Feminism." *Signs* 33.4: 809–832.

Chari, Sharad, and Katherine Verdery. 2009. "Thinking between the Posts: Postcolonialism, Postsocialism, and Ethnography after the Cold War." *Comparative Studies in Society and History* 51.1: 6–34.

Christensen, Hilda Rømer, Beatrice Halsaa, and Aino Saarinen (eds.). 2004. *Crossing Borders: Re-mapping Women's Movements at the Turn of the 21ˢᵗ Century.* Odense: University Press of Southern Denmark.

Cixous, Hélène, with Catherine Clément. 1986. *The Newly Born Woman.* Minneapolis: University of Minnesota Press.

Clarke, Adele. 2010. "In Memoriam: Susan Leigh Star (1954–2010)." *Science, Technology, and Human Values* 35.5: 581–600.

Collins, Patricia Hill. 1998. "It's All in the Family: Intersections of Gender, Race, and Nation." *Hypatia* 13.3: 62–82.

Cvetkovich, Ann. 2003. *An Archive of Feelings: Trauma, Sexuality, and Lesbian Public Cultures.* Durham: Duke University Press.

Dahl, Ulrika. 2004. "Progressive Women, Traditional Men: The Politics of 'Knowledge' and Gendered Stories of 'Development' in the Northern Periphery of the EU." PhD diss., University of California.

Dahl, Ulrika. 2010. "Rapport från vithetshavet." *Tidskrift för genusvetenskap* 31.1–2: 70–74.

Dahl, Ulrika. 2011. "Queer in the Nordic Region: Telling Queer (Feminist) Stories." In *Queer in Europe: Contemporary Case Studies,* edited by Lisa Downing and Robert Gillett, 143–157. Farnham: Ashgate.

Dahl, Ulrika. 2014. *Skamgrepp: Femme-inistiska essäer.* Stockholm: Leopard.

Dahl, Ulrika. 2015. "Sexism: A Femme-inist Perspective." *New Formations* 86: 54–73.

Dahlerup, Drude. 1998. *Rødstrømperne: Den danske Rødstrømpebevægelses udvikling, nytænkning og gennemslag 1970–1985.* 2 volumes. Copenhagen: Gyldendal.

Dahlerup, Drude. 2010. "Från rödstrumpa till professor." In *Föregångarna: Kvinnliga professorer om liv, makt och vetenskap,* edited by Christina Florin and Kirsti Niskanen, 31–58. Stockholm: SNS.

Darvishpour, Mehrdad. 1999. "Intensified Gender Conflicts within Iranian families in Sweden." *NORA* 7.1: 20–33.

Davis, Karen, Anita Göransson, and Anna Lena Lindberg. 1980. "Från redaktionen." *Kvinnovetenskaplig tidskrift* 1.1: 1–7.

Davis, Kathy. 2007. *The Making of Our Bodies, Ourselves.* Durham: Duke University Press.

Davis, Kathy. 2014. "Beyond the Canon: Travelling Theories and Cultural Translations." *European Journal of Women's Studies* 21.3: 215–218.

de los Reyes, Paulina. 1998. "Det problematiska systerskapet: Om 'svenskhet' och 'invandrarskap' inom svensk genushistorisk forskning." *Historisk tidskrift* 118: 335–356.

de los Reyes, Paulina, Diana Mulinari, and Irene Molina (eds.). 2002. *Maktens (o)lika förklädnader: Kön, klass & etnicitet i det postkoloniala Sverige: En festskrift till Wuokko Knocke.* Stockholm: Atlas.

de Lauretis, Teresa. 1987. *Technologies of Gender: Essays on Theory, Film, and Fiction.* Bloomington: University of Indiana Press.

Den jyske historiker: Historieteoretisk tidsskrift. 1997.

Deyanova, Liliana. 2014. "From Memory to Canon: How Do Bulgarian Historians Remember Communism?" In *Remembering Communism: Private and Public Recollections of Lived Experience in Southeast Europe,* edited by Augusta Dimou, Maria Todorova and Stefan Troebst, 439–458. Budapest: Central European University Press.

Duchen, Claire. 1992. "A Continent in Transition: Issues for Women in Europe in the 1990s." *Women's Studies International Forum* 15.1: 1–5.

Edenheim, Sara. 2008. "'The queer disappearance of Butler': När Judith Butler introducerades i svensk feministisk forskning, 1990–2002." *Lychnos* 145–173.

Edenheim, Sara. 2010. "Några ord till mina kära mödrar, ifall jag hade några." *Tidskrift för genusvetenskap* 31.4: 108–119.

Edenheim, Sara. 2012. "Att komma till Scott: Teorins roll inom svensk genushistoria." *Scandia* "Supplement: Genushistoriens utmaningar" 78.2: 22–32.

Eduards, Maud Landby. 1986. "Kön, stat och jämställdhetspolitik." *Kvinnovetenskaplig tidskrift* 7.3: 4–15.

Eldén, Åsa. 1997. "'The Killing Seemed to Be Necessary': Arab Cultural Affiliation as an Extenuating Circumstance in a Swedish Verdict." *NORA* 6.2: 89–96.

Evans, Mary, and Kathy Davis. 2011. "Introduction." In *Transatlantic Conversations: Feminism as Travelling Theory* edited by Mary Evans and Kathy Davis, 1–14. Farnham: Ashgate.

Essed, Philomena. 2004. "Cloning amongst professors: normativities and imagined homogeneities." *NORA* 12.2: 113–122.

Eyerman, Ron, and Andrew Jamison. 1991. *Social Movements: A Cognitive Approach.* University Park: Pennsylvania State University Press.

Fehr, Drude von der, Anna Jónasdóttir, and Bente Rosenbeck (eds.). 1998. *Is there a Nordic Feminism? Nordic Feminist Thought on Culture and Society.* London: UCL.

Florin, Christina, and Kirsti Niskanen (eds.). 2010. *Föregångarna: Kvinnliga professorer om liv, makt och vetenskap.* Stockholm: SNS.

Forskning om jämställdhet: Rapport från UHÄ:s konferens i Uppsala den 8 och 9 maj 1978. 1978. Stockholm: Universitets- och högskoleämbetet.

Frangeur, Renée (ed.). 2001. *Gråt gärna – men forska: Rapport från konferensen 6-7 mars 2001 om kvinnorörelse och kvinno/genusforskning.* Linköping: Forums skriftserie.

Fredriksen, Inge, and Hilda Rømer, eds. 1986. *Kvinder, mentalitet, arbejde: Rapport fra det 2. Nordiske kvindehistorikermøde 1985: Kvindehistorisk forskning i Norden.* Aarhus: Aarhus universitetsforlag.

Friedman, Susan Stanford. 1998. *Mappings: Feminism and the Cultural Geographies of Encounter.* Princeton: Princeton University Press.

Frykman, Jonas, and Orvar Löfgren. 1987. *Culture Builders: A Historical Anthropology of Middle-Class Life.* 2nd ed. New Brunswick: Rutgers University Press.

"Från redaktionen." 1985. Editorial. *Kvinnovetenskaplig tidskrift* 6.4: 1–3.

"Från redaktionen." 1990. Editorial. *Kvinnovetenskaplig tidskrift* 11.4: 1–3.

Funk, Nanette. 2004. "Feminist Critiques of Liberalism: Can They Travel East? Their Relevance in Eastern and Central Europe and the Former Soviet Union." *Signs* 29.3: 695–726.

Gal, Susan, and Gail Kligman. 2000. *The Politics of Gender after Socialism: A Comparative-Historical Essay.* Princeton: Princeton University Press.

Ganetz, Hillevi, Evy Gunnarsson, and Anita Göransson (eds). 1986. *Feminism och marxism: En förälskelse med förhinder.* Stockholm: Arbetarkultur.

Gapova, Elena. 2007. "Klassovyi vopros postsovetskogo feminizma, ili ob otvlechenii ugnetennykh ot revolyutsionnoi bor'by." *Gendernye issledovaniya* 15: 144–164.

Gapova, Elena. 2012. "Review of the anthology *Praktiki i identichnosti: Gendernoe ustroistvo.*" *Laboratorium* 1: 150–155.

Gemzöe, Lena et al. 1989. "Sex, genus och makt i antropologiskt perspektiv." *Kvinnovetenskaplig tidskrift* 10.1: 44–52.

Gendernye issledovaniya 2010 Roundtable discussion: 'Chto zhe takoe "gendernye issledovaniya chego by to ni bylo", 19: 70-91.

Glaeser, Andreas. 2000. *Divided in Unity: Identity, Germany and the Berlin Police.* Chicago: University of Chicago Press.

Gradin, Anita. 1984. "Forskning och politik går hand i hand." In *Organisering av jämställdhets-/kvinnoforskning i Norden*, 111–121. Oslo: Nordic Council of Ministers.

Gressgård, Randi, and Christine M. Jacobsen. 2003. "Questions of Gender in a Multicultural Society." *NORA* 11.2: 69–77.

Griffin, Gabriele (ed.). 2004. *Employment, Equal Opportunities and Women's Studies: Women's Experiences in Seven European Countries.* Königstein: Ulrike Helmer.

Griffin, Gabriele, and Rosi Braidotti. 2002. "Introduction: Configuring European Women's Studies." In *Thinking Differently: A Reader in European Women's Studies,* edited by Gabriele Griffin and Rosi Braidotti, 1–28. London: Zed.

Göransson, Anita. 1987. "Innovation och institution: Om receptionen av kvinnohistoria och kön som analytisk kategori." In *Manliga strukturer och kvinnliga strategier: En bok till Gunhild Kyle, december 1987,* edited by Birgit Sawyer and Anita Göransson, 45–59. Gothenburg: Historiska institutionen, University of Gothenburg.

Göransson, Anita. 1989. "Fältet, strategierna och framtiden." *Kvinnovetenskaplig tidskrift* 10.3–4: 4–18.

Göransson, Anita. 2010. "Att bygga ett vetenskapligt fält: Förutsättningar och utvecklingslinjer." In *Föregångarna: Kvinnliga professorer om liv, makt och vetenskap,* edited by Christina Florin and Kirsti Niskanen, 177–214. Stockholm: SNS.

Haas, Peter M. 1992. "Introduction: Epistemic Communities and International Policy Coordination." *International Organization* 46.1: 1–35.

Haavet, Inger Elisabeth. 2009. "Nyskapning og felleskap: Kjønnshistoriens historie sett gjennom de nordiske kvinnehistorikermøtene." *Tidsskrift for kjønnsforskning* 33.1–2: 110–123.

Haavind, Hanne. 2003. "Masculinity by Rule-Breaking: Cultural Contestations in the Transitional Move from Being a Child to Being a Young Male." *NORA* 11.2: 89–100.

Haavio-Mannila, Elina. 1985. "Kvinnogemenskap i forskningen: Reflektioner kring *Det uferdige demokratiet: Kvinner i nordisk politikk.*" *Kvinnovetenskaplig tidskrift* 6.2: 84–86.

Haavio-Mannila, Elina (ed.). 1983. *Det uferdige demokratiet: Kvinner i nordisk politikk.* Stockholm: Liber.

Haavio-Mannila, Elina (ed.). 1985. *Unfinished Democracy: Women in Nordic Politics.* Oxford: Pergamon.

Hadjimichalis, Costis, and David Sadler (eds.). 1995. *Europe at the Margins: New Mosaics of Inequality.* Chichester: Wiley.

Hagemann, Gro. 1994. "Postmodernismen en användbar men opålitlig bundsförvant." *Kvinnovetenskaplig tidskrift* 15.3: 19–34.

Hagemann, Gro. 2003. *Feminisme og historieskrivning: Inntrykk fra en reise.* Oslo: Universitetsforlaget.

Hallgren, Hanna. 2008. *När lesbiska blev kvinnor: Lesbiskfeministiska kvinnors diskursproduktion rörande kön, sexualitet, kropp och identitet under 1970- och 1980-talen i Sverige.* Gothenburg: Kabusa.

Halsaa, Beatrice. 1996. "I skjæringspunktet mellom fag og politikk." In *Hun og han: Kjønn i forskning og politikk*, edited by Harriet Holter, 117-140. Oslo: Pax.

Halsaa, Beatrice. 2001. "Finns det en nordisk feminism och en nordisk kvinno/genusforskning? Det norska svaret." In *Gråt gärna – men forska: Rapport från konferensen 6-7 mars 2001 om kvinnorörelse och kvinno/genusforskning*, edited by Renée Frangeur, 71-76. Linköping: Forums skriftserie.

Halsaa, Beatrice. 2002. "The History of the Women's Movement in Norway." In *Thinking Differently: A Reader in European Women's Studies*, edited by Gabriele Griffin and Rosi Braidotti, 351-360. London: Zed.

Halsaa, Beatrice. 2004. "No Bed of Roses: Academic Feminism 1880-1980." In *Crossing Borders: Re-mapping Women's Movements at the Turn of the 21st Century*, edited by Hilda Rømer Christensen, Beatrice Halsaa and Aino Saarinen, 81-98. Odense: University Press of Southern Denmark.

Halsaa, Beatrice. 2006. "Norsk kvinne- og kjønnsforskning – med tidsskriftet som prisme." *Tidsskrift for samfunnsforskning* 47.2: 225-258.

Harding, Sandra. 1986. *The Science Question in Feminism.* Ithaca: Cornell University Press.

Haraway, Donna. 1991. *Simians, Cyborgs and Women: The Reinvention of Nature.* New York: Routledge.

Haraway, Donna. 1997. "The Virtual Speculum in the New World Order." *Feminist Review* 55: 22-72.

Hearn, Jeff, and Emmi Lattu. 2002. "Gender, men and masculinities." NORA 10.1:3-5.

Heinämaa, Sara. 1994. "The Rhetoric of Positioning in Women's Studies." *NORA* 2.2: 83-94.

Hemmings, Clare. 2005. "Telling Feminist Stories." *Feminist Theory* 6.2: 115-139.

Hemmings, Clare. 2007. "What Is a Feminist Theorist Responsible For? Response to Rachel Torr." *Feminist Theory* 8.1: 69-76.

Hemmings, Clare. 2011. *Why Stories Matter: The Political Grammar of Feminist Theory.* Durham: Duke University Press.

Hillström, Magdalena, and Hanne Sanders. 2014. "Inledning: En rörelse och en idé under 1800-talet." In *Skandinavism: En rörelse och en idé under 1800-talet*, edited by Magdalena Hillström and Hanne Sanders, 9-14. Stockholm: Makadam.

Hirdman, Yvonne. 1988. "Genussystemet: Reflexioner kring kvinnors sociala underordning." *Kvinnovetenskaplig tidskrift* 9.3: 49-63.

Hirdman, Yvonne. 1991. "The Gender System." In *Moving on: New Perspective on the Women's Movement*, edited by Tayo Andreasen, 187–207 Aarhus: Aarhus University Press.

Hirdman, Yvonne. 2007. *Gösta och genusordningen: Feministiska betraktelser*. Stockholm: Ordfront.

Hirdman, Yvonne. 2008. "Han och hon och dom: Frågor i tidens töcken." In *Att göra historia: Vänbok till Christina Florin*, edited by Maria Sjöberg and Yvonne Svanström, 36–43. Stockholm: Institutet för framtidsstudier.

Hirdman, Yvonne. 2014. *Vad bör göras? Jämställdhet och politik under femtio år*. Stockholm: Ordfront.

Holli, Anne Maria, Eva Magnusson, and Malin Rönnblom. 2005. "Critical Studies of Nordic Discourses on Gender and Gender Equality." *NORA* 13.3: 148–152.

Holm Sørensen, Birgitte, and Bente Meyer. 2003. "Introduction: Gender and New Media." *NORA* 11.3: 125–129.

Holt, Alix. 1985. "The First Soviet Feminists." In *Soviet Sisterhood: British Feminists on Women in the USSR*, edited by Barbara Holland, 237–265. London: Fourth Estate.

Holter, Harriet. 1980. "Kvinnoforskning: Historisk utveckling och aktuella motsättningar." *Kvinnovetenskaplig tidskrift* 1.1: 8–21.

Honkanen, Kattis. 2004. *Historicizing as a Feminist Practice: The Places of History in Judith Butler's Constructivist Theories*. Meddelanden från Ekonomisk-statsvetenskapliga fakulteten vid Åbo Akademi Ser. A: 547.

Honkanen, Kattis. 2005. "'It is Historically Constituted': Historicism in Feminist Constructivist Arguments." *European Journal of Women's Studies* 12.3: 281–295.

Ingström, Pia (ed.). 2007. *Den flygande feministen och andra minnen från 70-talet*. Helsingfors: Schildt.

Isaksson, Emma. 2007. *Kvinnokamp: Synen på underordning och motstånd i den nya kvinnorörelsen*. Stockholm: Atlas.

Jegerstedt, Kari. 2000. "A Short Introduction to the Use of 'Sex' and 'Gender' in the Scandinavian Languages." In *The Making of European Women's Studies: A Work in Progress Report on Curriculum Development and Related Issues in Gender Education and Research*, Vol. 1, edited by Rosi Braidotti and Esther Vonk, 39–41. Utrecht: ATHENA.

Jensen, Elisabeth Møller. 1993. "Inledning: Historien om kvinnornas litteratur." In *Nordisk kvinnolitteraturhistoria: Vol. 1: I Guds namn, 1000–1800*, 11–15. Höganäs: Wiken.

Jónasdóttir, Anna. 1984. *Kvinnoteori: Några perspektiv och problem inom kvinnoforskningens teoribildning*. Högskolan i Örebro, Skriftserie 32.

Jónasdóttir, Anna. 1985. "Kvinnors intressen och andra värden." *Kvinnovetenskaplig tidskrift* 6.2: 17–33.

Khavlin, Tat'yana. 2010. "Gender v sotsiologii: Sravnitel'nyi analiz gendernykh sotsiologicheskikh kursov v universtitetakh Germanii i Ukrainy." *Gendernye issledovaniya* 19: 251–266.

Kaplan, Caren. 1994. "The Politics of Location as Transnational Feminist Practice." In *Scattered Hegemonies: Postmodernity and Transnational Feminist Practices*, edited by Inderpal Grewal and Caren Kaplan, 137–152. Minneapolis: University of Minnesota Press.

Kaplan, Caren. 2000. *Questions of Travel: Postmodern Discourses of Displacement*. Durham: Duke University Press.

Kashina, Marina. 2012. "Review of the Anthology *Praktiki i identichnosti: Gendernoe ustroistvo*." *Laboratorium* 1: 139–144.

Kašić, Biljana. 2004. "Feminist Cross-Mainstreaming within 'East-West' Mapping: A Postsocialist Perspective." *European Journal of Women's Studies* 11.4: 473–485.

Keskinen, Suvi (ed.) 2009. *Complying with Colonialism: Nordic, Race and Ethnicity in the Nordic Region*. Farnham: Ashgate.

Khotkina, Zoya. 2000. "Gendernye issledovanija v Rossii – desyat' let." *Obshestvennye nauki i sovremennost'* 4: 21–26.

King, Katie. 1994. *Theory in Its Feminist Travels: Conversations in U.S. Women's Movements*. Bloomington: Indiana University Press.

Knapp, Gunnel-Axeli. 2005. "Race, Class and Gender: Reclaiming Baggage in Fast Travelling Theories." *European Journal of Women's Studies* 12.3: 249–265.

Knudsen, Susanne V., and Bente Meyer. 2003. "Editorial." *NORA* 11.2: 66–67.

Knudsen, Susanne V., and Bente Meyer. 2004. "Editorial," *NORA* 12.3:126-126.

Knudsen, Susanne V., and Lotta Strandberg. 2004. "Introduction: Gender and Power 1." *NORA* 12.2: 67–71.

Knudsen, Susanne V., Bente Meyer, Mette Kunøe, and Kirsten Gomard. 2001. "Editorial." *NORA* 9.2: 75–79.

Knocke, Wuokko. 1997. "Problematizing Multiculturalism: Respect, Tolerance and the Limits to Tolerance." *NORA* 5.2: 127–136.

Koch, Nynne. 1975. *Kvindernes nye verden: Voksenundervisning*. Copenhagen: Fremad.

Kochkina, Elena. 2007. "'Sistematizirovannye nabroski.' Gendernye issledovaniya v Rossii: ot fragmentov k kriticheskomu pereosmysleniyo politicheskikh strategii." *Gendernye issledovaniya* 15: 92-143.

Kochkina, Elena. 2008. Review of *Rossiiskii gendernyi poryadok*, (2007) by E. Zdravomyslova and A. Temkina. *Gendernya issledovaniya* 17: 291–299.

Kvindeforskning i Danmark: Materialesamling 2: Seminar på Sandbjerg april 1978. 1978. Red. af Anna-Birte Ravn fra Kvindeforskningsgruppen ved Aalborgs universitetscenter. Aalborg: Aalborg universitetsforlag.

Kvinneforskning. 1999. "Min vei til kvinneforskning." 1.

Kvinneforskning i Norden. 1988.

Kvinnohistoria i teoretiskt perspektiv: Konferensrapport från det tredje nordiska kvinnohistorikermötet, 13–16 april 1989. 1990. Uppsala: Department of Economic History.

Kvinnovetenskaplig tidskrift. 1989. "90-talets kvinnoforskning." 3–4.

lambda nordica. 1996. "Queer theory: Vad är det och vad är det bra för?" 2.3–4.

Larsen, Eirinn. 2013. "Kvinne- og kjønnshistoriens fortellinger." In *Fortalt fortid: Norsk historieskriving etter 1970*, edited by Jan Heiret, Teemu Ryymin and Svein Atle Skålevåg, 148–175. Oslo: Pax.

Lemke, Thomas. 2011. *Biopolitics: An Advanced Introduction.* New York: New York University Press.

Lerner, Julia. 2008. "The Real Pseudo: Considering Post-Soviet Mimetic Culture through the Lens of Postcolonial and Symbolic Anthropology." Paper presented at Soyuz Annual Meeting: Contemporary Critical Inquiry through the Lens of Postsocialism, University of California, Berkeley, April 24–27.

Liinason, Mia. 2011. *Feminism and the Academy: Exploring the Politics of Institutionalization in Gender Studies in Sweden.* Lund University.

Liinason, Mia. 2014. "Maktens skiftningar: En utforskning av ojämlikhetsregimer i akademin." *Tidskrift för Genusvetenskap.* 35(1):75-97.

Liljeström, Marianne. 1990. "Institutionaliserad heterosexualitet och undersökning av könssystem." *Kvinnovetenskaplig tidskrift* 11.4: 18–29.

Liljeström, Marianne. 2005. "Poverkh bar'erov." *Gendernye issledovaniya* 13: 29–37.

Liljeström, Marianne. 2009. "Nordic Gender Equality and Finland." In *Challenges for Finland and Democracy: Parliament of Finland Centennial.* Part 12: 232–259. Helsinki: Edita.

Liljeström, Marianne, and Harriet Silius. 1996. "Editorial." *NORA* 4.1: 1-2.

Liljeström, Marianne, and Harriet Silius. 1998. "Editorial." *NORA* 6.2: 75–77.

Liljeström, Marianne, and Harriet Silius. 1999. "*NORA* in the Field of Feminist Journals." *NORA* 7.1: 4–5.

Lindén, Claudia. 2008. "Feministisk teorireception inom litteraturvetenskapen." *Lychnos* 201–226.

Lindén, Claudia. 2011. "Temporality and Metaphoricity in Contemporary Swedish Feminist Historiography." In *Rethinking Time: Essays on History, Memory, and Representation*, edited by Hans Ruin and Andrus Ers, 301–312. Huddinge: Södertörn University Philosophical Studies 10.

Lindén, Claudia. 2012. "Ur led är feminismens tid: Om tidsmetaforer, otidsenlighet och gengångare i feministisk historieskrivning." *Tidskrift för genusvetenskap* 33.3: 5–25.

Lindholm, Margareta. 1985. "*Signs* vol. 9, nr 4, 1984." *Kvinnovetenskaplig tidskrift* 6.4: 56–57.

Lundgren, Eva. 1987. "Feministisk teori: Grundval för nya vetenskapliga paradigm?" *Kvinnovetenskaplig tidskrift* 8.2–3: 36–52.

Lykke, Nina. 2001a. "Lesbian Studies, Lesbian Lives, Lesbian Voices." *European Journal of Women's Studies* 8.3: 275–279.

Lykke, Nina. 2001b. "Finns det en nordisk feminism och en nordisk kvinno/genusforskning? Det danska svaret." In *Gråt gärna – men forska: Rapport från konferensen 6–7 mars 2001 om kvinnorörelse och kvinno/genusforskning*, edited by Renée Frangeur, 77–82. Linköping: Forums skriftserie.

Lykke, Nina. 2001c. "Institutionalization: Between Successor-discipline and Transdisciplinary Challenge: Notes on Conceptual Frameworks." In *Women's Studies: From Institutional Innovations to New Job Qualifications*, edited by Nina Lykke, Christine Michel and Maria Puig de la Bellacasa, 17–25. Odense: University of Southern Denmark.

Lykke, Nina. 2001d. "Fra 'Os vs Dem' til en mangestemmig og dialogisk international feminisme." In *Svensk genusforskning i världen: Globala perspektiv i svensk genusforskning och svensk genusforskning i ett globalt perspektiv*, edited by Anna Johansson, 108–124. Gothenburg: Nationella sekretariatet för genusforskning.

Lykke, Nina. 2004a. "Between Particularism, Universalism and Transversalism: Reflections on the Politics of Location of European Feminist Research and Education." *NORA* 12.2: 72–82.

Lykke, Nina. 2004b. "Women's/Gender/Feminist Studies: A Post-disciplinary Discipline?" In *The Making of European Women's Studiess: A Work in Progress Report on Curriculum Development and Related Issues in Gender Education and Research*, Vol. 5, edited by Rosi Braidotti, Edyta Just Marlise Mensink, 90–108. Utrecht: ATHENA.

Lykke, Nina. 2005. "Towards a New Professional Organisation for Women's/Gender/Feminist Studies in Europe?" In *The Making of European Women's Studies: A Work in Progress Report on Curriculum Development and Related Issues in Gender Education and Research*, Vol. 6, edited by Rosi Braidotti and Annabel von Baren, 147–158. Utrecht: ATHENA.

Lykke, Nina, Anna-Birte Ravn, and Birte Siim. 1994. "Images from Women in a Changing Europe." *Women's Studies International Forum* 17.2–3: 111–116.

Lützen, Karin. 2010. "'Men hvad med hendes Anglo far?' Karin Lützen läser Cherríe Moraga." *Tidskrift för genusvetenskap* 30.4: 67–71.

Lützen, Karin, and Annette K. Nielsen (eds.). 2008. *På kant med historien: Studier i køn, videnskab og lidenskab tilegnet Bente Rosenbeck på hendes 60-årsdag.* Copenhagen: Museum Tusculanum.

Magnusson, Eva. 2005. "Gendering or Equality in the Lives of Nordic Heterosexual Couples with Children: No Well-Paved Avenues Yet," *NORA* 13.3:153-163.

Manns, Ulla. 2006. "På två ben i akademin: Om den tidiga kvinnoforskningens projekt." In *Blad till Bladh: En vänbok till Christine våren 2006*, edited by Monica Einarsson, 107–116. Huddinge: Södertörns högskola.

Manns, Ulla. 2008. "Rörelsens rum: Det lesbiska i nordisk kvinnoforskning 1975–1990." In *Att göra historia: Vänbok till Christina Florin,* edited by Maria Sjöberg and Yvonne Svanström, 69–82. Stockholm: Institutet för framtidsforskning.

Manns, Ulla. 2009. "En ros är en ros är en ros: Konstruktionen av nordisk kvinno- och genusforskning." *Lychnos,* 283–314.

Manns, Ulla. 2012. "Historiska rum." *Scandia* "Supplement: Genushistoriens utmaningar" 72.2: 65–69.

Manns, Ulla. 2014. "Methodological Feminism and the History of Feminism." In *Methods, Interventions and Reflections: Report from the X Nordic Women's and Gender History Conference Bergen, August 9-12 2012,* edited by Ulla Manns and Fia Sundevall, 51–56. Gothenburg: Makadam.

Manns, Ulla, and Ann-Cathrine Östman. 2008. "The Uses of Joan Scott: Concepts and Theories in Nordic Studies of Gender and Work in the 1990s." Paper presented at "Labouring Feminism and Feminist Working-Class History in Europe and Beyond," International Conference, August 28–31, Stockholm.

Markkola, Pirjo. 2001. "Lutheranism and the Nordic Welfare States in a Gender Perspective." *Kvinder, køn og forskning* 10.2: 10–19.

McDermott, Patrice. 1994. *Politics and Scholarship: Feminist Academic Journals and the Production of Knowledge.* Urbana: University of Illinois Press.

Melby, Kari, Anu Pylkkänen, Bente Rosenbeck, and Christina Carlsson Wetterberg. 2006. *Inte ett ord om kärlek: Äktenskap och politik i Norden ca 1850-1930.* Gothenburg: Makadam (i samarbete med Centrum för Danmarksstudier vid Lunds Universitet).

Mendoza, Breny. 2002. "Transnational Feminisms in Question." *Feminist Theory* 3.3: 295–314.

Metoder och problem i kvinnoforskningen: Rapport från ett seminarium i Göteborg 14–15/3 1981. 1982. University of Gotenburg: Forum för tvärvetenskapliga kvinnostudier 82: 1.

Meyer, Bente and Susanne V. Knudsen. 2002. "Editorial", *NORA* 10.1:2-2.

Meyer, Bente and Susanne V. Knudsen. 2003. "Editorial", *NORA* 11.3:123-124.

Meyer, Bente and Susanne V. Knudsen. 2004. "Editorial", *NORA* 12.2: 66-66.

Michel, Christine. 2001. "Reflections about the Comparability of Women's Studies in Europe." In *Women's Studies: From Institutional Innovations to*

New Job Qualifications, edited by Nina Lykke, Christine Michel and Maria Puig de la Bellacasa, 13–17. Odense: University of Southern Denmark.

Mignolo, Walter. 1995. "Afterword: Human Understanding and (Latin) American Interests: The Politics and Sensibilities of Geocultural Locations." *Poetics Today* 16.1: 171–214.

Mignolo, Walter. 2000. *Local Histories/Global Designs: Coloniality, Subaltern Knowledges, and Border Thinking*. Princeton: Princeton University Press.

Mignolo, Walter. 2009. "Epistemic Disobedience, Independent Thought and Decolonial Freedom." *Theory, Culture and Society* 26.7–8: 159–181.

Mignolo, Walter. 2010. "Cosmopolitanism and the De-colonial Option." *Studies in Philosophy and Education* 29.2: 111–127.

Mignolo, Walter, and Madina Tlostanova. 2006. "Theorizing from the Borders: Shifting to Geo- and Body-Politics of Knowledge." *European Journal of Social Theory* 9.2 205–221.

Mizielińska, Joanna. 2006. "Queering Moominland: The Problems of Translating Queer Theory into a Non-American Context." *SQS* 1:87–104.

Mohanty, Chandra Talpade. 2006. *Feminism without Borders: Decolonizing Theory, Practicing Solidarity*. Durham: Duke University Press.

Moisio, Sami. 2003. "Back to Baltoscandia? European Union and Geo-Conceptual Remaking of the European North." *Geopolitics* 8.1: 72–100.

Mortensen, Ellen. 1996. "Butches and Nomads: The Dynamic Imperative in Feminist Theory." *NORA* 4.1: 53–62.

Mulari, Heta. 2015. "New Feminisms, Gender Equality and Neoliberalism in Swedish Girl Films, 1995–2006." PhD diss., University of Turku.

Mulinari, Diana. 2001. "'Race'/Ethnicity in a 'Nordic' Context: A Reflection from the Swedish Borderlands." In *Svensk genusforskning i världen: Globala perspektiv i svensk genusforskning och svensk genusforskning i ett globalt perspektiv*, edited by Anna Johansson, 6–24. Gothenburg: Nationella sekretariatet för genusforskning.

Mulinari, Diana. 2009. "Drinking (Feminist) Mates." In *Friendship in Feminist Conversation: Festschrift for Ulla Holm*, edited by Mia Liinason, 131–151. Gothenburg: Acta Universitatis Gothoburgensis.

Mørck, Yvonne. 2003. "Narratives of the Intersections of Masculinities and Ethnicities in a Danish High School Class." *NORA* 11.2: 111–120.

Mørck, Yvonne, and Dorthe Staunæs. 2003. "Introduction: Gender and Ethnicity." *NORA* 11. 2: 67–68.

Nikolchina, Miglena. 2002. "The Seminar: 'Mode de'emploi': Impure Spaces in the Light of Late Totalitarianism." *differences* 13.1: 96–127.

NORA. 2015. 23.4.

Nordenstam, Anna. 2005. "Karin Westman Bergs könsrollsseminarium pionjäråret 1967-68." *Kvinnovetenskaplig tidskrift* 26.4: 55–65.

Nosova, Marina. 2004. "Feminizm/postfeminizm: Lokal'nye smysly global'nogo diskursa'." *Gendernye issledovaniya* 10: 235–241.

Nytt om kvinneforskning. 1980. 5.

Okin, Susan Moller, Joshua Cohen, Matthew Howard, and Martha Craven Nussbaum. 1999. *Is Multiculturalism Bad for Women?* Princeton: Princeton University Press.

Oleksy, Elzbieta. 1995. "Selected Proceedings of the Women's Studies Conference, Łódź, Poland, May 17–21, 1993." *Women's Studies International Forum* 18.1: 3–8.

Olsson, Jenny-Leontine. 2011. *Kön i förändring: Den svenska könsrollsforskningen 1959–1979.* Lund: Sekel.

Organisering av jämställdhets-/kvinnoforskning i Norden. 1984. Oslo: Nordiska Ministerrådet.

Oushakine, Sergei. 2002. "Chelovek roda on: Znaki otsutstvia." In *O muzhesvennosti,* edited by Sergei Oushakine. Moskva: NLO.

Oushakine, Sergei. 2005. "'Doing gender' na russkom pole: Kruglyi stol." *Gendernye issledovaniya* 13: 197–199.

Ousmanova, Almira. 2003. "On the Ruins of Orthodox Marxism: Gender and Cultural Studies in Eastern Europe." *Studies in East European Thought* 55.1: 37–50.

Outhwaite, William, and Larry Ray. 2005. *Social Theory and Postcommunism.* Oxford: Blackwell.

Penezic, Vida. 1995. "Women in Yugoslavia." In *Postcommunism and the Body Politic,* edited by Ellen E. Berry, 57–77. New York: New York University Press.

Pereira, Maria do Mar. 2011. "Pushing the Boundaries of Knowledge: An Ethnography of Negotiations of the Epistemic Status of Women's, Gender, Feminist Studies in Portugal." PhD diss., London School of Economics.

Peterson, Abby. 1987. "Makt och auktoritet i feministisk teori och praktik." *Kvinnovetenskaplig tidskrift* 8.2–3: 65–77.

Phillips, Sarah D. 2008. *Women's Social Activism in the New Ukraine: Development and the Politics of Differentiation.* Bloomington: Indiana University Press.

Plakhotnik, Olga. 2010. "'Razreshit' nel'zya zapretit': K voprosy ob institutsionalizatsii gendernykh issledovanii kak uchebnoi distsipliny v sovremennoi Ukraine." *Gendernye issledovaniya* 19: 156–165.

Pletsch, Carl E. 1981. "The Three Worlds, or the Division of Social Scientific Labor, circa 1950-1975." *Comparative Studies in Society and History* 23.4: 565–590.

Probyn, Elspeth. 2005. *Blush: Faces of Shame.* Minneapolis: University of Minnesota Press.

Pryse, Marjorie. 2000. "Trans/Feminist Methodology: Bridges to Interdisciplinary Thinking". *National Women's Studies Association Journal* 12(2):105-118.

Pushkareva, Natal'ya. 2007a. "Gendernye issledovaniya v istorii i etnologii: Poka tol'ko 'voobrazhaemoe'?" *Gendernye issledovaniya* 15: 165–173.

Pushkareva, Natal'ya. 2007b. *Gendernaya teoriya i istoricheskoe znanie*. St. Petersburg: Aleteiya.

Radhakrishnan, Rajagopalan. 1996. *Diasporic Mediations: Between Home and Location*. Minneapolis: University of Minnesota Press.

Rich, Adrienne. 1993. *The Dream of a Common Language: Poems 1974–1978* [1978]. New York: Norton.

Riles, Annelise. 2000. *The Network Inside Out*. Ann Arbor: University of Michigan Press.

Rosenbeck, Bente. 1997. "Intet nyt under solen: Refleksion over feministisk teori." *Kvinder, køn og forskning* 1: 18–28.

Rosenbeck, Bente. 1998. "Nordic Women's Studies and Gender Research." In *Is there a Nordic Feminism? Nordic Feminist Thought on Culture and Society*, edited by Drude von der Fehr, Anna Jónasdóttir and Bente Rosenbeck, 344–357. London: UCL.

Rosenbeck, Bente. 2000. "En lang tradition for samarbejde: Nordisk kvinde- og kønsforskning i et historisk og aktuelt perspektiv." In *Satsningar och samarbete: Nordisk kvinno- och könsforskning under 20 år*, edited by Solveig Bergman, 3-18. Oslo: NIKK småskrifter, 5.

Rosenbeck, Bente. 2012. "Mange veje, nye retninger." *Scandia* "Supplement: Genushistoriens utmaningar" 78.2: 70–75.

Rosenbeck, Bente. 2014. *Har videnskaben køn? Kvinder i forskning*. Copenhagen: Museum Tusculanum.

Royer, Michelle. 1992. "Women in a Changing Europe." *Australian Feminist Studies* 7.15: 99–103.

Said, Edward W. 1991. *The World, the Text and the Critic* [1983]. New York: Vintage.

Said, Edward W. 1994. *Culture and Imperialism*. New York: Vintage.

Sakwa, Richard. 1999. "Postcommunist Studies: Once again through the Looking Glass (Darkly)." *Review of International Studies* 25: 709-719.

Savkina, Irina. 2007. "Faktory razdrazheniya: O vospriyatii i obsuzhdenii feministskoi kritiki i gendernykh issledovanii v russkom kontekste." *NLO*. 86 (no pages).

Schmitz, Eva. 2007. *Systerskap som politisk handling: Kvinnors organisering i Sverige 1968 till 1982*. Lund Dissertations in Sociology, Lund University.

Scott, Joan W. 2011. *The Fantasy of Feminist History*. Durham: Duke University Press.

Scott, Joan W. (ed.). 2008. *Women's Studies on the Edge*. Durham: Duke University Press.

Scott, Joan W. 1986. "Gender: A Useful Category of Historical Analysis." *The American Historical Review.* 91(5): 1053-1075.

Shlapentokh, Vladimir. 1989. *Public and Private Life of the Soviet People: Changing Values in Post-Stalin Russia.* Oxford: Oxford University Press.

Shore, Chris. 1993. "Transcending the Nation-State? The European Commission and the (Re)-Discovery of Europe." *Journal of Historical Sociology* 9.4: 473–496.

Shore, Chris. 1995. "Inventing the 'People's Europe': Critical Approaches to European Community 'Cultural Policy'." *Man* 28: 779–800.

Silfwerbrand-ten Cate, Ragnhild, ed. 1975. *Feminology: Proceedings of the Dutch-Scandinavian symposium on the development and the significance of interdisciplinary research into woman's position in society in the past and at present.* Nijmegen: Katholieke Universiteit.

Sjöberg, Maria. 2000. "Från husbondekontrakt till jämställdhetskontrakt?" *Häften för kritiska studier* 33.2: 39–44.

Skrivelse från Nordiskt Forum. 1974.

Staunæs, Dorthe. 2003. "Where Have All the Subjects Gone?: Bringing together the Concepts of Intersectionality and Subjectification." *NORA* 11.2: 101–110.

Strandberg, Lotta and Susanne Knudsen. 2004. "Introduction: Gender and power 2," NORA 12.3:127-129

Stråth, Bo, and Øystein Sørensen. 1997. "Introduction: The Cultural Construction of Norden." In *The Cultural Construction of Norden*, edited by Bo Stråth and Øystein Sørensen, 1–24. Oslo: Scandinavian University Press.

Støren, Thordis, and Tone Schou Wetlesen (eds.). 1976. *Kvinnekunnskap: En artikkelsamling om kvinners situasjon i mannssamfunnet.* Oslo: Gyldendal.

Sullivan, Nikki. 2004. "Being-exposed: 'the poetics of sex' and other matters of tact. *Transformations*, 8.

Sullivan, Nikki. 2006. "Transmogrification: (Un)becoming Other(s)." In *The Transgender Studies Reader*, edited by Stephen Whittle and Susan Stryker, 552–564. New York: Routledge.

Thayer, Millie. 2010. "Translations and Refusals: Resignifying Meanings as Feminist Political Practice." *Feminist Studies* 36.1: 200–230.

Thomas, Alastair H. 1996. "The Concept of the Nordic Region and the Parameters of Nordic Cooperation." In *The European Union and the Nordic Countries*, edited by Lee Miles, 15–30. London: Routledge.

Thurén, Britt-Marie. 2002. "Genusforskning som en rymd genomkorsad av förståelsevägar." In *Genusvägar: En antologi om genusforskning*, edited by Britt-Marie Thurén, 5–23. Malmö: Liber.

Thurén, Britt-Marie. 2003. *Genusforskning: Frågor, villkor och utmaningar.* Stockholm: Vetenskapsrådet.

Tidskrift för genusvetenskap. 2010. "Vithet." 1–2.

Torr, Rachel. 2007. "What's Wrong with Aspiring to Find Out What Has Really Happened in Academic Feminism's Recent Past? Response to Clare Hemmings." *Feminist Theory* 8.1: 59–67.

Tsing, Anna Löwenhaupt. 1997. "Transitions as Translations." In *Transitions, Environments, Translations: Feminisms in International Politics,* edited by Joan W. Scott, Cora Kaplan and Debra Keates, 253–272. New York: Routledge.

van der Tuin, Iris. 2008. "Third Wave Materialism: New Feminist Epistemologies and the Generation of European Women's Studies." PhD diss., University of Utrecht.

Velásquez, Juan. 2007. "Förortsfeminismens villkor: Transversell politik." *Tidskrift för genusvetenskap* 28.3: 56–80.

Voronina, Olga. 2007. "'Angliiskii retsept' dlya rossiiskikh gendernykh issledovanii." *Gendernye issledovaniya* 15: 174–178.

Wahl, Anna. 1996. "Molnet: Att föreläsa om feministisk forskning." *Kvinnovetenskaplig tidskrift* 17. 3–4:31–41.

Weinbaum, Alys E. 2005. "The Global Politics of Feminist Knowledge Production." In chapter "Towards a New Feminist Internationalism" by Miranda Joseph, Priti Ramamurthy and Alys E. Weinbaum. In *Women's Studies for the Future: Foundations, Interrogations, Politics,* edited by Elizabeth Lapovsky Kennedy and Agatha Beins, 207–228. New Brunswick: Rutgers University Press.

Westman Berg, Karin (ed.). 1979. *Gråt inte – forska: Kvinnovetenskapliga studier.* Stockholm: Prisma.

Wetlesen, Tone Schou. 1976. "Innledning: Om kvinneforskning". In *Kvinnekunnskap: En artikkelsamling om kvinners situasjon i mannssamfunnet,* edited by Thordis Støren and Tone Schou Wetlesen, 9–13. Oslo: Gyldendal.

Wickman, Jan. 2005. "Introduction: Gender and Sexualities." *NORA* 13.1: 3–8.

Widerberg, Karin. 1985. "Finnes det en nordisk modell i kvinneforskningen?" In *Den samfunnsvitenskapelige kvinneforskningen fra mot år 2000.* Oslo: NAVFs sekretariat for kvinneforskning.

Widerberg, Karin. 1986a. "Har kvinnoforskning med jämställdhetspolitik att göra?" *Kvinnovetenskaplig tidskrift* 7.3: 36–47.

Widerberg, Karin. 1986b. "Från marxism till feminism, till könskamp till…: Ett könskampsperspektiv på arbetsdelning och rätten." In *Feminism och marxism: En förälskelse med förhinder,* edited by Hillevi Ganetz, Evy Gunnarsson and Anita Göransson, 170–201. Stockholm: Arbetarkultur.

Widerberg, Karin. 1987. "Till en teori om kvinnoförtryck: Barriärer och öppningar." *Kvinnovetenskaplig tidskrift* 8.2–3: 53–64.

Widerberg, Karin. 1992. "Vi behöver en diskussion om könsbegreppet." *Kvinnovetenskaplig tidskrift* 13.4: 27–31.

Widerberg, Karin. 1998. "Translating Gender." *NORA* 6.2: 133–138.

Widerberg, Karin. 2006. "Disciplinization of Gender Studies: Old Questions, New Answers? Nordic Strategies in the European Context." *NORA* 14.2: 131–140.

Wiegman, Robyn. 2000. "Feminism's Apocalyptic Futures." *New Literary History* 31.4: 805–825.

Wiegman, Robyn 2005. "The Possibility of Women's Studies". In *Women's Studies for the Future: Foundations, Interrogations, Politics*, edited by Elizabeth Lapovsky Kennedy and Agatha Beins, 40–60. New Brunswick: Rutgers University Press.

Wiegman, Robyn. 2008. "Feminism, Institutionalisation, and the Idiom of Failure." In *Women's Studies on the Edge*, edited by Joan W. Scott, 39–66. Durham: Duke University Press.

Wiegman, Robyn. 2010. "The Intimacy of Critique: Ruminations on Feminism as a Living Thing." *Feminist Theory* 11.1: 79–84.

Wiegman, Robyn. 2012. *Object Lessons.* Durham: Duke University Press.

Wiegman, Robyn (ed.) 2002. *Women's Studies on Its Own: A Next Wave Reader in Institutional Change.* Durham: Duke University Press.

Witt-Brattström, Ebba. 2006. "Nej tack till feministiskt kvinnohat." *Bang* 1.

Witt-Brattström, Ebba. 2007. "Lessing svär i feministkyrkan." *Dagens Nyheter,* December 8, Culture Section.

Witt-Brattström, Ebba. 2010. *Å alla kära systrar: Historien om mitt sjuttiotal.* Stockholm: Norstedt.

Women's Studies and Gender Research in Finland: Evaluation report. 2002. Helsinki: Academy of Finland.

Wuthnow, Julie. 1996. "Haole Dyke in Space: A Close Encounter with Phallic Nationalism and Queer Politics." *NORA* 4.2: 137–144.

Yanagisako, Sylvia, and Carol Delaney. 1994. "Introduction." In *Naturalizing Power: Essays in Feminist Cultural Analysis*, edited by Sylvia Yanagisako and Carol Delaney, 1-24. New York: Routledge.

Young, Iris Marion. 1997. "Asymmetrical Reciprocity: On Moral Respect, Wonder, and Enlarged Thought." *Constellations* 3.3: 340–358.

Yuval-Davis, Nira. 2011. *The Politics of Belonging: Intersectional Contestations.* London: Sage.

Zdravomyslova, Elena. 2014. In "Feministskie refleksii o polevom issledovanii," Anna Temkina. *Laboratorium* 6.1: 84–112.

Zdravomyslova, Elena, and Anna Temkina. 2000. "Vvedenie: Feministskii perevod: Tekst, avtor, diskurs." In Elane Zdravomyslova and Anna Temkina, *Khrestomatiya feministskikh tekstov: Perevody*. St. Petersburg: Izd. D. Bulanin.

Zdravomyslova, Elena, and Anna Temkina. 2003. "Gender Studies in Post-Soviet Society: Western Frames and Cultural Differences." *Studies in East European Thought* 55.1: 51–61.

Zdravomyslova, Elena, and Anna Temkina. 2007. "Avtonomizatsiya gender-nykh issledovanii v transnatsional'nom prostranstve: feministskie praktiki." *Gendernya issledovaniya* 15: 75–91.

Zdravomyslova, Olga. 2010. "Gendernye issledovaniya kak opyt publichnoi sotsiologii v Rossii." *Gendernye issledovaniya* 19: 121–128.

Zherebkina, Irina. 2003. *Gendernye 90-e, ili fallosa ne sushchestvyet*. St. Petersburg: Aleteiya.

Zherebkina, Irina. 2007a. "Totalitarnyi feminizm." *Gendernye issledovaniya* 15: 211–233.

Zherebkina, Irina. 2007b. *Sub'ektivnost' i gender: Gendernaya teoriya sub'ekta v sovremennoi filosofskoi antropologii*. St. Petersburg: Aleteiya.

Zubkovskaya, Olga. 2009. "Primenima li i kak zapadnaya postkolonial'naya teoriya dlya analiza postsovetskogo feminizma (na primere kategorii sovet-skogo i postsovetskogo 'vostoka')." *Gendernye issledovaniya* 18: 177–199.

Zvereva, Galina. 2005. "'Chuzhoe, svoe, drugoe': Feministskie i gendernye kon-cepty v intellektual'noi kul'ture postsovetskoi Rossii." *Adam & Eva: Almanakh gendernoi istorii* 2: 238–278.

Other sources

Interviews:

Eva Borgström, November 23, 2007

Drude Dahlerup, February, 2009

Kari Melby, August 18, 2008

Birgitte Possing, August 19, 2008

News from NIKK. 1996. 1

News from NIKK. 1997. 7

NIKK Magazine. 2000. 2

NIKK Magazine. 2001. 1.

Websites

www.nikk.no

http://en.wikipedia.org/wiki/Nordic_Gender_Institute (accessed 2016-01-04).

www.norden.org

http://www.rethinking-nordic-colonialism.org. (accessed 2016-05-05).

https://eu.spb.ru/en/gender-studies/courses

Balibar, Etienne. 2004. "Europe as Borderland." The Alexander von Humboldt Lecture in Human Geography, University of Nijmegen, November 10.

http://gpm.ruhosting.nl/avh/Europe%20as%20Borderland.pdf (accessed 2016-01-08).

Evaluation of "Centres of Gender Excellence." 2011. Vetenskapsrådets rapportserie, no. 5. https://www.vr.se/download/18.2ab49299132224ae106800051/Rapport+_gender_5.2011.pdf (accessed 2016-01-04).

Muharska, Ralitsa. 2006. "Silences and Parodies in the East-West Feminist Dialogue." *Eurozine* 3.2. www.eurozine.com/articles/2006-02-03-muharska-en.html (accessed 2016-01-14).

Oushakine, Sergei. 2012 Interview "Do i posle gendera."

http://polit.ru/article/2012/06/21/ushakin/(accessed 2016-01-14).

Russia Journal. 1999. "Maria Arbatova: Russia's Chief Feminist." 12.

http://russiajournal.com/node/856 (accessed 2015-10-01).

Index

Authors

Ulrika Dahl is a cultural anthropologist and Associate Professor of Gender Studies at Södertörn University, Sweden, where she currently leads the Baltic Sea funded research project *Queer(y)ing Kinship in the Baltic Region.* She is senior editor of *lambda nordica – Nordic journal of LGBTQ studies* and associate editor of *European Journal of Women's Studies.* Previous work includes the monographs *Skamgrepp: Femme-inistiska Essäer* (2014) and *Femmes of Power: Exploding Queer Femininities* (2008, with Del LaGrace Volcano) and a range of articles in *Gender, Place and Culture, Nora, New Formations, Journal of Somatechnics, Tidskrift för Genusvetenskap,* and *Feminist Theory* as well as in many anthologies.

Marianne Liljeström is Professor of Gender Studies at the University of Turku, Finland. She has published articles on Nordic and Russian/Soviet gender history, edited and written parts of several textbooks in Finnish on feminist theory and methodology. She is advisory board member for the journals *European Journal of Women's Studies* and *lambda nordica,* and member of the editorial board of *NORA, Nordic Journal of Feminist and Gender Research.* She is the author of *Useful Selves. Russian Women's Autobiographical Texts from the Postwar Period* (2004) and co-editor of *Working with Affect in Feminist Readings: Disturbing Differences* (2010, with Susanna Paasonen). Currently she is conducting research on the history of academic feminism in Finland.

Ulla Manns is Professor of Gender Studies at Södertörn University and was leading this research project, funded by the Baltic Sea Foundation. 2010-2015 she was in the steering committee for *Time, Memory and Representation: A Multidisciplinary Program on Transformations of Historical Consciousness* (Riksbankens jubileumsfond). Within that program she's completing a study on memory politics in Western 19th century feminism. She is the author of monographs as *Upp systrar, väpnen er!* (2005) and co-editor of *Etik, politik och historikerns ansvar* (Makadam förlag 2016), with Patricia Lorenzoni. Among articles: "För framtiden? Emancipatorisk forskning och glapp mellan text och tanke" in *Etik, politik...*, and "Silence and Sex in Feminist Memory Politics, or A methodology for beside" (under publication). Manns is member of the editorial board of *Lychnos*, of the advisory board of *lambda nordica* and *Tidskrift för genusvetenskap*.

Södertörn Academic Studies

1. Helmut Müssener & Frank-Michael Kirsch (eds.), *Nachbarn im Ostseeraum unter sich. Vorurteile, Klischees und Stereotypen in Texten*, 2000.

2. Jan Ekecrantz & Kerstin Olofsson (eds.), *Russian Reports: Studies in Post-Communist Transformation of Media and Journalism*, 2000.

3. Kekke Stadin (ed.), *Society, Towns and Masculinity: Aspects on Early Modern Society in the Baltic Area*, 2000.

4. Bernd Henningsen et al. (eds.), *Die Inszenierte Stadt. Zur Praxis und Theorie kultureller Konstruktionen*, 2001.

5. Michal Bron (ed.), *Jews and Christians in Dialogue, ii: Identity, Tolerance, Understanding*, 2001

6. Frank-Michael Kirsch et al. (eds.), *Nachbarn im Ostseeraum übwer einander. Wandel der Bilder, Vorurteile und Stereotypen?*, 2001.

7. Birgitta Almgren, *Illusion und Wirklichkeit. Individuelle und kollektive Denkmusterin nationalsozialistischer Kulturpolitik und Germanistik in Schweden 1928–1945*, 2001.

8. Denny Vågerö (ed.), *The Unknown Sorokin: His Life in Russia and the Essay on Suicide*, 2002.

9. Kerstin W. Shands (ed.), *Collusion and Resistance: Women Writing in English*, 2002.

10. Elfar Loftsson & Yonhyok Choe (eds.), *Political Representation and Participation in Transitional Democracies: Estonia, Latvia and Lithuania*, 2003.

11. Birgitta Almgren (eds.), *Bilder des Nordens in der Germanistik 1929–1945: Wissenschaftliche Integrität oder politische Anpassung?*, 2002.

12. Christine Frisch, *Von Powerfrauen und Superweibern: Frauenpopulär-literatur der 90er Jahre in Deutschland und Schweden*, 2003.

13. Hans Ruin & Nicholas Smith (eds.), *Hermeneutik och tradition. Gadamer och den grekiska filosofin*, 2003.

14. Mikael Lönnborg et al. (eds.), *Money and Finance in Transition: Research in Contemporary and Historical Finance*, 2003.

15. Kerstin Shands et al. (eds.), *Notions of America: Swedish Perspectives*, 2004.

16. Karl-Olov Arnstberg & Thomas Borén (eds.), *Everyday Economy in Russia, Poland and Latvia*, 2003.

17. Johan Rönnby (ed.), *By the Water. Archeological Perspectives on Human Strategies around the Baltic Sea*, 2003.

18. Baiba Metuzale-Kangere (ed.), *The Ethnic Dimension in Politics and Culture in the Baltic Countries 1920–1945*, 2004.

19. Ulla Birgegård & Irina Sandomirskaja (eds.), *In Search of an Order: Mutual Representations in Sweden and Russia during the Early Age of Reason*, 2004.

20. Ebba Witt-Brattström (ed.), *The New Woman and the Aesthetic Opening:Unlocking Gender in Twentieth-Century Texts*, 2004.

21. Michael Karlsson, *Transnational Relations in the Baltic Sea Region*, 2004.

22. Ali Hajighasemi, *The Transformation of the Swedish Welfare System: Fact or Fiction? Globalisation, Institutions and Welfare State Change in a Social Democratic Regime*, 2004.

23. Erik A. Borg (ed.), *Globalization, Nations and Markets: Challenging Issues in Current Research on Globalization*, 2005.

24. Stina Bengtsson & Lars Lundgren, *The Don Quixote of Youth Culture: Media Use and Cultural Preferences Among Students in Estonia and Sweden*, 2005.

25. Hans Ruin, *Kommentar till Heideggers Varat och tiden*, 2005.

26. Ludmila Ferm, *Variativnoe bespredložnoe glagol'noe upravlenie v russkom jazyke XVIII veka* [Variation in non-prepositional verbal government in eighteenth-century Russian], 2005.

27. Christine Frisch, *Modernes Aschenputtel und Anti-James-Bond: Gender-Konzepte in deutschsprachigen Rezeptionstexten zu Liza Marklund und Henning Mankell*, 2005.

28. Ursula Naeve-Bucher, *Die Neue Frau tanzt: Die Rolle der tanzenden Frau in deutschen und schwedischen literarischen Texten aus der ersten Hälfte des 20. Jahrhunderts*, 2005.

29. Göran Bolin et al. (eds.), *The Challenge of the Baltic Sea Region: Culture, Ecosystems, Democracy*, 2005.

30. Marcia Sá Cavalcante Schuback & Hans Ruin (eds.), *The Past's Presence: Essays on the Historicity of Philosophical Thought*, 2006.

31. María Borgström & Katrin Goldstein-Kyaga (ed.), *Gränsöverskridande identiteter i globaliseringens tid: Ungdomar, migration och kampen för fred*, 2006.

32. Janusz Korek (ed.), *From Sovietology to Postcoloniality: Poland and Ukraine from a Postcolonial Perspective*, 2007.

33. Jonna Bornemark (ed.), *Det främmande i det egna: filosofiska essäer om bildning och person*, 2007.

34. Sofia Johansson, *Reading Tabloids: Tabloid Newspapers and Their Readers*, 2007.

35. Patrik Åker, *Symboliska platser i kunskapssamhället: Internet, högre lärosäten och den gynnade geografin*, 2008.

36. Kerstin W. Shands (ed.), *Neither East Nor West: Postcolonial Essays on Literature, Culture and Religion*, 2008.

37. Rebecka Lettevall & My Klockar Linder (eds.), *The Idea of Kosmopolis: History, philosophy and politics of world citizenship*, 2008.

38. Karl Gratzer & Dieter Stiefel (eds.), *History of Insolvency and Bankruptcy from an International Perspective*, 2008.

39. Katrin Goldstein-Kyaga & María Borgström, *Den tredje identiteten: Ungdomar och deras familjer i det mångkulturella, globala rummet*, 2009.

40. Christine Farhan, *Frühling für Mütter in der Literatur?: Mutterschaftskonzepte in deutschsprachiger und schwedischer Gegenwartsliteratur*, 2009.

41. Marcia Sá Cavalcante Schuback (ed.), *Att tänka smärtan*, 2009.

42. Heiko Droste (ed.), *Connecting the Baltic Area: The Swedish Postal System in the Seventeenth Century*, 2011.

43. Aleksandr Nemtsov, *A Contemporary History of Alcohol in Russia*, 2011.

44. Cecilia von Feilitzen & Peter Petrov (eds.), *Use and Views of Media in Russia and Sweden: A Comparative Study of Media in St. Petersburg and Stockholm*, 2011.

45. Sven Lilja (ed.), *Fiske, jordbruk och klimat i Östersjöregionen under förmodern tid*, 2012.

46. Leif Dahlberg & Hans Ruin (eds.), *Fenomenologi, teknik och medialitet*, 2012.

47. Samuel Edquist, *I Ruriks fotspår: Om forntida svenska österledsfärder i modern historieskrivning*, 2012.

48. Jonna Bornemark (ed.), *Phenomenology of Eros*, 2012.

49. Jonna Bornemark & Hans Ruin (eds.), *Ambiguity of the Sacred: Phenomenology, Politics, Aesthetics*, 2012.

50. Håkan Nilsson, *Placing Art in the Public Realm*, 2012.

51. Per Bolin, *Between National and Academic Agendas: Ethnic Policies and 'National Disciplines' at Latvia's University, 1919–1940*, 2012.

52. Lars Kleberg & Aleksei Semenenko (eds.), *Aksenov and the Environs/Aksenov iokrestnosti*, 2012.

53. Sven-Olov Wallenstein & Brian Manning Delaney (eds.), *Translating Hegel: The Phenomenology of Spirit and Modern Philosophy*, 2012.

54. Sven-Olov Wallenstein and Jakob Nilsson (eds.), *Foucault, Biopolitics, and Governmentality*, 2013.

55. Jan Patočka, *Inledning till fenomenologisk filosofi*, 2013.

56. Jonathan Adams & Johan Rönnby (eds.), *Interpreting Shipwrecks: Maritime Archaeological Approaches*, 2013.

57. Charlotte Bydler, *Mondiality/Regionality: Perspectives on Art, Aesthetics and Globalization*, 2014.

58. Andrej Kotljarchuk, *In the Forge of Stalin: Swedish Colonists of Ukraine in Totalitarian Experiments of the Twentieth Century*, 2014.

59. Samuel Edquist & Janne Holmén, *Islands of Identity: History-writing and identity formation in five island regions in the Baltic Sea*, 2014.

60. Norbert Götz (ed.), *The Sea of Identities: A Century of Baltic and East European Experiences with Nationality, Class, and Gender*, 2015.

61. Klaus Misgeld, Karl Molin & Jaworski *Solidaritet och diplomati: Svenskt fackligt och diplomatiskt stöd till Polens demokratisering under 1980-talet*, 2015.

62. Jonna Bornemark & Sven-Olov Wallenstein (eds.), *Madness, Religion, and the Limits of Reason*, 2015.

63. Mirja Arnshav & Anna McWilliams, *Stalins ubåtar: en arkeologisk undersökning av vraken efter S7 och SC-305*, 2015.

64. Carl-Gustaf Scott, *Swedish Social Democracy and the Vietnam War* (forthcoming).

65. Jonna Bornemark & Nicolas Smith (eds.), *Phenomenology of Pregnancy*, 2016.

66. Ulrika Dahl, Marianne Liljeström & Ulla Manns, *The Geopolitics of Nordic and Russian Gender Research 1975–2005*, 2016.